Canadian
Mosaic II

Canadian Mosaic II

6 Plays

edited by

Aviva Ravel

Simon & Pierre
Toronto • Oxford

Simon & Pierre Publishing Co. Ltd.
A member of the Dundurn Group

Editors: Carl Brand & Nigel Wood
Designer: Sebastian Vasile
Printer: Best Book Manufacturers

Canadian Cataloguing in Publication Data

Main entry under title:

Canadian mosaic II
Plays.

ISBN 0-88924-274-7

1. Canadian drama (English) – 20th century.*   2. Canadian drama (English) – Minority authors.*   3. College and school drama, Canadian (English).*   I. Ravel, Aviva.

PS8315.C352 1996   C812'.5408   C96–932228–3
PR9196.6.C32 1996

Publication was assisted by the **Canada Council**, the **Book Publishing Industry Development Program** of the **Department of Canadian Heritage**, and the **Ontario Arts Council.**

Care has been taken to trace the ownership of copyright material used in this book. The author and the publisher welcome any information regarding references or credit for attribution in subsequent editions.

Printed and bound in Canada

Printed on recycled paper.

Simon & Pierre
2181 Queen Street East
Suite 301
Toronto, Ontario, Canada
M4E 1E5

Simon & Pierre
73 Lime Walk
Headington, Oxford
England
OX3 7AD

Simon & Pierre
250 Sonwil Drive
Buffalo, NY
U.S.A. 14225

CONTENTS

Editor's Note

The response to our first *Canadian Mosaic* anthology which focused on plays set in diverse cultural communities was so encouraging that *Canadian Mosaic II* follows just one year later. Featured in this volume are playwrights whose writings in this instance reflect their varied backgrounds, history and traditions: French/English, Irish, Chinese, Jewish, and Japanese.

Influenced by their ancestral past, the writers explore their roots which moulded and shaped them, and past and present fuse to become one. They share the conviction that their personalities, indeed their lives, are determined by events that occurred in the past — famine, poverty, separation from a parent, discrimination, alienation from the country in which their forebears were promised a haven. Acutely aware of their ancestors' struggles, they identify with them and recognize that their particular heritages have made them unique. As their exploration deepens, emotional and cultural ties are further strengthened. Occasionally this identification is so close, that in two of the plays (*Beautiful Deeds / De beaux gestes* and *The House On Hermitage Road*) the writers give the narrators their own names, electing not to fictionalize their stories. Each play is comprised of a unique texture woven by sound, language, rhythm, and sub-text, reflecting its culture in a spontaneous and natural way.

While Marie-Lynn Hammond in *Beautiful Deeds / De beaux gestes* probes the lives of her two grandmothers, one French, the other English, she discovers her own composite personality: "la tête anglaise and le cœur français." Employing dialogue, monologue and song, the writer relates her grandmothers' fascinating stories and unearths more similarities than differences between them.

In *Like the Sun*, Veralyn Warkentin recreates the well-known struggles of her immigrant Irish ancestors. With respect and compassion she describes their suffering from famine and disease that took countless lives. Fiercely proud of their endurance, the narrator notes at the end of the play that "the descendants of the Irish in Canada number 3.5 million."

Marty Chan's *"Mom, Dad, I'm living With a White Girl,"* approaches cultural identity by means of satire and comedy. On the one hand he explodes the grotesque myths that have been associated with the Chinese community through fantastical literature, while at the same time he writes with love and appreciation for his genuine roots and traditions. Although the protagonist has adopted "modern" Canadian ways, his own distinct personality has essentially been shaped by his culture, creating steadfast bonds with his family and community.

In *Gently Down The Stream*, the author explores the lives of two Jewish immigrant old men. They ritually evoke memories of their European misfortunes before immigrating to Canada, and recount experiences of their early poverty-stricken years in the new country. Detached from the indifferent strangers they observe in the park, they finally depart for the community centre for support and warmth.

Dirk McLean's personal history has made an indelible imprint on him, a fact that is reflected in his play *The House On Hermitage Road* which describes his childhood in Trinidad. While his mother left him for eight years in search of a better life, Dirk was raised in a loving family, participating in strong cultural traditions and bonding to his heritage. The writer brings with him to his new home in Canada these traditions which he describes with pride and pleasure.

The final play, *The Golden Door* by W. Ray Towle, recounts the discrimination against the Japanese community during World War II. Although loyal to Canada, they are treated as enemy aliens and ousted from their homes in a country they called home for forty years. This episode has left enduring scars on the community which subsequent generations continue to bear. The author relates historical events in detail while dramatically portraying one family's plight, the dynamics of a community and its traditions.

Following the pattern set in the first volume, each play is accompanied by a glossary and/or notes that translates and explains expressions, cultural references, and historical incidents. Questions at the end of the book are designed to provoke discussion. We hope this volume in which six playwrights express in the language of drama the experiences of six communities will reach theatre lovers, directors, producers and ultimately our Canadian stage.

The characters in the six plays often share similar experiences, aspirations and concerns. All the playwrights write with a sense of pride in their heritage and traditions, the past is part of the present whether the events recounted are pleasant or troubling. Canada, welcoming immigrants from many countries, encompasses many cultures. Our survival as a nation depends on our reaching out to each other with understanding, and in doing so, discovering the common attributes that unite us.

Beautiful Deeds/
De beaux gestes

by MARIE-LYNN HAMMOND

AUTHOR'S NOTE

Beautiful Deeds/De Beaux Gestes was my first play. Because I was then a singer-songwriter, I originally conceived of it as a simple one-woman show, with me singing songs and telling stories about my grandmothers. The grandmothers had other plans. Early on in the writing, they noisily insisted on being on stage with me. With no background in theatre, I figured I was in trouble.

Fortunately, several talented dramaturges came to the rescue. Nine drafts and four years later, I had a play, albeit an unconventional one.

For example: originally I felt this piece was so personal that it couldn't be performed without me. Later I saw that my part is indeed a "role" and could be played by another bilingual actor/singer. Still, I'd been hired to appear in the first two productions. Since I can't act to save my life, all my attempts to give my character spoken lines sounded awkward or sentimental. So I stuck to singing.

This doesn't mean, though, that my character is a passive Greek chorus of one. On the contrary: in one sense, all the action takes place inside the singer's head. My grandmothers both died before I began the play. Corinne and Elsie's conjured spirits, while largely true to what facts I could verify, are also the result of my imagination acting on what survived them: memories, stories, memorabilia, and the unsolved mysteries that allowed me, as a writer, to invent.

In past productions interaction between the characters has taken the form of a subtle web of gestures, glances, musical links and physical movement, which, if all were translated into stage directions, would make for a tedious text. So I invite readers to use *their* imaginations when reading this play: my character may only sing, but she is on stage the entire time. Try to see her there, watching, listening, reacting — her very presence the catalyst for the unfolding stories.

Marie-Lynn Hammond
June, 1996

PLAYWRIGHT

Marie-Lynn Hammond is a bilingual singer-songwriter and playwright. The daughter of an RCAF pilot and a Franco-Ontarian teacher, she grew up in such diverse places as Bagotville, Quebec, and Surrey, England.

In 1971 she moved to Toronto where she and partner Bob Bossin co-founded Stringband, one of Canada's seminal folk groups. By 1978 Marie-Lynn had also embarked on a solo performing and recording career that continues to this day.

In 1981, Ms. Hammond began work on *Beautiful Deeds*, a musical play about her grandmothers. First produced in 1984 in Toronto, the play was nominated for a Dora Mavor Moore award for Best New Play and has enjoyed several subsequent productions.

Since then Ms. Hammond has continued to produce works for theatre. From 1987 to 1991 she also hosted two national CBC radio shows and co-authored two screenplays, one of which, *The Circle Game*, has been made into a film.

A NOTE ON THE TEXT

This play was the first produced in a fully bilingual (and more true-to-life) version, with Corinne speaking only French until the last scene. The version included here is obviously more accessible, with only some phrases as well as a few songs entirely in French. We've used the following conventions to deal with them.

When French words or phrases are interspersed throughout a primarily English text we have italicized them. When French is the dominant language of a song or speech (e.g., in Corinne's text in the prologue) we have not italicized.

To avoid endless footnotes, we have translated only those phrases essential to understanding the story whose meanings might not easily be deduced through context. Many expressions (e.g. "Eh misère!" — literally, "oh misery!") don't have obvious English equivalents and are not included largely to keep reminding the reader that English is not Corinne's mother tongue.

The italicization of English words simply indicates emphasis.

ORIGINAL PRODUCTION

This play was first co-produced by Le Théâtre du P'tit Bonheur in Toronto (now called Le théâtre français) and the Manitoba Theatre Centre in Winnipeg. It opened November 27, 1994, in Toronto, where it ran in a fully bilingual version, and then went to Winnipeg in January 1995.

ORIGINAL CAST AND PRODUCTION TEAM

ELSIE	Diana Belshaw
MARIE-LYNN	Marie-Lynn Hammond

CORINNE   Louise Philippe

Musicians   Claude Allard
                       Marilyn Lerner
Direction   Jackie Maxwell and John Van Burek
Set and costumes   Francine Tanguay
Lighting   Elizabeth Asseltine and Louise Guinand
Stage manager   Janet Speigel

PRODUCTION HISTORY

Théâtre du P'tit Bonheur, 1994

Manitoba Theatre Centre, 1995

Blyth Festival, 1995

National Tour, 1987 (including National Arts Centre, Ottawa, and Persephone Theatre, Saskatoon)

Théâtre de la quinzième, Vancouver, 1990

Théâtre Lac Brome, 1995

REVIEWS

"[The] two solitudes come together beautifully … a very personal, engaging piece …" — *Toronto Star*, Dec. 2, 1984

"The conflict [in the climactic] scene is subtle but savage … It is a tribute to the playwright's skill that the play remains at this point personal and specific to her family situation, yet seems to take on universal implications." — *Winnipeg Free Press*, January 11, 1985

"Moving and lyrical" — *Toronto Globe & Mail*, July 1985

"*Beautiful Deeds*" is a love song across the solitudes that divide nations, families, and individuals. Its beauty, finally, lies in its power to heal." — *Kitchener-Waterloo Record*, Oct. 29 1987

"Moving and evocative … an intelligent and sensitive evening of theatre that provokes laughter, tears and conversation — but never anything less than fascination." — *Ottawa Citizen*, Nov. 11, 1987

BEAUTIFUL DEEDS

A MUSICAL PLAY IN TWO ACTS

THE CHARACTERS

CORINNE: a Franco-Ontarian woman about 60
ELSIE: an English Canadian woman in her late 50's
MARIE-LYNN: their grand-daughter, mid 30's

THE SETTING

CORINNE is in her kitchen in lowertown Ottawa; ELSIE is in the living room of her Montreal apartment. For the last scene they are in the Montreal apartment of one of CORINNE's daughters. But while these spaces can be hinted at, the set shouldn't attempt realism. It should be a relatively abstract space in which the three characters can move about freely. There is, however, to one side, a piano or keyboard setup for the accompanist and a guitar stand, if the MARIE-LYNN character plays. Ideally the pianist is a woman, as she is sort of an extension of MARIE-LYNN. (If there is a separate synthesizer player, ideally this person should be in the wings or balcony i.e. not visible, but s/he needs to have a view of the action.)

The grandmothers are on stage and visible when the audience enters. CORINNE is knitting. ELSIE is scribbling poems in a large hard-bound notebook and sipping scotch.

THE TIME

For CORINNE and ELSIE, the spring of 1944 (except for the phone call section of the prologue which is a flash forward to about one year later). For MARIE-LYNN it is the present.

PROLOGUE

(MARIE-LYNN appears and begins to sing hesitantly *a capella* as though making up the song as she goes.)

> perdu sur une mer vaste et profonde
> c'est pas qu'il manque de côtes pour atterrir

mais me voici encore entre deux mondes
je me demande comment il faut choisir

car j'ai la tête anglaise, j'ai le coeur français
pris au milieu, entre les deux,
je voyage sans fin
j'ai la tête anglaise, j'ai le coeur français
l'âme en conflit, toute ma vie
me voilà triste marin[1]

(The piano suddenly plays a trill to imitate telephone rings. We see ELSIE and CORINNE. Their speeches overlap slightly, although each woman is carrying on a separate telephone conversation.)

ELSIE: Hello? Yes. Barney?

CORINNE: Allo? Thérèse? Oui?

ELSIE: Speak up dear, bad connection.

CORINNE: Pas vrai! Quoi? Une petite fille?

ELSIE: A girl? How delightful!

CORINNE: Pas un garçon? Okay, okay, j'voulais juste —

ELSIE: Pardon?... The boy can wait till next time? But of course!

CORINNE: *Oui, oui, c'est très beau quand-même. Félicitations!*[2] As-tu choisi son nom?

ELSIE: What are you calling her?

CORINNE: Marie *quoi?*

ELSIE: Well, it's certainly original ... imagine, my first grandchild! My love to all of you. Oh Barney, just one thing —

CORINNE: Ah je comprends là. Est-ce que Barney y'est content? Bon ben, moi aussi.

---

1   N.B. Translations of French lyrics can be found at the end of the play.
2   It's very nice anyway. Congratulations!

ELSIE: I'm feeling ancient enough as it is these days — so I want you to promise me something.

CORINNE: Imagine, ma fille, là là, *j'ai quatorze petits-enfants qui vont m'appeler "grand'mère"!*[1]

ELSIE: *Don't* let her call me grandmother!

CORINNE: Marie-*Lynn*??

ELSIE: *Marie*-Lynn??

ACT ONE, SCENE ONE

MARIE-LYNN: (sings) scrapbooks and albums of pictures and photographs
            a handful of jewelry, these few souvenirs
            letters and papers, a bundle of poems
            and whose are these voices that call through the years

CORINNE: *Franchement, là, c'est trop.* Oh I wanted her to wait, but she wouldn't listen …

ELSIE: Damn this wedding. I thought I'd resigned myself to it …

CORINNE: So. Tomorrow we're going to bring out *le confetti-là*, and we've just put away the funeral wreaths...

ELSIE: I don't know how I'm going to make it through tomorrow. If only Ted were still here …

CORINNE: *Pauvre Moïse.* Oh, it wasn't a big surprise. I knew it had to happen sooner or later …

ELSIE: I still don't believe he's gone. I know it's been a while now but I can't get used to it. It was just too sudden.

CORINNE: *Malgré que des fois,*[2] I thought he'd live forever. Ninety-two years old, and in all the years we were married, I never once saw him take to his bed because he was sick.

---

1   now I've got fourteen grandchildren who'll call me grandma!
2   Even though sometimes

ELSIE: I mean, he wasn't even fifty. Such a stupid accident. Oh God! Why can't I remember what happened? One minute he was standing beside me, and the next — . We should have come straight home after the theatre ...

CORINNE: That's why, that Friday morning when he said he was tired, that he wanted to sleep late, I knew. *J'le savais.* He never got up again ...

ELSIE: Shouldn't have gone down to Rockhead's. But the bands are so good there — give me a coloured band any time when it comes to dancing. But we'd all had one too many and then he started in, accusing me of flirting ... No, that's wrong.

CORINNE: On Monday, *le père* Lemieux he comes to give *le sacrament* and Tuesday night the whole family is praying around the bed ...

ELSIE: It was him, Ted making eyes at that woman — then people shouting, stumbling towards the door, smoke so thick you couldn't see, the band playing "Bye Bye Blackbird" Barney, — Terry? someone yelling at Ted — a fist striking out at the top of the stairs and then Ted, falling and falling and falling ...

CORINNE: He died like he was falling asleep, *ce pauvre vieux*[1] — he got weaker and weaker and then he lets out one last breath like a long sigh, *pis ça y'est, c'était fini* ...[2]

ELSIE: And then just when I needed to be alone, days of questions: doctors, the police, that obnoxious reporter. "Of course we had the odd fight," I told them, "doesn't every couple? Look, it didn't *mean* anything. What do you mean, foul play?"

MARIE-LYNN: *(sings)* half-whispered stories whose endings will vary according to who might be telling the tale

CORINNE: Tch Tch Tch. Moise is dead. *C'est ben triste,* but we all have to die sometime. Like this marriage, I've done my best to accept that too. But what I can't understand *c'est Thérèse,* who comes to me this afternoon the day before her wedding, with some story she heard I don't know where about *j'sais pas quoi* ...[3]

---

1   that poor old man
2   and that was that, it was over
3   I don't know what

MARIE-LYNN: *(sings)* and just as one reaches the heart of the matter
— memory that suddenly stubbornly fails

ELSIE: The nerve! To suggest that someone might have pushed Ted down those stairs — that *I* might have! But that's monstrous! "Listen," I said, "if you knew what this man and I have been through together!"

CORINNE: My own daughter, *imagine-toi*, she wants to know if it's true that — oh! Is she trying to say I wasn't a good wife? All my life I do nothing but work to look after the family. Ten children, two husbands — not at the same time of course, *mais tout de même*[1]— and then for years, *maman* and *papa* living here and I have to take care of them on top of everything else!

ELSIE: And then those looks when I admitted to being a little older than him — all right, I'm eight years older. What of it? Even he didn't know. Look back then, there was enough talk without dragging our ages into it. Besides, it didn't make any difference. We really were kindred spirits.

CORINNE: Does she think it was easy being married to a man so much older than me? Huh! After *maman* died, *papa* would spend all his time in the kitchen, here, and Moïse would be there, and me, I'd look up from my work and see those two white heads and for a minute I'd have to think — which one is my husband, which one my father? Two old men, never wanting to go out, so me I can't leave to go to the cinema or visit a friend! Two old men, always getting in my way, using up all my baking soda for their stomach aches …

ELSIE: It didn't matter what we did, whether it was flying into the wilderness and camping out for days on end, or hitting all the clubs and partying like mad when we got back into town, it didn't matter, as long as we were together … And I swear, right up until the end, he still cared. The passion was there. We always had that.

MARIE-LYNN: *(sings)* but it isn't the pictures it's the spaces between them
the moment that followed, the moment before —

---

1   but all the same

that cry out for answers but the voices grow fainter
until I can't hear them at all anymore
and these lives gone to dust with their secrets and silence
by leaving the puzzle and taking the key
perhaps in their own way are graciously making
some room for all we who come after
and sifting these clues now I'm starting to see
what can never be known must perhaps be imagined
and maybe the piece of the puzzle that's missing is me ...

ACT ONE, SCENE TWO

(MARIE-LYNN looks at CORINNE and begins to sing "L'Esclave," tentatively at first, as though improvising a way to set CORINNE in motion. Gradually her singing becomes stronger and more rhythmic.)

MARIE-LYNN: lundi c'est le lavage
mardi le raccommodage
mercredi le repassage
jeudi c'est le tissage
vendredi le grand menage
partout dans la maison
samedi c'est l'magasinage
suivi par le cuisson —

(CORINNE stirs and starts to speak. MARIE-LYNN stops singing abruptly and watches CORINNE.)

CORINNE: (To herself) *Mon dieu, faut qu'j'me grouille.*[1] I have to finish getting the food ready — because tomorrow, after the wedding, they'll all be here to eat, *encore,* just like after the funeral. (To audience) *Ah, ça arrète jamais, hein?*[2] *Et pis,* on top of everything else, Thérèse and her stories. *Ben, je comprends,* she's upset — she was very close to her father that one. And now she's feeling a little bit guilty, *hein?* I warned her. When she came to me with her big news — she's in love, she's fiancée with some young pilot, *imagine-toi donc,* they want to get married *tout de suite.* "Thérèse," I said to her, "ce jeune homme-là, Barney — euh — Hammond: he's English, *ben okay.* But — Protestant! Your father

---

1   I've got to get going
2   it never stops, eh?

there, he's going to — !" *"Mais maman,"* she says, "weren't you ever in love? What about when you married Papa?" *"Ecoute, Thérèse,"* I said to her, *"l'amour,* that's a luxury I could never afford. Don't forget, before I met your father, I was a widow with no money and two little babies! That's why we had to go to Sudbury to stay with *ma tante* Rose while I looked for a job. Then one day Rose, she introduced me to a young man, Edmond — Eddy — Allard. *Y'éait fin, Eddy, pis y'était beau …*[1]

MARIE-LYNN: (sings to CORINNE) *quand Corinne était jeune*
she dreamed of love *et toutes les belles affaires* —

CORINNE: (interrupts) But he was studying *la médecine,* and he had no money! Now his father, Moïse Allard — *he* owned the biggest store in all of Sudbury. He was a widower, fifty-four years old, thirty-one years older than me. But one day I saw him light his cigar with a five dollar bill. Well, after that things changed, I can tell you! I remember the next time Eddy came to see me. (Corinne as Eddy:) *"Bonjour Corinne, bonjour. R'gardez,* I brought you a little present, it's the music for the waltz that everyone's playing right now." *"Merci Eddy, vous êtes bien gentil.* Sit down, sit down. *Ecoutez Eddy,* I have to tell you something. It's very nice that you bring me some sheet music, but your father has offered to buy me the piano!" *Ben, pauvre Eddy,* he nearly fell off his chair. *"Mais Corinne!"* he says. "What about the night when we walked in the moonlight? And what about — ?" *"Ben, écoutez, Eddy,"* I said to him, "your father, he's old, but he's not crippled! I can walk with him in the moonlight too. *Oubliez-pas* — I have two little boys to feed! *Pis une autre affaire, Eddy.* You know what they say — better to be an old man's doll than a young man's slave!" *Ah misère!* (chuckles ruefully) At first it was fine. Moïse, he built me a nice big house, I had a maid, and he let my buy lots of pretty dresses too. Mais je te dis, that didn't last long, because the year after we got married, Sir Wilfrid Laurier himself asked Moïse to run for Parliament, and, for Moïse, there was God — and the Liberal party. Thousands of dollars he spends on that election, only to lose. He was a proud man, Moïse. He took it very bad. He even began to drink. So he lost more money and had to sell the store, then the house, and finally we have to move into a little old shack in the middle of nowhere. And me I have to work like a

---

[1] he was nice, that Eddy, and handsome too.

slave to feed and take care of everyone, because, *oubliez-pas,* Moïse he gave me *eight more babies!* So — maybe he bought me the piano, but he sure didn't leave me much time to play!

(MARIE-LYNN sings to CORINNE and audience and accompanies herself on the spoons. The piano comes in half-way through song.)

MARIE-LYNN: lundi c'est le lavage
    mardi le raccommodage
    mercredi le repassage
    jeudi c'est le tissage
    vendredi le grand menage
    partout dans la maison
    samedi c'est l'magasinage
    suivi par le cuisson —
    dimanche c'est pour prier
    ensuite le grand diner
    mon dieu j'aimerais donc
    juste deux minutes pour m'reposer
    car demain lundi matin
    ça va tout recommencer!

(Piano holds the last chord as CORINNE shakes her head and exchanges a rueful smile with MARIE-LYNN.)

CORINNE: Eh misère!

ACT ONE, SCENE THREE

(MARIE-LYNN turns from CORINNE to ELSIE.)

ELSIE: (ELSIE begins to speak to audience as piano chord fades. Attempts a tone of amused condescension.) French Canadian. Tomorrow my son is marrying a French Canadian — a girl he hardly knows, someone he met on leave of course. And even if he survives that, as soon as he's finished training he'll be flying fighters over Germany ... God I'm losing everyone — damn this war! Well of course I'm for it, but if it weren't for the war, surely none of this would be happening? I didn't want to leave the coast, didn't want to move to Montreal, but Ted insisted. "I'm too old to enlist," he said, "but if they want me out east as a test pilot, by god, I'll leave tomorrow." Hmm. (shakes her head) It's too ridiculous. We spend twenty years in British Columbia where he flies those flimsy planes into the wilderness, wings icing up over the mountains, ploughing through fog so thick that TCA was grounded and even the ducks were walking. All that and no fatal tumble out of the sky. Instead, we come out here and six months later he falls down two flights of stairs at Rockhead's Paradise club and cracks his skull open like an egg at the bottom. And he must have fallen — I mean, who would have pushed him? "Look," I told that reporter, "you can ask Barney. He's my son — the older one. Terry's the younger. They were both there that night and — I beg your pardon? Married? I told you, twenty years together ... Barney's last name? (Reluctantly) Well, yes, Hammond, that's correct. And Ted? Yes, Dobbin, Ted Dobbin because — . *My* name? I told you I'm Elsie — " (she halts suddenly)

MARIE-LYNN: (sings to ELSIE) Elsie was a beauty, and she was a wild
one the only time she pleased the family
was when she married a banker's son

ELSIE: All right, it's true. I was married before, to Douglas Hammond. He — died when the boys were very young, and — look, I don't think of that part of my life very much anymore. I mean, I didn't even want to marry him in the first place! As soon as I realized my mistake, I tried to break it off. Douglas wouldn't hear of it, despite some rather drastic measures on my part. So in desperation I turned to my mother.
(ELSIE alternates between playing her younger self and her mother for the rest of this monologue.)
"Mama," I said, "I have to break it off. I don't love him." (As mother) "I beg your pardon? You'll do no such thing, my girl. Especially after what happened last week. Now Elsie, showing up two hours late to a party thrown in honour of your engagement to Mr. Hammond is extremely bad manners. But to walk in on the arm of another man — ! Fortunately Douglas is willing to overlook your appalling behaviour, because remember, Elsie, you've already had one broken engagement. And then, this *other* business with George Archer!" (as Elsie) "But mama, I'd have married George in an instant! It's just that he didn't ask *me*. That's why when Douglas proposed, I — " (As mother) "I don't care to listen to excuses, Elsie. Douglas Hammond is a quiet, steady, responsible sort ..." (As Elsie, under her breath) "And that's precisely the problem." (As mother) "I beg your

pardon?" (As Elsie) "I said I'm not in love with him." (As mother) "Love? What about your *reputation*? You *shall* marry Douglas Hammond, is that clear? Because one broken engagement is barely excusable, but two — that's a *scandal!*"

(ELSIE rolls her eyes, gestures, and exchanges a laugh with MARIE-LYNN as the piano plays a brisk instrumental tag based on the "Elsie" song.)

ACT ONE, SCENE FOUR

ELSIE: So there I was you see —

CORINNE: Imagine-toi donc.

ELSIE & CORINNE: (together) Twenty-three years old!

CORINNE: Already on my second marriage!

ELSIE: And still single!

CORINNE: *"Bon, d'accord,"*[1] Thérèse says to me, "now I understand why you married *papa*. But what about Calixte Vaillant, your first husband? You married so young, you must have been in love with him?"

ELSIE: I got engaged to Douglas Hammond because there was simply nothing else to do. Well, what options besides marriage did a woman in my position have?

CORINNE: As if I had any choice about my first marriage either! It all started when I was sixteen and *papa*'s store burned down — in the great fire of Hull! *Ah misère!* We lost everything we had. Well, they can't afford to keep me at home no more, and in those days, there was only three things a girl could do: teach school —

ELSIE: Working was out of the question.

CORINNE: Get married —

ELSIE: So was attending university.

---

1   well okay

CORINNE: Or become a nun.

ELSIE: I mean jobs were for girls who didn't have money, and degrees were for girls who didn't have beaus. I had plenty of both.

CORINNE: So, first I teach school. And it's hard work, some of the boys as old as me and twice as big. But one night they had *une danse carrée*[1] at the schoolhouse. *Eh misère,* there's nothing like a dance to make you forget your troubles, *hein?* And I noticed Calixte Vaillant because he was a good dancer. Like me.

ELSIE: No, up until a girl married, life was a series of balls, riding parties, Mediterranean cruises (ELSIE reads from postcards as though she is writing them. Music begins. All ELSIE's "postcards" are underscored with humorous variations on "The Lady is Bored" which is sung at the end of this scene. This one is tinkly and Bach-like …)
Dear Hattie,
Arrived in London last night. Mother found the crossing rough but I met some very lively people on board and I was never at loss for amusement. The captain was Hungarian, of all things, and incidentally, the biggest devil of the lot!
Affectionately, Elsie.

CORINNE: *Eh bien!* The next thing I know, *maman* and *papa* they come to tell me that Calixte has a big farm, and it's all arranged for me to marry him. So. I don't stop to ask if I am in love because I must obey *maman* and *papa*. Besides, I don't want to become a nun, and what else is there left to do?

ELSIE: (Piano plays theme as sweeping romantic waltz.)
Dear dear dear dear George,
After a week in Paris, here we are on the Riviera where it is deliciously hot. I can't say I miss little Brockville at all — oh, except for you and Hattie of course! Father is complaining there are unusually large numbers of soldiers about, there is even talk of war, but I don't mind, they look quite dashing! (ELSIE looks up) Oh dear! Shouldn't have put that. (appears to cross out last phrase and add the following:) Pining for you, Elsie.

CORINNE: *Ben là là,* on our wedding night he wants to get into bed with me! *Jamais de la vie!*[2] *Ben,* I thought that if he lay down beside

---

1   a square dance
2   not on your life!

me, just lay down, that I would have a baby. And I didn't want one just yet. So, Calixte says, *"Ecoute, ma Corinne, faut qu'j'texplique queq'chose"* — and he explained it all to me. And, I had a baby! Then I find out it's not *his* farm at all, it's his stepfather's, and in the winter Calixte he has to go off to *les chantiers*.[1] So, there I am, stuck with two little babies — two, because after the first I have another one — and all the farm chores as well!

ELSIE: (Piano plays theme with "Italian" mandolins-in-the-moonlight feel: many trills and embellishments.)
Dear Cousin Beryl,
Firenze and Roma are wonderful cities, but Venice is surely the most romantic! We lunched with the Harringtons today and later Jack Harrington and I went out on a gondola, where he said some very silly, charming things which I — think I shall disregard. Should you see George, do tell him to write me!
Your cousin, Elsie.

CORINNE: And then Calixte he gets very sick, he can't walk. I have to bathe him, and dress him, and take care of the babies too, and after three, four years like that I think I am going to die. My brothers, they say, Corinne, you have to put Calixte *dans un foyer*.[2] So I go to the *curé* — and he says, "Madame Vaillant, when you married you promised before God to take that man for better or for worse, in sickness and in health. It is your duty to stay by him as long as he lives!" But my brothers came and said, *"Laisse-faire le curé."*[3] And they took Calixte to Ottawa and put him in a home. He died five days later.

ELSIE: (Piano plays very simple, modal version of melody in octaves only — no chords, with "Arabic" feel. Stops somewhere at, or during, the P.S.)
Dearest Hattie,
Here is a picture of me with an Arab in Algiers — isn't he a striking fellow in his caftan! We are heading back north now and shall be home in a month.
Love, Elsie
(short pause)
P.S. We met some people in Gibraltar who claim to know the

---

1   the lumber camps
2   in a nursing home
3   never mind the priest

Archers, and they said George had gotten engaged to Marjorie Lyons, of all people. Isn't that the silliest story? I told them they must be mistaken.

(MARIE-LYNN begins to sing. ELSIE sings or speaks the lines indicated. CORINNE joins in the last verse for a cointerpoint section, weaving the melody of "L'Esclave" around the "The Lady Is Bored" melody.)

THE LADY IS BORED/L'ESCLAVE

MARIE-LYNN: Straw hats and tennis and tea
            lacy white dresses and long summer days
            she has everything leisure and riches afford

ELSIE: but oh I'm so terribly — bored!

MARIE-LYNN: London and Brussels and Rome
            dining in style on the Champs Elysées
            her mother is hoping she'll marry a lord

ELSIE: oh but the lady is bored!

MARIE-LYNN: who is that smoking there out on the yacht?

ELSIE: well it's me of course darling, but I'll never get caught

MARIE-LYNN: she is pampered and coddled, admired, adored

MARIE-LYNN & ELSIE: oh but the lady is bored!

CORINNE: (lundi c'est le lavage, mardi le raccommodage)

MARIE-LYNN: straw hats and tennis and tea

CORINNE: (mercredi le repassage, jeudi c'est le tissage)

MARIE-LYNN: lacy white dresses and long summer days

CORINNE: (vendredi le grand menage et le cirage)

MARIE-LYNN: she has everything leisure and riches afford

CORINNE: (samedi l'magasinage, dimanche le grand diner)

MARIE-LYNN & ELSIE: oh but the lady is bored!

CORINNE: (mon dieu j'aimerais donc m'reposer!)

ACT ONE, SCENE FIVE

(Piano segues from "The Lady Is Bored" into "Battle to Fight" melody. MARIE-LYNN sings first verse quietly. ELSIE begins to speak over the music around the second line of the song.)

MARIE-LYNN: there's a battle to fight, will you fight it?
there's a debt to be paid, will you pay?
there are grave wrongs to right will you right them?
then join as a man in the fray!

there's the cry of an outraged Belgium
and above that the voice of our slain

ELSIE: Now the first war — somehow that was different. Oh, it was an awful, awful time — so many dead ... But it was also a very stirring, inspirational time, especially for me. Why, I even began to write poems, something I'd certainly never done before.

(Now, as though prompted by MARIE-LYNN, ELSIE joins in, reciting as MARIE-LYNN continues singing. She is hesitant at first, then becomes highly enthusiastic.)

MARIE-LYNN & ELSIE:
those men who have died for our freedom
will you let all their striving be vain?

let the slacker hang back if he wants to
but if manhood's not dead you will go
to the aid of a country who needs you
to help battle a crime-ridden foe

(By now MARIE-LYNN and ELSIE are marching in place centre stage, shamelessly exhorting the audience.)

there's a battle to fight, will you fight it?
there's a debt to be paid, will you pay?

there are grave wrongs to right, will you right them?
then enlist for your country, today!

ELSIE: That was the first one I ever wrote — they did get better as I went along. I wrote dozens — couldn't help it. You see, Douglas Hammond and I had been married two years by then, and we'd moved to Ottawa, where my life consisted of tea with the ladies, dinner with Douglas's stuffy friends from the bank, and, oh, let's not forget — church on Sundays. So that when war broke out it was almost a relief — because at last something *real* was happening. I wanted desperately to go overseas and nurse, but the family wouldn't hear of it. Douglas of course signed up immediately — anything less in our set would have been considered treason. I didn't see him again for three years. So, I behaved decorously, as befits a young wife with a husband at the front. I stayed home and wrote my poems. I sent Douglas long letters and food packages. I did all sorts of volunteer work. Why, I even —

MARIE-LYNN: (interrupting her, sings) Elsie knit mufflers for the men at the front
And slept with the ones on leave

ELSIE: (defensive) — well, I began to pine for a little fun! Now don't misunderstand me — I was very keen on the war. We all were. But really, one can only roll so many Red Cross bandages. So, I began to go out a bit.

MARIE-LYNN: (sings questioningly) And slept with the ones on leave?

ELSIE: (irritated) Dancing, and so on! There were still men in Ottawa you see, on account of the government, and some of them were quite lively, for civil servants. Besides, I really did my best to restrict my activities to the — patriotic realm. Which is how I came to be at the Victory rally one fine spring afternoon with a fellow from External Affairs — whose name I don't recall because something happened that day which made everything else unimportant. There were speakers at the rally, and a band, but best of all, they had a fellow flying an airplane. I don't think I'd ever seen one so close before. First, he did all sorts of fancy loops and rolls, swooping low over the crowd and making people duck and cry out, but not me. I was mesmerized! Couldn't take my eyes off the plane, or the pilot. And then damned if he didn't fly right under the Interprovincial Bridge! God, what nerve! The next moment (quiet piano underscoring begins) he was a tiny speck in the sky. And suddenly, more than anything, I wanted to be up there with him, climbing and climbing, free of the crowd, free of the pull of the earth. I watched until I couldn't see him anymore, and I swore right then and there that I would learn to fly too.

MARIE-LYNN: (sings) Over Queen Charlotte Sound
the lichen-covered rocks below
are grey and rust-brown
foam on the water like filigree
sun scatters sequins
of gold on the sea
and Ted with the log book
and his head bent down
while I'm holding her steady over Queen Charlotte Sound

over the mountains now
valley after valley
of smokey jade and shadow
snowy range rises against the blue
like a fantasy magic lantern view
and we're as tiny as a speck
of dust on the screen
lost in world no one's ever seen
over the mountains now

Bridge: engine droning
landing on some nameless lake
pontoons rocking gently
on the water
drift in silence
when we cut the motor
drift in silence
drift in silence

over Queen Charlotte Sound

ACT I, SCENE 6

CORINNE: (to audience and MARIE-LYNN) Weddings. Puh! Weddings are easy. But marriage — *c'est une autre paire de manches.*[1] Even these last few years with Moïse I lose patience, I close my heart, and Thérèse, she gets upset with me. Well, at her age, it's easy to love. But me, so many people to take care of for so long — *c'est trop. J'peux pu, moi! L'amour — fini, parti!* All used up, like the baking soda! (she crosses herself) *Pardonnez-moi, Seigneur,*[2] maybe I complain a little too much, *hein? Le bon Dieu là,* he sends us joy and sorrow, and it's not for us to question, only to accept … *Mais quand-même,* sometimes I wonder why he has to send everything at once! A war that never ends, last week my husband's funeral, and tomorrow my daughter marries a Protestant! *"Ecoute Thérèse,"* *j'ai dit,* "what about the children? That's no example for them, a father who never goes to Mass. *Pis le français? Ils vont-tu parler le français au moins?"* But she's got an answer for everything that one. "What about Jean-Marie?" she says. "Okay, *c'est vrai,* your brother he's engaged to an English girl, but Joanne (she uses the French pronunciation) at least, she's Catholic!" (Corinne "becomes" Thérèse:) "But *maman,* her name isn't Joanne, it's Joan. *Mais ça fait rien,* because Jean Marie can do whatever he wants and you never say anything. But don't worry, my children will speak French. Because I'm not going to have *ten, maman,* only two or three, and I'll have time — lots of time to teach them, and to play games and sing songs, and to put my arms around them whenever they want — *pauvre maman!* — all the things you were too busy for — except with Jean Marie!" *Ah! Me parler de même!*[3] Her, she doesn't know what it's like! "Maman, I'm hungry!" *"Maman* it hurts!" *"Maman* I'm scared." *"Maman,* please hug me!" *"Assez, assez, j'ai pas le temps!*[4] *J'ai pas le temps — !"...*

(A pause, as she realizes THÉRÈSE may be right.) *Ben, justement,* with Jean Marie, I *had* the time. He was my last one, my baby. I can't help it if I have a special place in my heart for him. Besides, when he was growing up, it was maybe the happiest time in our lives. *Le bon Dieu là,* he sent us ten hard years in Sudbury, and ten hard years during the depression, but

---

1   (literally) that's another pair of sleeves, i.e., that's a whole different thing
2   Forgive me, Lord
3   To talk to me like that!
4   Enough, enough, I don't have time!

in between, we had almost ten good years — in Windsor. Now I know some people think you can't even have *one* good year in Windsor. But anyway, we were not really in the town. *Moïse, lui,* he bought the general store in Loiselleville, (piano underscoring begins, based on "La jeune mariée") a little village a few miles out in the country. But that was good, because we had a big house over the store, and behind, a big big vegetable garden. And we had a pony for the children, and a little dog, and about twenty-five cats. *J'te dis qu'on avait des chats! Partout des chats! Ah, c'était le bon temps!*[1] The winters were mild, the summers were long and hot, the children would play out in the fields all day. Saturday night, I'd put on my good dress, and *Moïse puis moi là,* it's off to the schoolhouse *pour les danses carrées!* (Smiles) Windsor. Loiselleville ... (piano out). I remember when I found out I was going to have another baby. It's true I was only forty-one years old but *Moïse lui,* he was seventy-two! Madelaine, our youngest, she was already six, so I thought at last it was *fini. Ben non!* I had to start knitting the little layettes again. Anyway, when Jean-Marie was born, it was *une accouchement très difficile*[2] — very long and very hard. Finally, the doctor left, and I fell asleep, the baby beside me. Sometime later I wake up — no baby! He's gone! Me, I'm all confused, I think maybe he's dead! (she crosses herself) I call for help — no one comes. Just then I hear noise from downstairs, and I remember, there is a grate in the floor near the bed and I can see through it into the store. *Ça fait que,* I lean over, *pis-ben oui!* Right under is the counter and Moïse is behind it. In front of him are the children and three or four customers. And there in the big scale on the counter is Jean Marie, *mon p'tit! Pis là* I hear Moïse saying — *ah, qu'y était fier!*[3] "*R'gardez bien, mesdames et messieurs,* ten pounds and a quarter! And me, I'm seventy-two years old!" Imagine! And me so tiny! I wanted to yell at him: "*Garde-le donc,*[4] *ton* ten pounds and a quarter! Me, it almost killed me!"

(Introductory piano chord, then MARIE-LYNN begins to sing "La jeune mariée" *rubato,* settling into a brisk tempo by the end of the first verse. This song follows a traditional folk form where a new name gets added with every verse. CORINNE begins to join in with the *"ben oui"*s and *"ben non"*s in the second verse.)

---

1   Boy did we have cats! Cats everywhere! Ah, those were good times!
2   a very hard labour
3   my, he was proud!
4   You can keep it

MARIE-LYNN: quand j'étais jeune mariée,
diddl'aille don
mon mari m'a dit,
"viens ici t'coucher"
pis neuf mois plus tard,
voilà un petit bébé
c'est une fille? Ben oui!
pas un garçon? ben non diddl'aille don
pis faut choisir son nom
pis faut l'appeler Marie queq'chose
Marie Cecile c'est un beau nom
appelle-la donc Marie Cecile
Marie Cecile diddl'aille don

quand j'étais jeune mariée, diddl'aille don
mon mari m'a dit,
"viens ici t'coucher"
pis neuf mois plus tard,
voilà un petit bébé
encore une fille? Ben oui
pas un garçon? ben non! diddl'aille don
pis faut choisir son nom
pis faut l'appeler Marie queq'chose
Marie Yvonne c'est un beau nom
appelle-la donc Marie Yvonne
Marie Yvonne et pis Marie Cecile
de diddl'aille don

(Third verse as above, with MARIE-LYNN playing spoons and adding "Marie Colette". Then a short instrumental section where CORINNE gets up and does a little jig, followed by a chorus that adds "Marie-Thérèse" and "Marie-Madeleine." Then back to *rubato* for the last verse, as above for first four lines, then, still singing:)

MARIE-LYNN: encore une fille?

CORINNE: ben non!

MARIE-LYNN: c'est un garçon?

CORINNE: ben oui diddl'aille di! (Music stops, CORINNE now speaks.)
Un garçon! Enfin un autre garçon! Bon ben, we have to pick a

very special name for him. *Voyons …* Dosithé Aldéric Marie, after his grandfather? (MARIE-LYNN looks uncertain) *Non? Eh bien,* what about Nicéphor Eusèbe Joseph Chrysologue, for his uncles? (MARIE-LYNN shakes her head) *Non plus?* Okay. H-mph. *Ah! Je l'ai!* We are going to call him Joseph Jésu Marie! That way, the entire Holy Family has to look out for him!

MARIE-LYNN: *Ben non!*

CORINNE: Ah, I cannot call him Jésu, *en? T'as raison, t'as raison …*[1] *Ah! Là, je l'ai!* We're going to call him Joseph *Jean* Marie!

MARIE-LYNN: *Bon!!!*

CORINNE: *Ben oui! C'est beau, ça!*

MARIE-LYNN: (sings) pis faut choisir son nom
pis faut l'appeler queq'chose de beau
appelle-le Joseph Jean Marie
j'ai dit appelle le Jean Marie
(et pis) Marie Madelaine etc.

(CORINNE joins in for a grand *rubato* finale)

Joseph Jean Marie
c'est un garçon diddl'aille don!

(As the last piano chord fades we see ELSIE upstage, glass of liquor in hand, looking at MARIE-LYNN and CORINNE. She looks somewhat disdainful but is perhaps also feeling left out of the merriment.)

BLACK OUT — END OF ACT ONE

ACT TWO

(ELSIE's decanter of liquor is now half empty. She is leafing through her notebook, glass in hand. CORINNE has her sewing things out and is mending a black dress. MARIE-LYNN begins to sing, guitar and voice only. Piano enters softly on "Beautiful deeds" line and fades out before ELSIE speaks. Once again,

---

1   You're right

the grandmothers begin speaking as if to themselves and gradually shift to include MARIE-LYNN and the audience.)

SCENE ONE

MARIE-LYNN: as I sit and watch I long to be
　　　　　out where the grey sky meets the sea
　　　　　where the grey sky meets the sea
　　　　　for I know there's a place where dreams come true
　　　　　where smiles are many and tears are few
　　　　　where the grey sky meets the sea
　　　　　and the beautiful deeds that we wish to do
　　　　　will be given birth and we start anew
　　　　　in that land of our dreams beyond the blue
　　　　　where the grey sky meets the sea
　　　　　where the grey sky meets the sea

ELSIE:　　How am I going to get through tomorrow without him? How will I survive all the smiles, the handshakes, the toasts to the happy couple? Surely it's a dream — it's got to be a dream! Any minute now Ted's going to walk in and … God, if we could just go back to that moment at the top of the stairs and this time — he was only flirting! — this time I'll hang onto his arm I won't get jealous I won't …

CORINNE:　(gets up, then sits down) Normalement this time of night I would make Moïse his tea — he always liked a cup of tea before going to bed. Every night for forty years. First the whole family would say the rosary, and then I'd bring him his tea.

ELSIE:　　But it wasn't just me that night! Because Ted had to flirt with Rockhead's girl of all people! So Rockhead jumped in too — and then everyone's shouting and pushing and somebody — I can't remember — it *was* an accident!

CORINNE:　It's so quiet in the house! One by one, they're all leaving, or dying … *Je me sens drôle.*[1] I'm not used to being on my own …

ELSIE:　　Oh I don't want to be alone! Don't know how to be alone! … But we can't go back, can we, can't take it from the top just one more time. There is no starting over. He's gone.

1　I feel strange

33

MARIE-LYNN: (sings, with music accompaniment)
and the beautiful deeds that we wish to do
will be given birth and we start anew
in that land of our dreams beyond the blue
where the grey sky meets the sea

ELSIE: "And we start anew" — but that's impossible now! I mean what am I going to do with myself? Can't write bloody poetry twenty-four hours a day! No, no you see, I've had my second chance, when Ted and I went out to the coast. That — that reporter who was hanging around a few weeks ago — where is he? Here's what he should be writing about! Not one drunken chance moment in a smokey nightclub, but the twenty years we lived through before that. There's your story! Romance and adventure, yes, but hard times too, dangerous times! Oh, the first few years were fine. It was the twenties and British Columbia was the place to be, everyone clamouring to get over the mountains to the interior, and the only way to do it was to fly. So, men like Ted, they were gods! But the thirties — it got tough. Suddenly, no more putting on the Ritz. Money was scarce. Sometimes Ted would go a month without work. So, we stayed home, played a lot of cribbage, danced to Benny Goodman on the radio — God we could dance together ...! I couldn't help out much. Hmmf — people think I'm rich — if only they knew! I can't even buy a new dress for the wedding!

CORINNE: *Mon dieu,* this poor old dress! It's not in style anymore! But anyway, it's a wedding, it's not a fashion show. For some people it's important to be in style, but me, I was never like that.

MARIE-LYNN: (sings) *quand Corinne était jeune* she dreamed of love
et toutes les belles affaires that a girl thinks of

CORINNE: *Ben okay, c'est vrai,* at first with Moïse he bought me anything I wanted: hats, dresses, beautiful shoes. And I wasn't going to say no, not after those hard years with Calixte. Hmm. You marry a man, you promise to honour and obey because you think *he* will take care of you. Hah! The same thing happened with Moïse, after he lost the election. For a while he drank so much, he had to go in the hospital — *ah misère!*

ELSIE: I never expected him to die before me! How awkward to find oneself at my age, with no means of financial support. I've really no choice but to return home, home to my aged parents. Because it's *mother* who's rich you see, and I hardly saw a penny from her after Ted stepped into the picture. Poor Ted. They refused to let him set foot in the house.

(MARIE-LYNN looks at ELSIE questioningly.)

ELSIE: Well, he was a pilot, he, ah, wasn't good enough for me, he … Douglas of course, they had adored.

MARIE-LYNN: (sings) Elsie took a notion
in nineteen twenty-five
left her husband for the man who taught her
how to sail the skies

ELSIE: All right! Douglas didn't die. I left him. So my parents blamed the whole thing on Ted, because they didn't want to blame me, though God knows everyone else did. Look, back then, running off with another man wasn't exactly the sort of behaviour to garner citations from the Imperial Order of the Daughters of the Empire. And then the messy business of trying to get a divorce. The only grounds of course was adultery, and only the innocent party could sue. Well. I was obviously not the innocent party. And to top it off, divorces were handled only through some Senate Committee, so talk about washing one's dirty linen in public! I mean there it was, laid out for everyone to see, in Hansard for Godsake! No wonder Douglas put up such a fuss. Now it wasn't as if I didn't try with him — I stayed for ten years! But when Ted came along it was like flying up through a bank of cloud and suddenly coming out into a blue, summery sunlit space … Oh, I knew precisely where lay the path of duty. I saw it stretch out before me like a noble highway, straight, narrow, and infinitely oppressive. So I summoned up all my strength and nerve — and deliberately turned my back on it. And all of a sudden, people I'd counted on as good friends would cross over to the other side of the street to avoid me …

CORINNE: *Ça fait qu'encore une fois,*[1] it's me who has to care for the children, keep an eye on the store, make trips to the hospital to see Moïse. And then Lucien, my second one, he gets sick, and I have to

---

1 So once again

watch him die … So if back then one day — a day when I thought I would never smile again, the door opens and (pause) *ben*, okay, Thérèse is right about that part, there — was this man who use to come to the store — *un petit commis-voyageur*[1] — and one day he walks in whistling with his suitcase full of ribbons and lace and he says, *"Bonjour Madamoiselle*, I think we've met before but in case you don't remember, *ici Jean Joseph Arthimis Samuel Robitaille*, but everyone calls me Joe *pis c'est* fine by me, especially on a beautiful day like this. Just look at the sky! And of course it's always nice to see a pretty girl too! M-m-h-m-m. *Et puis*, is Monsieur Moïse Allard here by any chance?" "No, my husband is away right now." (Corinne as Joe) "Oh! The old man is your husband! *Ben pardonnez-moi madame*, I thought for sure you were his daughter. I didn't know he'd married again. *Y'est ben chanceux, c'vieux-là.*[2]" Then he opens his suitcase and says (piano begins soft underscoring, waltz chorus from "Le coffre a jouets.") — *"Regardez, madame*, beautiful laces and ribbons and trims" and he winds them round my neck and in my hair, "all the latest styles, just like they are wearing at the balls in Paris!" (Corinne gets up and begins to slowly waltz around the stage as though dancing with Joe) And now he is singing and waltzing me around the store … Me, I try to pull away: (laughing) *"Assez, assez, Monsieur Robitaille!"* (As Joe) *"Appelez-moi Joe. Tout le monde m'appelle Joe!*[3] But why stop? You dance very well, Madame Allard!" (She stops dancing.) And then he tells me funny stories, so the tears run down my face, and he is young, his hair so dark and curly and he looks at me — (with sudden, almost stricken intensity) ah! *J'oublierai jamais ses yeux!*[4] (The piano stops. CORINNE collects herself and looks at MARIE-LYNN who has been watching intently.) *Pis après* — was that so wrong? It was just a little bit of fun! But I don't want to think about this — it was much too long ago.

(CORINNE turns abruptly and walks away. MARIE-LYNN makes as if to follow her, then changes her mind.)

MARIE-LYNN: (sings) *quand Corinne était jeune* she dreamed of love
et toutes les belles affaires that a girl thinks of

---

1   a little travelling salesman
2   That old guy's really lucky
3   Call me Joe. Everyone calls me Joe!
4   I'll never forget his eyes!

but as the years went by *les rêves ont disparu*
until all of a sudden, *voilà l'imprévu …*

who is that smiling at the door
à qui ce visage qui hante sa mémoire
ribbons of laughter, *les dentelles d'amour*
it's a shadow, it's a dream, *ce n'est qu'une histoire*

CHORUS: lundi c'est le lavage, mardi le repassage
chaque jour de la semaine poignée dans l'esclavage
on fait de son mieux, on fait ce qu'on peut
et quand c'est pas assez ben on prie le bon Dieu

Corinne's still knitting mittens *à quatre-vingt dix ans*
a grey-haired *grand'maman* to her many *p'tits enfants*
où est la jeune fille? the young girl is gone
mais dans son cœur the secrets and the dreams live on

lundi c'est le lavage, mardi le repassage
chaque jour de la semaine poignée dans l'esclavage
on fait de son mieux, on fait ce qu'on peut
et quand c'est pas assez ben on prie le bon Dieu
toujours faut travailler, souvent on veut brailler
mais chaque fois qu'on a la chance bien sur qu'on va danser
mais chaque fois qu'on a la chance bien sur qu'on danser

ACT TWO, SCENE TWO

ELSIE: But it wasn't just my running away of course, or even running away with a flyer. No. What people found really galling was the fact that I myself had decided to learn to fly. And flying was about the last thing someone of my position was expected to take up. Women had barely earned the right to wear trousers in public, let alone *fly*. Back then, flying was adventurous, glamorous too, but also considered rather — how shall we say — bohemian? Well, it was the flyers you see. They swaggered. They drank. They wore silk scarves and wonderful boots. They were — oh let's face it they were damned *sexy*, and that was the problem. Still, that day, when I saw the pilot fly under the bridge, I didn't care a fig for what anyone thought. I'd made up my mind to learn and that was that. Shortly after though, the war ended. Douglas came home, I became pregnant and had a baby instead. Arthur

Barnard. Barney. A lovely baby, all dark curls and blue eyes. For a while I thought he'd be enough. But then one evening, (piano begins underscoring with a tango theme) Douglas and I went to a party. It was rather a dull affair, and I'd already caused a flap simply by showing up in a cerise-coloured dress. But I had the devil in me that night, so at one point I said quite loudly: "By the way Douglas, did I mention that I've decided to learn to fly?" There was dead silence for a moment, then the men began to snort and chuckle. "Hey Elsie," laughed one of them, "in that case you ought to meet Lieutenant Dobbin here. He's a flyer." Douglas later accused me of flirting, but I swear I wasn't, because at first glance this fellow Dobbin wasn't my type at all. He was short, almost stocky, with a rough and ready manner and an insolent grin. (Elsie plays both Ted and her younger self. As Ted:) "Pleased to meet you, Mrs. Hammond. I've been admiring your outfit. It isn't everyone that can carry something like that off." (as Elsie) "Why, thank you. I'm afraid we women must seek adventure in whatever small ways are open to us." (As Ted) "Listen, are you serious about this flying business? It's dangerous — a lot more dangerous than wearing a red dress." (As Elsie) "I don't care. I think flying is the most marvellous thing on earth!" Then I told him about the pilot I'd seen flying at the Victory rally. "Well," he said, grinning, "Under the bridge you say? That was none other than myself." (As Elsie) "I don't believe you! You're just like all the other men here, you don't take me seriously at all." Then he stopped smiling and looked me straight in the eye. (As Ted) "On the contrary, I take you very seriously. In fact, I'm going to make you an offer. Some fellows and me we've bought a couple of Curtiss Jennies, and we keep 'em out near Brown's Pasture. If you want to come out someday, I'll take you up for a ride. And if you still want to learn to fly after that, I'll teach you."
(Piano tango finishes with a flourish.)

Well, I was thrilled. The next day Ted just turned up out of the blue, took me by the arm and said, "Come along Elsie — today I'm giving you your first flying lesson." And I should have learned then, shouldn't I? But I didn't. Why? Because I made the mistake of falling in love with my instructor. And once you fall in love with a man, they'll never teach you anything. First they get critical, then they lose their patience, and finally, they become so insulting that you're scared they won't love you anymore and you cry out, "Stop! You're right. I'm slow, I'm stupid, and we needn't do this again, ever! Now let's go and have a drink at the Chateau, please!" Then they take you in their arms and murmur, "Darling,

I didn't mean to be hard on you. I just hate to see you wasting your time, that's all!" Men. Well it doesn't matter. What matters is that Ted loved me and I loved him. Besides, I went with him on countless flights, and saw the world in ways I could never have imagined. Sometimes he'd let me take the controls — swearing of course that we'd all be killed — but planes were a lot simpler in those days, and I did just fine. (MARIE-LYNN begins soft vamp on guitar based on "Elsie" song theme.) So I never did get my license. I never did fly solo. Because once I was with Ted I didn't care to anymore ... I mean, why go alone when you can go together? Never did fly solo. But really, I've — no regrets.

MARIE-LYNN (sings) Elsie was a beauty
and she was a wild one
the only time she pleased the family
was when she married a banker's son

he enlisted in the Great War
there wasn't time to stop and grieve
Elsie knit mufflers for the men at the front
and slept with the ones on leave

CHORUS: Restless spirit dance, dance on
maybe if you'd lived today
all that drive and passion
might have found a way
Elsie won't you dance

Elsie took a notion
in nineteen twenty-five
left her husband for the man who taught her
how to sail the skies

tea time at the Empress
oh how the scandal runs wild
my dear I hear she's in the family way
and they say it's the flier's child

(repeat chorus)

BRIDGE: Together like outlaws into the heart of the north
Skeena mountains, Bellacoola
Gypsy Moth flying where no one had flown before

Peace River, South Nahanni
hard drinking, fast living, throttle wide open
till the fast life laid him low
it was never the same again after he'd gone
no, it seemed there was no place left to go …

hand-tinted photograph
of Elsie in her younger days
they say my sister's got her eyes
but I've got her wilful ways

(repeat chorus)

ACT II, SCENE 3

CORINNE: So me what I want to know is, what is it really like in Heaven? What are they doing there right now, Moïse, Calixte, *maman, papa,* my babies Lucien and Isabel? No one seems to know that much about it, *hein,* except that people are very happy there because at last they are with *le bon Dieu. Mais l'enfer!*[1] *Monsieur le curé là,* he can talk for hours about the eternity of pain and torture, the flames so hot they would make your furnace seem like a block of ice, and the terrible screams of the damned because the devils force them to eat hot coals — ah! (She shudders). But one thing I don't understand — how come the nuns and priests know so little about heaven, and so much about hell? *Ça a pas d'bon sens, ça!*[2] Anyway, it frightens me to hear them talk like that, because ever since I saw the angel (She crosses herself) I know heaven and hell are as real as this — table! *Bien sûr,* you don't believe me, no one did, they said I was dreaming, but I was never the kind to have my head in the clouds. *H-mf! Sainte Thérèse d'Avila* can well have seen her visions, what else does a nun have to do all day? But me — I was much too busy for that. Oh — I knew there were angels, I just never thought *I* would see one! But that summer night, there was *mon p'tit Lucien* — he was very sick, so crippled he could not walk, lying in a cot at the foot of my bed, so if he made a sound I was by his side, et *tout d'un coup*[3] I find myself wide awake and

---

1   But Hell!
2   That doesn't make any sense!
3   all of a sudden

sitting up in bed, for no reason, because everything is quiet. Then I see a pale light at the window, and something moving there. The light becomes a shape, like a man, a woman, or both together, and all silvery, the colour of moonlight. At its back, wings like a swan, and the face — ah! So strong, so peaceful. The angel moves over to the cot and gently, tenderly, he picks up Lucien, and oh! I will never forget as long as I live the sight of his poor little legs dangling over the angel's arm as they flew out into the darkness! Night filled the room again, I ran to the little bed, and oh I was so glad to see that Lucien was still there. (Pause) But when I touched him, *mon Dieu! Y'etait mort!*[1] *Y'etait mort!* Ah, when your mother or your husband dies, it is terrible, yes! But your own child! *Ca c'est le pire, ça.*[2]. For a while, all I could think of was the moment when I touched that cold, still little body. But then, I thought about the angel and I knew — Lucien is in heaven, and in heaven he can run and play like he could never do here on earth. So there is a real heaven, and my son is there. I saw the angel. And I know.

MARIE-LYNN: (sings) hier j'ai regardé dans leur coffre à jouets
ah si j'avais su tout ce qui m'attendait

une poupée endormie, étouffée de caresses
un ourson de velours tout bourré de tristesse
une étoile à la page de tous leurs cahiers
mon vieux coeur fait naufrage comme ce pauvre voilier

CHORUS:

et un rayon de soleil
une poignée de tristesse
adieu mes petits, adieu mes amours
adieu jeunesse

et des billes de cristal, souvenirs lumineux
coulent entre mes mains, comme des bijoux précieux
ensuite des timbres de tous les pays
venus par milliers se coller dans leurs vies
et les roses séchées de leur premières amours
un chapelet oublié qui attend leur retour

---

1   He was dead.
2   That's the worst

(repeat chorus)

> et un carnet fané qui retient ses secrets
> un peu comme on a fait
> et enfin un casse-tête qui manque des morceaux
> un peu comme entre nous

(repeat chorus twice: the first time *rubato,* with simple, childlike piano accompaniment, then in time, with full accompaniment)

ACT TWO, SCENE FOUR

ELSIE: (ELSIE is sorting bits of jewelry in her jewelry box.) What on earth am I going to wear to this wedding? I still think Barney's making a mistake. "Look," I told him. "Take that French girl out if you like, but do you have to marry her?" "Mother," he said, "you're being a snob. Besides, you introduced us." Well, that's not quite true. I'd met her sister Colette because she lives across the street. Of course, we'd never be in this part of town if it weren't for the housing shortage, but it seemed only polite when Ted and I threw a party for Barney to invite Colette. It turns out her sister is up visiting for the weekend so Colette brings her along and the next thing I know, Barney's sneaking down to Ottawa every chance he gets. We had quite a row about it.

CORINNE: (Finishes sewing dress.) *Bon, c'est fini.* Too late to change anything now. *Pauvre Moïse. Réellement,*[1] he took the news quite well, because he was fond of Thérèse, but maybe, deep down, who can tell? *Pis imagine,* me, I said to her, "Thérèse — ! You know how he is about the Church, your father! That's going to kill him, *certain, certain!*" (imitating Therese:) *"But maman, he's ninety-two years old! He's going to die of something, sometime!"* *"Thérèse, "là, là, tu blasphême!"* Of course, me I didn't mean really kill him, and she didn't mean it either, but — (she crosses herself) who could have known? *"Pardonnez-moi maman,"* she says. "You know how much I love *papa.* But I love Barney too …"

ELSIE: Well it's clear from the letter that arrived last week (she finds the letter) that my arguments had an effect — the effect of a red flag on a bull. "Dear Mother — hmf — he knows I prefer Elsie.

---

1   Actually

"Dear Mother,
Frankly, I'm surprised at the vehemence of your reaction. You spoke of differing backgrounds and cultures. You imply that her family has no position, no money, no style. What about you and Ted — talk about opposite worlds!" But that was different! Ted and I, we created our own!

CORINNE: *"L'amour, Thérèse"*, j'ai dit, "that's not the only thing to think about in marriage." "Yes, but what about the others," she says. "Yves, Cécile, Madeleine, Yvonne — they all married for love!" "Okay, okay, *c'est vrai, ça*, but at least they fall in love with Catholics!"

ELSIE: And then at the end he says, "I know you're also concerned about the long run. But mother, the long run doesn't count in wartime. I could be dead in two months." Oh god! I know he'll make it back, but I don't want him to come home to an unhappy marriage!

CORINNE: But she thinks Barney and her can be happy. Hmm. So, when she asks *"Alors maman,* you will come then to meet his mother?" I had to say yes.

ELSIE: But he wouldn't listen, so what could I do? I had to give the happy couple my blessing.

CORINNE: So Thérèse and me we take the train last Saturday to Montreal. Colette had invited Barney's mother for Sunday lunch, but she never showed up.

ELSIE: Meeting Thérèse's mother was a bit of an ordeal. And to make matters worse, I showed up late — a day late to be exact.

CORINNE: Thérèse and Colette they say, well she's been feeling very bad since her husband died, maybe she'll come tomorrow.

ELSIE: I don't quite know what happened. I was missing Ted terribly, so I had a few drinks, and the next thing I knew, I woke up and it was pitch black outside ...

CORINNE: Thérèse, she goes back to Ottawa on the train Sunday night, because she has to work the next day, *mais que voulez-vous,* I have to stay.

ELSIE: Well, it was too late to telephone so I had another drink and went back to bed. Woke up the next morning with the worst hangover of my entire life. However, I did feel awful about not showing up the day before so with shaking hands I dressed and put on my makeup. (Synthesizer underscoring begins here. Slightly dissonant, angular improvisation reinforcing the text and based loosely on "The Lady is Bored" melody.)

CORINNE: Anyways the next day Colette is at work, so, me, to pass the time I decide to make some pies, when I happen to look out the window and and I see this lady crossing the street. She's wearing a fancy hat, long gloves, earrings, bracelets, *pis une grande cape mauve*[1] — *imagine-toi!*

ELSIE: I had a small drink to steady myself, and then I set out to cross the street. The traffic was rather heavy …

CORINNE: And horns are honking, drivers are slamming on their brakes, but she keeps moving slowly, her head held up high, you would have thought she was the Queen of England, that one …

ELSIE: I was wearing very high heels and I remember at one point, it was quite embarassing, I stumbled …

CORINNE: Then oh! She falls. But quickly she's up again, like nothing has happened. And suddenly me, I think — *mon Dieu, c'est elle* — Elsie! All dressed up like that just to cross the street!

ELSIE: But I collected myself, and made it to the door.

CORINNE: *Ben moi,* I'm up to my elbows in flour, I can't even think what to do, when the doorbell rings …

(synthesizer underscoring ends here with a doorbell sound)

ACT TWO, SCENE FIVE

(Although the actors may each have used the whole stage at times before now, one should get the sense that ELSIE has now crossed into Corinne's territory.)

---

1   a big mauve(or purple) cape

CORINNE: (Wiping her hands on her apron.) Ah — *bonjour Madame*, excuse me, I —

ELSIE: Not at all. I take it you're Mrs. Allard.

CORINNE: *Oui*, Corinne Allard. And you are —

ELSIE: Elsie — Elsie … Dobbin.

CORINNE: (Looks puzzled but says nothing.)

ELSIE: (In accented but Parisian French and extending her hand.) *Je suis très enchantée.*[1]

CORINNE: *Et moi aussi, madame. Alors comme ça vous parlez français?*[2]

ELSIE: Well, I think it's a beautiful language. I even sent Barney to French camp the summer he was fourteen. But I'm afraid I speak — *seulement un peu.*[3]

CORINNE: Ah well, we speak English then.

ELSIE: Thank you.

CORINNE: Please, may I take your, euh, *cape*? ("cape" in French is pronounced like "cap" in English. Confused, ELSIE reaches for her hat) *Non*, your *cape* (gestures to ELSIE's cape) … And your hat, Mrs. — *euh* —

ELSIE: Dobbin. Mrs. Dobbin. Didn't Barney tell you? Mr. Hammond — died when Barney was very young, but he kept his father's name after I remarried and … (to audience) God, I hate lying so early in the day …

CORINNE: Ah, I understand now. We have a lot in common then.

ELSIE: We do?

CORINNE: Yes. Me too I was married before, and my first husband died. And now of course, we are both widows again.

---

1 I'm delighted
2 And so am I. So it seems you speak French ?
3 only a little.

ELSIE: Ah! I see what you mean. Yes, it's an appalling coincidence. When I heard that Mr. Allard had just died, I was shocked.

CORINNE: Well, he was a very old man. I knew it had to happen sooner or later. Anyway, sit down please. Would you like some tea?

ELSIE: Tea? Why, that would be lovely. Listen, Mrs. Allard, I want to apologize for not coming yesterday. But ever since Ted died, I …

CORINNE: Please it's all right. Thérèse told me about Mr. — *euh* — Dobbin, and I know it's always harder when these things are unexpected.

ELSIE: Nothing could have been more unexpected, believe me. I'm afraid I'm still in shock.

CORINNE: I understand. Barney said he was a flyer too?

ELSIE: Oh yes, a tremendous pilot! Such a waste, he was still very much in his prime.

CORINNE: Did he die in a crash?

ELSIE: Well, not exactly. Though it was an accident. (pause) Have you ever flown, Mrs. Allard?

CORINNE: (busy with tea things) Flown? In a plane you mean?

ELSIE: Yes, of course in a plane.

CORINNE: Oh I never wanted to. It frightens me.

ELSIE: But it's glorious — such a feeling of wildness and freedom …

CORINNE: Well anyway, it's not for me. Me I take the train. Besides, it's cheaper. (aside) If *le bon Dieu* had wanted us to fly he would have given us wings. (To ELSIE) Would you like some cream?

ELSIE: No thank you.

CORINNE: Sugar?

ELSIE: No. No thank you.

CORINNE: How about some pie? *Tarte au sucre?* There's one just out of the oven.

ELSIE: *Tarte au sucre?* Sugar pie? Well I'd love to, but I, uh, had a late breakfast.

(An awkward silence. Then they begin to speak simultaneously.)

CORINNE: And so Thérèse and — *excusez* —

ELSIE: Well, Barney tells me — sorry!

ELSIE: (nods graciously to CORINNE) Please.

CORINNE: And so your son he is marrying my daughter.

ELSIE: Yes. That's right. Your daughter is marrying my son. Thérèse is a lovely girl. When Barney told me, I was delighted.

CORINNE: And Barney is a very nice young man. Such — nice manners.

(CORINNE sips tea, ELSIE plays with hers.)

CORINNE: More tea, Mrs. Dob — ah! But you have not touched your first cup!

ELSIE: Well, I, ah —

CORINNE: You would like something else instead? Coffee perhaps, or, uh …(awkward pause)

ELSIE: Well to be quite honest Mrs. Allard — I suppose I'm rather nervous — what I'd really like right now is a drink.

CORINNE: (taken aback) A drink? Well, *bien sur* … I think Colette has some — some sherry. *Une minute, s'il vous plait.*

(As she crosses behind ELSIE to fetch the sherry and glasses she throws a disapproving look back over her shoulder.)

ELSIE: You are going to join me, I hope, Mrs. Allard.

CORINNE: (as she pours) *Oh non, non merci.* Me, I never drink.

ELSIE: Oh come now, a little won't hurt you. Good for the nerves, you know.

CORINNE: That's what my doctor tells me. But *my* nerves are fine. (She gives ELSIE a glass of sherry.)

ELSIE: (slightly cowed) Thank you. (rallying) But still, we really ought to toast this marriage.

CORINNE: Well — perhaps.

ELSIE: (Seizes bottle and CORINNE's glass.) Allow me. (She pours liberally)

CORINNE: (alarmed) Only a little please, *madame!* (Takes the glass from ELSIE) Thank you.

ELSIE: To the wedding of our dear children.

CORINNE: To the wedding.

(ELSIE drinks, CORINNE takes a sip)

ELSIE: Mrs. Allard, you do know we are not Roman Catholic?

CORINNE: (Taken aback but recovers fast.) Yes. Thérèse told me.

ELSIE: But doesn't your church frown on mixed marriages?

CORINNE: Well, yes. This is the first time in our family someone marries a Protestant. But you know Barney has to sign a paper saying the children will be — *voyons!*[1] — brought up in the church?

ELSIE: But won't it be confusing, one parent Catholic, the other one not?

CORINNE: Oh yes! That is why Mrs. Dobbin, I'm praying that Barney will

---

1   literally, "let's see." A French expression of frustration or annoyance — Corinne is trying to find the right words in English.

convert.

ELSIE: I wouldn't count on it. Like most flyers, he's not exactly the religious type.

CORINNE: Well, in that case, I shall just have to pray a little harder.

(They drink. ELSIE refills her own glass.)

ELSIE: Mrs. Allard — to be perfectly frank — I'm not sure this marriage is a good idea.

CORINNE: *Mon Dieu,* I did not know *les Protestants* cared so much — une *minute s'il vous plait.* Is religion really the problem for you?

ELSIE: That's just part of it. What I mean is, Barney and Thérèse come from such different worlds, different cultures, that, ah —

CORRINE (interrupts) Ah! You mean we're *canadien français?*

ELSIE: Well yes — I mean NO! That in itself is no problem, but in *this* situation — I mean, don't you think they're being rather precipitous?

CORINNE: *Pardon?*

ELSIE: Don't you think they're rushing into it? They're both fine people, but they've only known each other a few weeks. And without some common bond of shared experience, I don't think they stand a chance. Surely this is the same reasoning behind the discouraging of mixed marriages. I'd say your church is quite wise in that respect.

CORINNE: *Mon Dieu, un vrai sermon!*[1]

ELSIE: But to sum up my feelings, I'm afraid I have to say — this marriage absolutely *must* be stopped!

CORINNE: And me, I agree with you one hundred percent.

ELSIE: Good heavens, you do?

---

1   My God, a real sermon!

CORINNE: *Mais oui! Certainement!*

ELSIE: But I thought you'd accepted it — all that praying for Barney and so on ...

CORINNE: Mrs. Dobbin, in this case, praying was a — a last resort. Of course they should think about it more. Marriage is a big step — especially when there's no divorce.

ELSIE: Right! ... Well then, how do we stop them? Have you tried talking with Thérèse?

CORINNE: *Ah oui, ah oui, ah oui!* But you know how it is, after a certain age they won't listen to you! (ELSIE nods in understanding) "Thérèse," I said, "you mean we're going to have a wedding ten days after your father's funeral?" "Well," she says to me, "there's a war on, we can't wait." (piano enters softly) Barney's going overseas. Besides, it will be a very quiet affair, just the family, I'll wear my little grey suit ..." *"Mais écoute,"* I told her, "you hardly know each other!"

(MARIE-LYNN sings first verse of "Flying/Spring of '44." While she sings this and the following verses there should be a sense of time passing in the conversation between ELSIE and CORINNE.)

MARIE-LYNN: he had twelve days leave when she met him in Montreal
            they courted and then they were married
            he wore his uniform
            she wore her grey silk suit
            and a hat with a veil
            her mother shook her head and said
            you hardly know the boy

            but it was spring of '44
            it was such a crazy time
            and he seemed so brave, so full of glory
            and his eyes shone blue as the sky
            when he talked about flying

            "oh flying
            well the Hurricane is a damn fine plane
            and I wish you could see all the boys and me

doing loops and dives in tight formation
chasing the wind like eagles in the sun"

(Piano continues to underscore quietly during the following:)

ELSIE: (she has Barney's letter out) The trouble with Barney, as you can
           see, is he's so damn stubborn. Well, then he goes on, "I must try
           one last time to make you understand about Thérèse and
           me. You spoke of different backgrounds and cultures —."
           (breaking off, slightly embarassed) Et cetera ... "But Thérèse and
           I are very much in love, and we believe that love can transcend all
           the differences." Well of course it can, when it's real! But this (she
           indicates the letter), Mrs. Allard — I'm inclined to think it's just
           another wartime romance ...

MARIE-LYNN: it was spring again when she went to meet his train
           they sent him home a hero
           with medals and that look in his eye and a cane —
           she hardly knew him
           and most nights he'd wake up shaking and scared
           but he'd never tell her what he was seeing

           but it was spring of '45
           it was such a hopeful time
           when he was finally on the mend
           they'd sit on the porch and he'd watch the sky
           like he was looking for something

           oh flying
           sun on the silver wing
           it's so silent out there
           like a blue cathedral
           you can climb and climb till the earth falls away
           and you're finally alone now
           you've finally come home

(By now ELSIE and CORINNE appear quite at ease with each other. Piano
continues to underscore quietly during the following:)

CORINNE: (refilling *both* their sherry glasses!) Now when we were young, we
           would listen to our parents, we did as we were told. Isn't that right?

ELSIE: God, we certainly did ...

CORINNE: But nowadays, young people do as they please, and everything is for love. They don't think about the rest.

ELSIE: True, very true. But you know, Corinne, love's not such a bad thing when you've got it.

CORINNE: Perhaps you're right, Elsie. Anyway, there's nothing more we can do. Now it's all up to Thérèse — and her young man.

MARIE-LYNN: well the doctors told him he could never fly again
but a hero's a hero
and the Air Force takes care of its own
oh they let him fly a desk for thirty years
and except for the drinking nothing much has changed
ah, he's still got his medals and his aches and pains
still got his bad dreams
he's still the same stranger she met
at the train

but there was a boy in '44
he always talked of flying
and one day his plane took off
and you know, they've never come down
they're still somewhere flying

oh flying
sun on the silver wing ...

(Piano holds last chord until ELSIE begins to speak.)

ELSIE: Corinne, there's just one thing. What — what if it doesn't work out? What I mean is, sometimes — people make mistakes. They marry, and then later fall in love with someone else. I mean *really* fall. You know what I mean — it must have happened at least once in your life.

CORINNE: *Ecoutez,* Elsie, I married at sixteen to please my parents, and at twenty-three because me and my boys we needed a home. Then, eight more children, no money — when was there time for love?

ELSIE: Yes, but wasn't there ever someone who you, ah —

CORINNE: (agitated) *Oui mais, quand-même,* even if there was, what was I going to do? I was married! L'amour, that's for a day, a month ... but we both know, Elsie, that marriage, that's forever!

ELSIE: Forever? Nothing is forever ... (silent for a moment, then, more to herself and audience than to CORINNE) God, I'm tired of pretending. Twenty years of love, and twenty years of lies. But not by choice. "Douglas," I said, "I'm in love — I want a divorce." He refused. So I played what I thought was my trump card. "I'm pregnant again, but it's not your child — it's Ted's." But he wouldn't give in. In his own quiet way he got even, because all these years he's never changed his mind. So, we lied, Ted and I. But people knew we weren't married, that we were living in sin, as they so quaintly put it. And I, of course, was the scarlet woman, corrupting innocent youth. Ted even lost work on account of me, but he never complained. On the contrary. I remember one day out at the airfield he said, "Come over here, I've got a surprise for you." And there was Ted's brand new Gypsy Moth, with my name painted on the side in big bold letters for all the world to see! "I named her for the spunkiest woman I know," he said ... Well I don't know about that any more. Because being scandalous can wear you down. Takes energy, takes nerve, to ignore the unkind voices. As long as Ted was there, it was worth it, but now he's gone, and they're still talking! "Foul play," "crime of passion" — passion yes, but crime! (shakes her head) Whatever happened that night, I loved him! That's what matters! ..."Spunkiest woman I know ..." Well, maybe it's true? After all I am still here. Despite the pain I haven't done away with myself. It's just that I'm not sure what to do now ...

CORINNE: (More to herself and audience than to ELSIE.) I'm not sure what to do either. I'm too old to start a new life, but not so old that I should be preparing for death. Still, I am afraid, afraid of dying, because — I can't forget. Why? I made my confession, I did my penance. I said my rosary a thousand times to ask forgiveness ...! But then, there's Cecile, her hair curly, curly like a little lamb, and all the others — hair so straight you put a curler in and it springs right out again. Still Moïse, he don't say nothing because two weeks after, he comes out of the hospital and right away, of course, I'm pregnant again ... And who can say? Not even me, I don't know for sure. But either way it was a mortal sin. I made my confession, but for that to be forgiven, the

Church says we must be *pénitente,*[1] and I have tried, tried to be sorry... but that day, a day when I thought my life was over, he led me outside and oh! *l'été des indiens,*[2] such a blue sky, the sun so hot, and the smell from the apple trees behind the store...we stood under them, eating apples like children! And then Joe stopped laughing for a minute and took my hand and said, *"Corinne, ma belle Corinne"* ... *Mon Dieu!* No matter how hard I try, there is a part of me, that cannot, will not be sorry, for that *one* afternoon, I did exactly what pleased me ...

(Soft piano underscoring begins just after ELSIE starts speaking.)

ELSIE: Alright then, let people talk — what do they know of it? — Ted and I and that brave little plane, the wind rushing past us high over the mountains, the light so dazzling we seemed to be on fire — the truth is, I don't regret a thing.

CORINNE: That day ... the sun and the smell of apples ... his hair against my face ... yes, it was a terrible sin! But in my heart, it felt like ... only ... joy!

(ELSIE and CORINNE remain facing the audience. MARIE-LYNN moves to centre stage to sing. In the second verse, when she mentions *"maman,"* CORINNE turns towards her, smiling. ELSIE does the same at the word *"papa".*)

MARIE-LYNN: (sings) perdu sur une mer vaste et profonde
c'est pas qu'il manque de côtes pour atterrir
mais me voici encore entre deux mondes
je me demande comment il faut choisir

CHORUS: car j'ai la tête anglaise, j'ai le coeur français
pris au milieu, entre les deux,
je voyage sans fin
j'ai la tête anglaise, j'ai le coeur français
l'âme en conflit, toute ma vie
me voila triste marin

au clair de la lune, mon ami Pierrot
maman sang all the old French songs to me
papa would listen, though he never understood

1   penitent, i.e., repentant
2   Indian summer

yet to a child the world seemed as it ought to be

(repeat chorus)

then after childhood faded like a distant lullaby
the world broke into two with no clear path in view
but now time has turned me circles
turned me round again to see
two voices can become a single heart that speaks as one
and their songs still echo down through time to me

oui, j'ai la tête anglaise, j'ai le cœur français
ici au milieu, entre les deux,
je voyage sans fin
j'ai la tête anglaise, j'ai le coeur français
l'âme partagé, j'ai tellement voyagé
je serais toujours marin

(As the music plays out the last bars instrumentally, MARIE-LYNN smiles first at CORINNE, then ELSIE. The music segues into the "Elsie" song for the curtain.)

THE END

GLOSSARY

ACT I

SCENE 1
Rockhead's — Rockhead's Paradise Club, one of a handful of Montreal night clubs at that time that featured exclusively black music.

SCENE 3
TCA — Trans-Canada Airlines, the first federally operated passenger airline in the country. Incorporated in 1937, it became known as Air Canada in 1964.

SCENE 4
Firenze and Roma — the Italian names for Florence and Rome.

SCENE 5
"roll so many Red Cross bandages" — these bandages were long, wide strips of cotton that had to be rolled up by hand before being shipped overseas. It was common for women on the home front to volunteer for such tasks at the Red Cross Society.

Victory Rally — these rallies were designed to drum up support and raise money for the war effort.

Interprovincial Bridge — at the time the main bridge spanning the Ottawa River between the cities of Ottawa and Hull.

pontoons — a word commonly used at the time to mean the floats on seaplanes.

SCENE 6
Re "La jeune mariée": it was traditional in Quebec when naming a girl to include "Marie," (i.e. Mary, in honour of the Virgin Mary) among her given names. It was not uncommon for boys to have "Marie" as part of their first names too, and they were often given "Joseph" as one of their names in honour of St. Joseph.

ACT II

SCENE 1
The Imperial Order Daughters of the Empire — Now known as the IODE, this Canadian charitable women's organization was founded in 1900. In Elsie's time and long after it tended to be made up of women from established Anglo

families. Elsie uses them here to symbolize the conservative and "stuffier" elements of upper-class society.

Hansard — the official publication of the Government of Canada. I'm not sure Senate committee hearings would have been reported in Hansard; Elsie is no doubt exaggerating to make the point, that, given the circumstances, details of divorces quickly became embarrassing public gossip in a time when divorces were still considered shocking.

cerise-coloured dress — "cérise" means "cherry" in French. A cherry-red dress would have been considered flashy, loud, or "common" in Elsie's set at the time, especially in conservative Ottawa.

Curtiss Jennies — the Curtiss JN-4 (nicknamed a "Jenny") was a small biplane used to train pilots during WW I. After the war surplus Jennies could be purchased relatively cheaply.

the Château — the Chateau Laurier Hotel in downtown Ottawa.

The Empress — the Empress Hotel in Victoria, B.C., where they still, to this day, serve 4 o'clock tea in the British style.

Gypsy Moth — a biplane built by De Havilland that could be fitted either with wheels or floats.

SCENE 3
Sainte Thérèse d'Avila — a medieval nun famous for her mystical visions.

SCENE 4
Hurricane — fighter plane used by the Allies in WW II. By 1944 it had largely been supplanted by Spitfires and Mustangs in combat but was still used to train pilots.

"fly a desk" — ironic air force expression meaning that a flyer was (usually reluctantly) assigned to a desk job.

mortal sin — Roman Catholicism holds that dying with a mortal sin on your soul condemns you to hell. Mortal sins can be "erased," as it were, through the sacrament of confession, but confession requires sincere repentance. Corinne is troubled because she cannot fully repent.

"Au clair de la lune, mon ami Pierrot" — the first line of a well-known traditional French lullaby.

TRANSLATIONS AND CREDITS FOR SONG LYRICS

PROLOGUE

La tête anglaise, le coeur francais
music and lyrics: Marie-Lynn Hammond

adrift on a vast deep ocean
it's not for lack of shores I do not land
but I am caught in the gulf between two worlds
wondering how I can ever choose

for I have an English head and a French heart
trapped in the middle between the two
with my soul in conflict all the days of my life
I am a sad sailor

L'esclave (The Slave)
lyrics: Marie-Lynn Hammond and Marie-Thérèse Hammond
music: Marie-Lynn Hammond

Monday is wash day
Tuesday it's mending
Wednesday it's ironing
Thursday's for weaving

Friday's for heavy cleaning
all through the house
Saturday's shopping
followed by cooking
Sunday's for praying
followed by a big Sunday dinner
my God I'd like just two minutes to rest
because tomorrow, Monday morning,
it's all going to start again!

The Lady is Bored
lyrics and music: Marie-Lynn Hammond

There's A Battle to Fight
Lyrics (originally a poem): Elsie Hammond
Music: Marie-Lynn Hammond

Over Queen Charlotte Sound
lyrics and music: Marie-Lynn Hammond

La jeune mariée
music and lyrics: Marie-Lynn Hammond

When I was a young bride
(diddle-aille don)
my husband said to me
come along to bed
and nine months later
there's a little baby
is it a girl (another girl?) well yes
not a boy? well no (diddle-aille don)
So we have to choose her name
and we have to call her Marie something
Marie Cecile's a nice name
so call her Marie Cecile
Marie Cecile (diddle-aille don)

last verse:
another girl? well no!
it's a boy? well yes!
so we have to chose his name
and we have to call him something special
call him Joseph Jean Marie, etc.

Joseph Jean Marie — it's a boy! (diddle-aille don)

Where the Grey Sky Meets the Sea
Lyrics (originally a poem): Elsie Hammond
Music: Marie-Lynn Hammond

La chanson de Corinne
music and lyrics: Marie-Lynn Hammond

when Corinne was young she dreamed of love
and all the pretty things that a girl dreams of
but as the years went by those dreams disappeared
until all of a sudden, the unexpected happened
who is that smiling at the door
whose face is this that haunts her memory

ribbons of laughter, the lace of love
it's a shadow it's a dream, it's only a story

CHORUS: Monday is wash day
        Tuesday is ironing
        every day of the week we're trapped like slaves
        you do your best
        you do what you can
        and when that's not enough
        you pray to God

Corinne's still knitting mittens at ninety years old
a grey-haired grand'maman to her many grandchildren
where's the young girl? the young girl is gone
but in her heart the secrets and the dreams live on

CHORUS
tag:
you can't stop working
often you want to weep
but whenever you have the chance
you dance

Elsie
music and lyrics: Marie-Lynn Hammond

Le coffre à jouets
lyrics: Marie-Lynn Hammond and Marie-Thérèse Hammond
music: Marie-Lynn Hammond

yesterday I looked in their toy chest
Ah, if I had known what awaited me there
a sleeping doll, smothered with caresses
a velvet teddy bear, stuffed with sadness
a star on every page of their school books
and a sorry toy sailboat, shipwrecked like my old heart

CHORUS:
and a ray of sunlight
a handful of sadness
farewell my little ones, farewell my loves
farewell to youth

and crystal marbles, like luminous souvenirs
flow through my fingers like precious stones
next, stamps from all over the world
come by the thousands to glue themselves in their lives
and the dried roses of their first loves
a forgotten rosary that awaits their return

CHORUS

and a faded notebook withholding its secrets
somewhat the way we have done
and finally a jigsaw puzzle with pieces gone missing
somewhat the way it has been between us

CHORUS

Like the Sun

by VERALYN WARKENTIN

PLAYRIGHT

A writer, director, performer and playwright, Veralyn has worn many hats in both amateur and professional theatre. She has written for stage, screen and radio. Her works have been produced by CBC Radio, the Manitoba Association of Playwrights, the Winnipeg Mennonite Theatre, and the Tara Players.

Scripts include the one-woman plays *Chastity Belts, Family Rebellion* and *We'll Do Lunch.* as well as several educational dramas. Veralyn has a Master's degree in English (University of Manitoba) for which she wrote the play *Mary & Martha*, set in a home for domestic servants in 1950's Winnipeg, as a creative thesis. Her fiction and poetry have appeared in *CV2, Zygote* and *Absinthe*.

Veralyn has taught acting and creative writing in Winnipeg and on Vancouver Island. She has directed for Manitoba Theatre for Young People, (*Pandora's Box*) and *The Merry Wives of Windsor* for Winnipeg's "Shakespeare in the Park" (1995). She has been assistant director on numerous productions including Craig Lucas' *Reckless* (University of Manitoba) and at the Manitoba Theatre Centre (*Our Town, Lost in Yonkers, Hamlet*). The production which received the most media attention was *Hamlet*, starring Keanu Reeves.

Like the Sun was commissioned in 1995 by Winnipeg's Irish theatre, the Tara Players, as part of the international recognition of the 150th Anniversary of "The Great Hunger," the tragic Irish Famine of the mid 1840's. Veralyn was asked to write a play on the subject with a distinctly Canadian flavour. The play premiered in Winnipeg at the multicultural festival of *Folklorama*, and then was re-mounted at Irish Fest '95 in Milwaukee, Wisconsin, the largest Irish festival in North America. In Milwaukee the play caught the attention of companies from the United States and Ireland. *Like the Sun* received its first American production in Chicago by the Gaelic Park Players in May 1996. Then in June, with assistance from the Canada Council, Veralyn attended the international premiere of the play in Lough Gur, Co. Limerick, Ireland. Productions are also planned in Montreal and Toronto in 1996/97 as part of the ongoing world-wide Famine commemorations.

NOTES: THE IRISH FAMINE

The Irish have a long history that includes many hardships and struggles. Just before the Famine, the potato single-handedly fed over one third the population. In the 1840's, a potato blight and the starvation and disease that followed caused the deaths of approximately one million people and at least as many people left their homeland. Between 1841 and 1851 Ireland's population dropped by about two and a half million people. After this famine, a shortage of jobs and political and economic problems caused emigration to continue. As a result, little more than half as many people live in Ireland today as lived there in 1845.

The popular imagery of the Famine remains vivid even today. Mass graves, wholesale evictions, emaciated people helplessly and hopelessly searching a barren land for potatoes, desperate and diseased masses flocking to the ports in an effort to be anywhere but Ireland, and the so-called "coffin ships" leaving the country alongside corn-laden vessels — these are powerful and enduring images of the Famine.

Christine Kinealy, *This Great Calamity*

The imprint of Ireland made the Irish immigrants what they were, and when they brought that to America ... they passed on parts of the imprint to their children, their grandchildren, even to their great-grandchildren. Every Irish immigrant's story is unique and intensely personal. Usually, the details of these stories were stored away in the hearts and minds of the individual immigrants. There they were cherished, yet kept hidden for fear of reliving the pain of immigration or of conveying it to others who might not care or understand.

Kerby Miller and Paul Wagner, *Out of Ireland*

ORIGINAL CAST AND PRODUCTION TEAM

Like the Sun was first produced by the Tara Players on August 14, 1995 at the Irish Club Theatre in Winnipeg, Canada with the following cast:

John O'Sullivan	Tony Cohen
Kathleen Walshe O'Sullivan	Maureen Taggart
Father O'Shaughnessy	Brendan Carruthers
Thomas	Thomas O'Rourke
Granny	Mary MacMartin
Courtney	Rachael Niekamp
British Officer	Peter Bowes
Beggar Child	Alanna Cunningham
Patrick O'Brien	Stephen Meehan
Sea Captain	Paddy O'Rourke
Doctor	Pat Dunne
French Canadian Soldier	Stephen Kennedy

Directed by Carol McQuarrie & Pat McAvoy
Stage Management by Brad Sawatsky & Lyle Skinner

Lighting by Peter Roche
Sound by Stu Loeb
Costumes by Lucille LaPorte
Set by Ted McMartin, Joe Cunningham & Eirann Cunningham
Make up by Harlyne Muys

ACKNOWLEDGEMENTS

The playwright is grateful for the invaluable assistance of Maureen Taggart and Brendan Carruthers in the research and writing of this play. Heartfelt thanks to the Tara Players and all the cast and crew for their support and creative input in the original production. Thanks also to historian Dr. Michael Quigley of Hamilton.

For performance rights please contact:
Veralyn Warkentin
806 Preston Avenue
Winnipeg, Manitoba
R3G 0Z3
Phone: (204) 772-2701

DEDICATION

This play is dedicated to the memory of the thousands of Irish men, women and children, who emigrated to the abundant shores of Canada, but did not journey past Grosse Ile. May they be remembered as long as love and music lasts.

LIKE THE SUN

THE CHARACTERS

In the present (Canada):
COURTNEY KATHLEEN: early teens
GRANNY O'SULLIVAN: 55+

In the past (Ireland):
KATHLEEN (KATIE) WALSHE O'SULLIVAN: 35-40 years old
THOMAS O'SULLIVAN: 8-10, very thin.
WILLIAM JOHN O'SULLIVAN: 35-40
FATHER MATHEW O'SHAUNESSEY: over 50

The following roles may be double cast:

English Soldier: 30-40
Patrick O'Brien, friend of John O'Sullivan: 35-40
Captain James Samson, British seaman: 45-55
Dr. George Douglas, British-Canadian doctor: 35-50
French Canadian Soldier: 20's

All of these characters speak with Irish accents except:
English Soldier (the former an upper class accent, the latter a more lower class accent); the Captain and the Doctor also have British accents; French Canadian Soldier.

The past and present scenes take place in different areas of the stage. Lighting plays a large role in isolating the different scenes.

During the wedding, taped music may be used, but live musicians are preferable. These musicians also play the wedding guests, are part of the procession to the emigrant ships, and sing the spalpeen song with John.

Note: Quotation marks indicate when Courtney is reading directly from her history project.

SCENE ONE — THE LESSON

(As the play opens in the "past" side of the stage, perhaps in silhouette, we see the young boy, THOMAS, skipping stones as if on a lake. Dream-like, traditional Irish music of harp and strings underscores the moment.

Shift to: the present. A typical Canadian living room. COURTNEY & GRANNY. GRANNY knits, while COURTNEY pencils in last minute corrections to her project. The stage is strewn with history books, papers and an old family photo album.)

GRANNY: I'll be your audience, Courtney. Sure you can practice on me.

COURTNEY: "The Great Famine: 1845-1849." Nineteen-ninety-five marked the 150th Anniversary of the Great Famine in Ireland.

GRANNY: "The Great Hunger" t'was called.

COURTNEY: The Great Hunger. My history project is based on books I have read, and conversations with my Irish grandmother.

GRANNY: Here I sit, straining to hear.

COURTNEY: (louder) Her stories helped bring the lives of my ancestors to life.

GRANNY: You haven't heard half of them yet, child.

COURTNEY: (Handing Granny a small gift box.) I almost forgot. This is for you, Granny. To thank you for helping me.

GRANNY: (opening box) A shamrock is it?

COURTNEY: Symbolic of our people. Let me pin it on.

GRANNY: Away with you with that thing, Courtney Kathleen. The Irish have given a fine sight more than just to be thought of by shamrocks, leprechauns and Irish coffee! The Feast of Saint Patrick is celebrated the world over because we left Ireland. We gave the world our music, our dance and our stories. Sure we gave the world ourselves.

COURTNEY: I know, Granny. That's what I wrote about. (Returning to her paper.) "No other country has lost so high a proportion of its people to emigration. Today many times more Irish live outside their homeland than in it." Potato crops failed all over Europe. But only Ireland lost one quarter of its population. Over five years, one million people starved to death or died from disease. Another 1.5 million left Ireland.

GRANNY: And not because we wanted to. If God gives us the right to listen to an Irishman's heart, the first word to be heard would be "land."

COURTNEY: The land hasn't been Irish land since Cromwell. "Ireland's fate was sealed in 1801 with the Act of Union uniting Ireland and England."

GRANNY: It was more of a rape than a marriage.

KATHLEEN: The land wasn't owned by the Irish after that. And the rents were eighty to a hundred percent higher than in England—

GRANNY: Payed to the English landlords who didn't even live there.

COURTNEY: "In 1835, well over two million Irish labourers were without any kind of work except for the thirty weeks in the year when the land was cultivated." Granny, a family of five would starve unless an Irishman could have a patch of land for potatoes.

SCENE TWO — UP WITH THE SUN

(September, 1845. Lights up on a peasant's plot of land near Edenderry, Ireland. It is early morning, sound effects of birds. THOMAS enters carrying a bundle of kindling tied with rope. His clothes are clean, but ragged. He is met by FATHER MATHEW O'SHAUGHNESSEY.)

O'SHA: *Dia dhuit*[1], Thomas.

TOM: Good morning, Father O'Shaughnessey.

O'SHA: Where is your Father?

TOM: He's above in the half acre, Father.

O'SHA: Up with the sun, was he?

TOM: Yes, Father. We got the loan of a spade! My Dad, brought it home yesterday. He walked nearly fourteen miles for it, so he did.[2]

O'SHA: A spade you say!

TOM: Sorry, Father. Did I sound too proud?

O'SHA: You didn't indeed, Thomas. Sure that's grand. In this part of the country there aren't even twenty spades between 900 Irishmen.

TOM: And there's only one national school. But no hope of using that.

O'SHA: Don't let your mother hear that prayer, son. And where is she while your father is above with the digging?

TOM: She's washing the potatoes.

O'SHA: And your sisters?

TOM: Peeling the potatoes.

O'SHA: And what might you be doing?

TOM: Waiting to eat them. I'm gathering a few cipins[3] for the fire, to start the pot boiling.

O'SHA: Thanks be to God for the Blue Month, when that first pot of blessed praties[4] is set before us.

TOM: They were two long months, Father. I'm famished with the hunger.

O'SHA: I know, son. July and August — the Hungry Months — are always crosses to bear. All the praties eaten and the new ones not yet dug. Only the Lord and the Saints themselves preserve us.

TOM: Then why can't they preserve the praties, too, Father?

SCENE THREE — A FEARFUL MALADY

(WILLIAM JOHN O'SULLIVAN enters.)

JOHN: Well, Father O'Shaughnessey! I didn't expect to see you 'til month's end, for Michaelmas.[5]

O'SHA: True enough. But I came for two reasons. The Brennan boy and young Anna Hennessey from Mullingar are having their bans read on Sunday.

JOHN: And the child not yet seventeen. Sure and when they have the amount of marriage fees, a stool and pot to boil potatoes in — our children marry. Are they not too young, Father?

O'SHA: At least they'll have a companion in their suffering. If the hope for an Irish Catholic cannot be to get ahead of his parent's generation, at least he can strive to keep from going back. As you have, William John. I see you've fixed the roof.

JOHN: I did indeed — and the landlord raised my rent!

O'SHA: I've heard tell of that. A shame it is.

JOHN: You take some pride in your own home — and they make you pay for it! It's to take away our incentive, Father. To steal our dignity. But I don't regret it. Katie's happy. If I can't give her a wooden floor, at least I can give her a decent roof.

O'SHA: Aye.

(KATHLEEN O'SULLIVAN'S voice offstage calling THOMAS.)

JOHN: Thomas! Your mother'll be awaiting on them sticks. Off with you, now. I'm after telling you that.

(exit THOMAS)

You'll be joining us for "the bit and the sup?"[6]

O'SHA: Aye. And I'll already say the Grace: *Go mbeirimid beo ar an am seo arís.*[7] "May we all be alive and happy this time twelve month."

(They cross themselves.)

JOHN: But you say you came for two reasons, Father.

O'SHA: I did, John. Young Thomas said you've a spade to harvest the croker. Now tell me, man, how are they looking?

JOHN: A mite on the small side, but plentiful, thanks be to God.

O'SHA: Thanks be to God for that.

(KATIE enters)

KATIE: Father Mathew! I'm delighted to see you! You're just in time to share in the new potatoes.

O'SHA: God bless you, Katie. You're looking as fresh and young as the day I wed you! I'm glad you're here, Kate. I was just going to tell John. You've heard of a "fearful malady" in the potato fields in Europe? I had hoped to God Ireland would be spared. We've hardships enough as it is.

KATIE: The blight?

O'SHA: It's the front page of the newspapers. The crops about Dublin are suddenly perishing.

JOHN: It can't be. Take a look at my field, Father. It'll be a bumper of lumpers I tell you! It's just English propaganda — and they say we spin yarns.

O'SHA: I hope for all our sakes you're right. If the potatoes fail, it'll be longer than a few Blue Months of hunger. And how will the rent be paid?

KATIE: Rack-rent, Father. Sure 'tis a scourge to us and already stretching us as far as we can go.

JOHN: And just gone as high as my roof!

O'SHA: I don't want to nay-say, William John, but remember the Consolidations.[8]

KATIE: Fancy name they have for throwing families off the land the
             English wanted for grazing their cattle. For the sake of livestock,
             they'd leave an Irish family for dead!

JOHN: Don't be talking about evictions. We've breakfast waiting and a
             wedding on the horizon. (to Katie) The Brennan Boy — what's
             this his name is —

KATIE: Young Dermid? Sure wasn't he just last year out there hurling[9]
             with our Thomas? Next thing it'll be my young lad.

(THOMAS protests)

             Maybe John is right, Father. Do you feel that lovely warm breeze?
             It'll be another glorious day, thanks be to God. Sure isn't it a
             grand time for a wedding.

TOM: And for breakfast!

SCENE FOUR — MORNING, NOON & NIGHT

COURTNEY: The Irish had more names for the potato than the Inuit have for
             snow! "By 1845 the population of Ireland swelled to eight
             million. So many people, so little land, so much poverty. It only
             seemed to make matters with England worse. England's difficulty
             was Ireland's opportunity."

GRANNY: And Ireland's difficulty was England's opportunity! But I suppose
             I should't be saying "was."

COURTNEY: But the harshest blow wasn't English. It came from South
             America, across the sea hidden deep in the cargo hold of a ship:
             "Phytophthora infestans."[10]

GRANNY: Grand language for the blackest truth: The Blight. I remember
             my Granny telling me *her* granny said that every time the skin of
             a potato turned red, a child had died and been taken away by the
             fairies. But when the skin turned black … God help the nation
             that lives on potatoes.

COURTNEY: But Granny, why a famine when blight didn't affect corn, turnips and grain? It says here that "Pre-Famine Ireland was the granary for the remainder of the kingdom."

GRANNY: Grain couldn't be eaten. It had to be sold to pay rent to the absentee landlords. Indeed, in the west of Ireland, the Irish had forgotten even how to grind grain into meal. They knew no ploughing or sowing, only the "lazy beds."

COURTNEY: But what about the Indian Corn the government brought in? I read they bought over £100,000 worth.

GRANNY: There were no iron mills to grind grain or corn. And where there were mills, the task was so complex, it took days for proper grinding. In the end, if improperly cooked, it would only make the hungry sicker.

COURTNEY: So without the potato, the peasants were left with nothing.

GRANNY: At the start, everyone hoped the blight would die out before the crops did. Despite all their hopes and prayers the warm winds carried the blight through fields and villages fast as a March hare — or an invitation to a wedding.

SCENE FIVE — THE BLIGHT

(The wedding. Solemn sacred music, gradually shifts to lively, jig music of an Irish fiddle. KATIE, THOMAS, FATHER O'SHAUGHNESSEY & PATRICK O'BRIEN on stage. FATHER O'SHAUGHNESSY makes the sign of the cross.)

O'SHA: May God be with them and bless them.
May they see their children's children.
May they be poor in misfortune, rich in blessings.
May they know nothing but happiness from this day forth.
Amen.[11]

KATIE: It was a fitting blessing, Father Mathew. And if my poor grandmother were here she'd say, "May the Little People bring them good fortune."

O'SHA: Aye, Amen.

KATIE: She always said the Little People are never far away — and she was right. Sure they love to dance as much as I do myself.

O'SHA: That they do. And they love the drink as much as I do! Eh, Patrick? (PATRICK takes a swig from his whiskey bottle.)

KATIE: Do you believe in the Wee Folk, Father?

O'SHA: I do not. But they're there. And where is John gone to? Have you worn him out with all your dancing, Kate?

KATIE: No chance of that, Father. John said he'd be off at the flight of night to check the fields. And would you look at that, Father. It's the sun rising already.

O'SHA: And what of your fields?

KATIE: Not a sign of it, Father, thanks be to God. John was out there before we came to the wedding. All's well.
(lively jig music swells)
The sun is shining, the fields are glorious, we're here at the wedding — will you dance a jig with me, Father?

O'SHA: Sure you'd dance me off my feet, Katie Walshe O'Sullivan.

(KATIE AND FATHER MATHEW dance. THOMAS joins in. The dance is in full swing when JOHN enters. The look on his face stops them all.)

KATIE: John? You look like as if you've seen Lazarus raised from the dead.

JOHN: Tell me it's cold enough for frost, Kate.

KATIE: Frost, John? Sure, where would the frost come from? Wasn't it a lovely evening when we were coming?

JOHN: It must be cold enough for frost, Kate. For they're black. The fields. As far as the eye can see. Black.

SCENE SIX — VOICES

GRANNY: The potato harvest of 1845 was a miserable omen.

COURTNEY: It was just the beginning. "In 1846, the overnight rampages of the galloping blight made the harvest a total loss."

(Spotlight on O'SHAUGHNESSEY. Mournful music, mixed with moans and the voice of a woman keening underscores the following monologues.)

O'SHA: On the 27th of last month, I passed from Cork to Dublin. The doomed plant bloomed in all luxuriance of an abundant harvest. Returning on the 3rd, I beheld with sorrow one wide waste of putrefying vegetation. The wretched people were seated on the fences of their decaying gardens, wringing their hands and wailing bitterly the destruction that had left them foodless.[12]

(BEGGAR CHILD enters)

CHILD: If you please, Father. My mother and father told me to throw myself at the mercy of decent people.

O'SHA: Where are your parents, child?

CHILD: I have no parents no more.

O'SHA: Where are they?

CHILD: They dragged themselves to the graveyard, dug holes and laid themselves down. And now they're just ... waiting.

O'SHA: I confess myself unmanned by the extent and intensity of the suffering I have witnessed. Especially among the women and little children. Crowds of them were scattered over the turnip fields, like a flock of famishing crows, devouring the raw turnips. The conditions of the Irish poor at the best of times have been disturbing, but now this! I beg of her Majesty's government to attend to this. Pray do something.[13]

(Shifts back to:)

GRANNY: Legend in Ireland has it that in a December act of generosity, the young Victoria, Monarch of Great Britain, donated £5 for famine relief in Ireland. 'Twas a generous amount back then. The same day, the Queen also donated £5 to the Battersea home for dogs.[14]

SCENE SEVEN — THE EVICTION

(KATHLEEN screams. She and THOMAS cringe from the BRITISH OFFICER who is throwing JOHN out of their house.)

OFF: Get out, you Irish bastard!

JOHN: We've no food and I swear to God, no more money. How can I be paying you rent? We've nothing. Open your eyes, man! I've a wife and four children. My daughters are out begging on the road. For the love of decency —

OFF: William John O'Sullivan, as tenant of this property number 22 in the County Offaly, you are legally bound and obligated to make your payments. To date, you are ten months in arrears. Therefore we must exercise the Landlord's legal right of eviction —

KATIE: Extermination is what it is!

JOHN: Katie, please …

KATIE: We're not crows to be scattered out of a corn field!

OFF: You'd do well to silence your wife, O'Sullivan. Before we hold her in contempt.

(KATIE retreats)

JOHN: We've no where to go. Please. Think of my children. You'll be leaving us with nothing but the Irish sky over our heads. I vow, I pledge upon my honour —

OFF: The "honour of an Irishman" — that's rich!

JOHN: If you can just give me a bit more time, I will pay all back — three-fold. Please, sir. For the love of all that is holy —

KATIE: No, John! Don't beg. Such as these will not be swayed by compassion.

(OFFICER gives her a threatening look, then orders:)

OFF: Set the roof ablaze!

            (lighting effects simulate fire)

TOM: The peelers[15] are burning our house! Stop them, Dad!

JOHN: I cannot.

OFF: Take your belongings, but come nightfall, you're to be cleared off.
            And you're not to set foot on this land again.

(OFFICER exits. Suddenly THOMAS breaks free and tries to throw a stone at
the exiting OFFICER. In the nick of time, JOHN prevents this)

JOHN: No, Thomas! They'd think nothing of answering your stone with
            a bayonet! God as my witness, I'll not forget this day.

(KATIE falls to her knees and watches the fire for a time. JOHN timidly
approaches)

KATIE: I'm sorry, John.

JOHN: *Mavourneen dheelish*.[16] What could you possibly be sorry for? It's
            all their doing.

KATIE: I know. I'm sorry I was always after telling you to fix the roof.

(a bittersweet moment)

JOHN: We'll make it through, Kate. As we always have. You gather up
            your brood and I'll find us a place to lay our heads. We're used to
            no beds, but I'll find a ditch, out of the wind and fashion a roof
            out of straw.

KATIE: Almighty God may have allowed the blight — but the English
            created a famine!

SCENE EIGHT — THE COST

COURTNEY: In 1847, a British newspaper reported: "Sixty thousand men, including British soldiers and policeman were needed to enforce Irish emigration, collect rent, evict and level the houses of truant tenants." It also reported that the collection of those rents cost more than the British Government was taking in.[17]

SCENE NINE — THE STONE

(THOMAS & JOHN huddle together in a ditch. Sound effects of thunder, wind.)

THOM: Daddy … ?

JOHN: Yes, *vick machree?*[18]

THOM: What's that mean, Daddy?

JOHN: "Son of my heart," it means. I forget that the old tongue is dying out just like — (stops himself)
          (THOMAS takes a stone from his pocket.)
          What's that you've got there?

THOM: It's the stone I wanted to throw at the peelers.

JOHN: 'Tis a "cursing stone." From a cursed land. Cursed by the landlord that stole it from us. Let this be on that Englishman's head.

THOMAS: I'll keep it, Father, and think of the man who burnt our house and made my Mother cry.

JOHN: I'll not soon forget this day. Try to sleep now.

THOMAS: I'll keep this so *I* won't forget. Now, tell me again — as Granny did — of the Little People.

JOHN: 'Tis your Granny who knows the stories, Thomas, not I.
          (a pleading look from THOMAS) Aye, the Good People. I shall

79

tell ye, again then. The grass is full of them. But, you know, *vick machree,* they'd rather you call them "the gentry" — they're a bit peevish that way.

THOMAS: They're not like the gentry that smashed our house though, are they, Dad?

JOHN: No, no. Your granny'd say they protect us. And that they like to play games, to sing and dance. As we did at the wedding, remember? (THOMAS brightens) And they say, the Wee Folk are so little that when they dance on a drewdrop it trembles — but it won't break.

THOMAS: I want to dance on the dewdrops, too! If we can't grow anymore spuds, I'll soon be able to dance on dewdrops, too, won't I, Daddy?

JOHN: Try to sleep, now. And may the angels send you happy dreams this night.

(JOHN rises and moves downstage. KATIE enters, places her shawl over Thomas, feels his forehead, and then joins JOHN.)

KATIE: The girls are with my sister. There's a bit of weaving they can do, for their food. Did you hear me?

(JOHN is overcome with emotion.)

JOHN: We've nothing, Kay. I've not even a patched roof to cover your head. My son will soon be as thin as the twigs he gathers. But the only fire is that burning in his empty belly! I curse the landlord! And, God help me, I'm teaching my son to hate. What evils will come when I can only pass along a heritage of misery and unforgiveness?

KATIE: Sure haven't the English ill-treated us for 700 years.

JOHN: No. Six hundred and seventy-two.[19]

KATIE: Then it's time to leave this land.
(he stares at her in disbelief)
Eileen got a letter from her cousin that emigrated to New York. You should hear it, John. She says that "Everyday is like

Christmas Day for meat!" She says if she were back in the Old Country, she'd go back to America again. Sure all others, they say it's the best country in the world.

JOHN: It's fine for Eileen's cousin. How could we ever pay for passage to America? And we've no friends[20] there.

KATIE: I have! I've my father's brother in Quebec.

JOHN: Canada? It's just another England — with more space! We'll not be going to Canada.

KATIE: No. We won't. But I will.

JOHN: *Katie!*

KATIE: It's the only way through this, John. You'll earn enough as a spalpeen to get by and look after the children. The girls will be alright. With the help of God, they won't starve. I'm to go to Uncle Bill. They say there's plenty of work in Quebec City for maid servants. I'll make enough to support myself and send the remainder home to you until you've all enough for passage.

JOHN: My wife — traveling over the sea alone? I'll not have it.

KATIE: I'm to journey with Father Mathew. If I'm not safe to travel with my priest — then sure and the world is Sodom and Gomorah.

JOHN: Father Mathew is it? We've not money enough.

KATIE: Thanks be to God, there was a skill I learned besides peeling potatoes with my fingernails. Like a good Irish girl I learned to cut corners.

JOHN: Aren't you always after telling me that. "John, save a farthing where a farthing can be saved."

KATIE: And I learned to cut corners on the quiet. (Lowering her voice) At the foot of the Great Oak, on the north side, I've a small dowry buried deep in the earth.

JOHN: Would you go away with that! You're spinning me a yarn! Buried teasure? Woman, you've not had enough nourishment to keep your head working.

KATIE: All we need now is that spade of yours.

JOHN: We've no more spade. The police must have taken it for I found it nowhere amidst the wreck of our house.

KATIE: It wasn't in the house. When I heard the sounds of their old boots quaking up the road, I went to the field and buried it.

JOHN: You buried the spade?

KATIE: Aye. But it was easier than digging it up will be. But with spade in hand, we'll go get that money.

JOHN: If this is the God's truth, why did you never tell me? How much is there?

KATIE: Enough. We've £4 15s.[21] (JOHN makes the sign of the cross & murmurs "Jesus, Mary & Joseph" under his breath.) Enough for a bit of food and passage for myself … and young Thomas.

JOHN: Thomas! He's too weak to stand — let alone travel.

KATIE: That's why I won't leave him here. You'll be wandering from town to town as a spalpeen,[22] and he's too much for my sister with all the others. The girls will be all right. With the help of God they won't starve. I'll tend to Thomas myself. He needs the nourishment he can only get in a new and healthy land — a golden land.

JOHN: I don't want you to go, Kate. The idea chills me to the marrow of my soul. It just feels wrong.

KATIE: It's hunger that feels wrong! It's the weeping of my children from the hunger that feels wrong! The spade that split my heart like a rotten potato when they burnt down our house — that feels wrong! You tell me one thing in Edenderry that's right anymore — that's right in all of Ireland? I'm going with Thomas to that Golden Land. So don't try to stop me.

SCENE TEN — RAINBOW PROMISES

(Solemn, traditional Irish music begins quietly under following:)

COURTNEY: "In 1847, my great-great grandmother and her Thomas along with so many others, left Ireland. Driven from the land that long before had been taken from them. Impoverished, and degraded, they journeyed only on rainbow promises of a Golden Land where they wanted to believe, though it was often winter, it was always Christmas."

SCENE ELEVEN — EMMIGRATION AND EXPORT

(Music swells as we see procession of emigrants. FATHER O'SHAUGHNESSY enters, followed by KATIE in a travel cloak, her arm around THOMAS, JOHN follows carrying a small satchel, PATRICK O'BRIEN and other MUSICIANS complete the procession. They are accompanied by the sounds of the village church bell. The FATHER turns to the crowd making the sign of the cross and this blessing:)

O'SHA: *Slan agus beannacht Dia oirbh go leir.*[23] Good bye and God's Blessing on you all.

(KATIE and JOHN embrace. There is a trace of awkwardness between them. Then JOHN embraces THOMAS. He is reluctant to let him go. FATHER MATHEW draws THOMAS from him. Exit FATHER MATHEW, followed by KATIE and THOMAS and one or two musicians. JOHN stands alone with his spalpeen friend, O'BRIEN at the dockside. Sound effects of ships, water, seagulls.)

JOHN: What desperation drives men from the soil of their nativity and the land of their fathers' graves?[24]

(Faint music of an Irish jig.)

O'BRIEN: You'll be seeing them again before you can say Ballyclare and Carrickfergus.

JOHN: Where's that music coming from?

O'BRIEN: They're playing on the ship, to ease the pain of leaving.

JOHN: As if you can ease the pain of a people leaving their homeland. Are we not a study in contrasts, Patrick O'Brien? The sun beaming down overhead, the birds in the hedges, serenading as my wife and child leave their home and leave my heart like stone. (O'BRIEN is distracted and looking in another direction.) Are you not listening to me?

O'Brien: Look at those ships, John. They're guarded by armed soldiers.

JOHN: They're bound for England, aren't they?

O'BRIEN: Aye. But there's twice the usual number of guard.

(They exchange a look. Then move stealthily. Absolute disbelief appears on their faces.)

JOHN: Meat! Vegetables! Eggs! They're taking the food out of our mouths and shipping it to England! They're shipping out our food, while the people here starve.

O'BRIEN: I wouldn't believe it if I hadn't seen it with the two eyes in my own head! In the name of God, what's going to become of us all?

JOHN: The food that would give my young lad nourishment and keep my family together is being exported, while the Irish people die.

O'BRIEN: This is a sight I shall never forget.

JOHN: As long as grass grows and water runs, I'll not forget this day.

SCENE TWELVE — FACTS

COURTNEY: "In all the famine years Ireland was actually producing enough food, wool and flax to feed and clothe not eight million people — but eighteen million." [25] Eighteen million!

GRANNY: What's the use of that knowledge, child? What can't be changed, must be endured. And even if it can't be understood — still it must be forgiven. If not, hatred will rot you from the inside out, as sure as the blight did the potato.

SCENE THIRTEEN — LETTERS

(Spotlight on KATHLEEN. She recites a letter home.)

KATIE: My dear and loving husband and daughters. We've not been out to sea more than a day but already I miss ye. It was all I could do yesterday not to run up on deck and try to swim ashore. I thought I was alright in small spaces, after the ditches, but in the heart of the vessel, you can't stand up straight. Thomas says he feels like Jonah in the belly of the whale. But alas, it broke my heart to tell him we'll be here longer than three days and three nights. Your loving wife and mother, Kathleen.

(Spot shifts to:)

O'SHA: Like vultures, the shipowners have packed us aboard. We're little more than paying ballast. Double tiers of berths hold four adults, leaving each soul only the barest eighteen inches demanded by law. As I lay in my bunk, arms at my side, struggling for breath, I thought I was aboard an "ocean hearse."[26]

(Spot shifts to:)

KATIE: We've been over a fortnight at sea. The heavy waves add to the misery of the sick. They've battened down the hatches to keep us from a drenching, but many have been overtaken by a powerful fever. There's not food and water enough. It made my heart bleed to hear the cries of "Water, for God's sake water" in the hold. It troubles me most to hear the cries of the little children. I'm doing my best to keep Thomas safe, but there is no escaping those with the fever. Thanks be to God and His Blessed Mother, I am still strong, so do not worry yourself about me.

(Shift to:)
O'SHA: I thought I had witnessed all the horrors of this life watching my people starve in their wracked homeland. Now this. Bodies wrapped in white blankets, tied with rope, looking like small masts, slid down a ramp into the sea. At least six bodies have I seen in this way go to their Maker. The heavy weather and storm has left the rest of us frantic with despair. Many are giving up hope. But I have confidence in the Lord that He will not see us perish. In last night's tempest, I went round to all my friends and neighbours for a last farewell. But our cries were loud enough to

rise above the storm and reach heaven. Thanks be to God, the ship made it through. It is now only this galloping fever I worry over. I have seen this at home. The "Black Fever" — Typhus. It killed so many, the English have called it "Irish Fever." Now young Thomas O'Sullivan has taken ill.

(KATIE and FATHER MATHEW exit as SEA CAPTAIN enters. He tips his hat, KATIE snubs him, rushing past.)

(Spotlight shifts to:)
BRITISH SEA CAPTAIN: Ship's Log, The Pandora, Captain James Samson, Day 47, Port of Departure, Liverpool en route to Quebec City.
It is the worst case of ship's fever I have ever witnessed in fifteen years as Captain of a vessel. Hundreds of poor people, men, women, and children of all ages, from the drivelling idiot of ninety to the new born babe. Huddled together without light, wallowing in filth and breathing a fetid air, sick in body, dispirited in heart, fevered patients lying beside the sound. It's little wonder the Canadian officials say they can smell an emigrant ship at the distance of a gunshot. No food or medicine, with only the quiet voice of spiritual consolation from Father O'Shaughnessy, who cannot minister to all the dying.
They came aboard my ship ghastly, yellow looking spectres, unshaven and hollow cheeked. Evicted from their homes, debilitated by lack of nourishment from the potato failure, demoralized in spirit, they're indifferent to death. It has cleft my heart in twain to know I am commander of a coffin ship. [27]

(CAPTAIN exits. General lights up.)

SCENE FOURTEEN — THE BLUE FLAG

(KATIE is on board. O'SHAUGHNESSY enters.)

O'SHA: There you are, Katie. What are you doing out on deck, alone?

KATIE: Don't scold me, Father, but I thought I would smother down below. Thomas finally fell asleep, so I stole up here. I'm dying to set foot on land — Ireland more than anywhere else — but I'll settle for the shores of Canada.

O'SHA: You'll soon have your wish, Katie. We're sailing up the St. Lawrence River now. Quebec City is not more than thirty miles upstream.

KATIE: I saw two other ships.

O'SHA: Other shiploads of immigrants. (Pointing) The Captain said that one is from the Continent, carrying Germans, and he thought the other held Scots.

KATIE: They'll be as happy as ourselves to set foot on land. Father, is that Quebec?

O'SHA: It's an island. We're entering what they call an archipelago. The Captain was telling me. There are some twenty odd islands in this part of the river — that one is the largest.[28]

KATIE: They must soon take the sick ashore, before we lose anymore poor souls to the sea.

O'SHA: How they'd ache at home if only they knew.

KATIE: Ah, leave me alone, Father. Sure John is already out of his wits about us. He was against this from the first. But it can't be as bad as the Ireland we left behind.

O'SHA: A father has a right to know about the condition of his son, that's all I'm saying on the subject.

KATIE: There's medicine in the cities. My Thomas just needs nourishment and he'll be alright. The motto of my family — the Walshe's — Father, is: "Pierced but not slain."

O'SHA: Is it? I thought it said "Don't cross me"!

(Shouts of sea men preparing to dock. Sound effects of the boat docking.)

KATIE: We're pulling in to that little island. Why are they hoisting a blue flag?[29] Quebec City is still up the river, you said.

O'SHA: The immigrant ships must make a stop here first.

KATIE: But look, Father, the other two ships — the Scots and the

Germans — they're sailing on.

O'SHA: The Captain said it's only the Irish and British based ships must stop here.[30]

KATIE: But what's "here," Father?

O'SHA: It is called Grosse Ile. It's an island. A quarantine island.

(KATIE stares at him in fear.)

SCENE FIFTEEN — CHOLERA BAY

(Grosse Ile. The CAPTAIN carries the limp body of THOMAS across the stage. KATIE, is frantic and held back by FATHER MATHEW.)

KATIE: No! Let me go! I must go with Thomas. Stop! You've got to stop the launch!

O'SHA: They're keeping the healthy passengers apart from the sick until the ship's fever abates.

KATIE: Where are they taking him?

O'SHA: The western part of the island. It's called the "Cholera Bay sector."

(KATIE fights even more.)

KATIE: Cholera! Let me go! They're not going to take him there!

O'SHA: KATIE, stop it! They'll not hear you.

KATIE: Sure, he's only a child. I don't care about the Fever. I haven't caught it yet. Tell, them, Father, tell them. They'll listen to you.

O'SHA: I'm just a man of the cloth. I have no jurisdiction here.

KATIE: If **you** don't then what's to become of us? Where is God, then? Where is God on this island where they keep a child from his mother?

O'SHA: Will you calm yourself, woman. I'm sure he'll be taken care of. God is with him — even if you can't be.

SCENE SIXTEEN — REPORT FROM GROSSE ILE

Spotlight on DR. GEORGE DOUGLAS:

June 10th, 1847, Weekly report from Grosse Ile: We are sorely ill-prepared for the number of immigrants fleeing the Famine and the rampage of the fever. In April, the new hospitals were equipped to care for 200 sick, and there was space for another 800 "healthy". Now we've already 530 sick and — God help us — 40-50 deaths per day; the like of which I've never seen. The hot weather is increasing the evil. With the typhus epidemic, both the hospitals in the western part of the island and the shelters and tents in the east are not enough. I am still able to supervise the medical work, but I fear my health is failing. I go from one end of this two and a half kilometre island to the other. We are recording the names of the immigrants; and the names of the dead. A Father Mathew has joined the other priests, some of whom are Anglican, but still serving the ill Catholics. We are already using both of their chapels as hospitals. The nurses are loyal, but near exhaustion and there are workers who desert for fear of infection. We don't know how to keep the healthy as they are. The army has been brought in to police the island, but the more determined still visit their sick friends and relatives in the lazarettos. Your servant, Dr. George Douglas, Medical Superintendent at Grosse Ile. [31]

Shift to:

GRANNY: You can be sure it was my granny, Kathleen Walshe O'Sullivan, who was one of those to sneak past the army. She had to be near her Thomas. So the nurses let her stay outside his room. Through a window she sang to him and told him stories from the homeland.

(Mournful music. In silhouette we see FATHER MATHEW making the sign of the cross.)

COURTNEY: "In the year known as 'Black '47,' on a small Canadian island, the terrible wails of loss that had echoed through every Irish village since 1845 were heard once more." [32]

SCENE SEVENTEEN — "MY SUNSHINE YOU WERE"

(Lights up on FATHER MATHEW and a Canadian soldier upstage, behind KATIE who kneels beside THOMAS' grave, marked by two spades, formed into a cross.)

KATIE: My sunshine you were. I loved you better than the sun itself; and when I see the sun go down, I think of my boy and my black sorrow. Like the rising sun, he had a red glow on his cheek. He was bright as the sun at midday. But a storm came, and my sunshine was lost. My sunshine will never come again. Cold and silent is his bed.[33]

(Awkwardly, trying to be gentle, the FRENCH-CANADIAN SOLDIER steps forward.)

SOLDIER: *Madame, pardon.* Forgive me, but we must move along now. You must go …

KATIE: Where is there for me to go?

SOLDIER: It is very sad about your son, *Madame,* but there are others …

KATIE: Three daughters, yes. But Thomas was our only son. (She breaks down.)

SOLDIER: *Oui, Madame.* There are others I must attend to. This is not usually what I see. On Grosse Ile there are so many children left alone, so many orphans. They don't know where to go, either. *Excuse, Madame.* We must escort you back to Cholera Bay. We have orders to unload soil from Montmagny. On Grosse Ile, the earth is too thin. Six men are always needed to dig the mass—

(FATHER MATHEW angrily steps forward and cuts him off.)

O'SHA: We understand, Soldier. I'll be sure this woman gets back. Leave us for a few moments, please. You must follow your orders, as I must follow mine.
(The SOLDIER bows and exits. After a moment of silence, FATHER MATHEW places his hand on her shoulder.)
We must go, now Katie. I must get back myself. I've been called back to Ireland. I'm to sail tomorrow.

KATIE: He doesn't know, Father. I picked up my pen countless times to tell him. But I couldn't.

O'SHA: Of course you couldn't.

KATIE: Father, there's a chill in my heart as cold as the wind off the sea.

O'SHA: I know there is, child.

KATIE: I know Thomas is at peace, but it's John I'm worried about now. I'm afraid he'll never forgive me for taking Thomas away from him. He had a terrible fear of us leaving — but I wouldn't listen.

O'SHA: I'll tell him in person.

KATIE: You'll tell him. You'll tell him everything?

O'SHA: Aye, everything.

KATIE: You're my strength, Father.

O'SHA: You're our strength, Katie. You're our rock. I'll send word back to you at your Uncle Bill's as soon as I arrive home.

KATIE: No, Father. I'll be staying here where I am needed. Sure I was used to caring for my own brood. I will be a mother to those that need me — and they'll all be my Thomas. This island is where I'll stay until John and my girls come.

SCENE EIGHTEEN — MESSAGE FROM GROSSE ILE

(JOHN O'SULLIVAN rests on his spade. He is listless and exhausted. In the distance we hear a song, as song by the spalpeen workers. FATHER MATHEW enters and listens to the last few measures of the song before recognizing JOHN.)

O'SHA: John — is that you, John?

JOHN: Father Mathew! I didn't think I'd see you till I arrived in Canada! She's not come back with you has she? Is that why I haven't heard from either of you in a fortnight? Kate said she'd be a servant

91

there, but I can't imagine her letting any Colonist tell her what to do.

(FATHER MATHEW steps to him and places both hands firmly on his shoulders.)

O'SHA: It's not Katie, John.

JOHN: (breaking away) *No!!*

O'SHA: We never reached Quebec City. It was on the quarantine island. The Fever. He was too weak from the first to fight it. He went quietly, in his dreams. Will you come out to the chapel with me and we'll light a candle —

JOHN: Don't talk to me about the Church, Father. I swear I'll not rest till I see the landlord who drove us from our homes hanged! It was the night air in the ditches that finished him. It was the landlord that murdered my Thomas, not the Fever.[34]

O'SHA: Katie's afraid you won't forgive her for taking Thomas away from you.

JOHN: Kate? How is she?

O'SHA: She said to tell you that she is "Pierced but not slain." And she made a vow to Thomas that she would give you this —
            (he hands JOHN the small white stone)
            Thomas said he kept the cursing stone in his pocket ever since he left Ireland. It would dig into his leg while he tried to sleep, but he wouldn't part with it. He kept it close to help him remember what his father had said. But in the fever shed, on the last night, he asked one of the Canadian nurses to take the stone and place it beside his pillow instead. When he opened his eyes in the morning, he told the nurse that when he put aside the cursing stone, for the first time, he could truly rest. Thomas said to be sure and tell his father to do the same.

(Quick fade as JOHN stares at the stone in his hand and begins to sob.)

SCENE NINETEEN — THE CELTIC CROSS

[COURTNEY: "Today, wooden crosses still mark mass graves in four cemeteries. Grosse Ile became the final resting place of over 13,000 Irish men, women and children. Outside of Ireland, it is the most important and profound Great Famine site on earth. "

GRANNY: Some say it's "the most westerly graveyard in Ireland."

COURTNEY: "In 1992, Parks Canada announced a plan to turn Grosse Ile into a theme park: 'Canada: Land of Welcome and Hope.' The backlash and outcry from Irish Canadians stopped them in their tracks."

GRANNY: And that Brian lad Prime Minister at the time, too. A fine Irishman he turned out to be!

COURTNEY: "An international storm of protest, ranging from Canada, the U.S. and Ireland insisted Grosse Ile not be turned into a playground for boaters, but a shrine to their Irish ancestors, and a testament of the generosity of the Canadians who took them in."

GRANNY: Sure the Irish harp itself is part of Canada's national seal, recognizing our contribution to the foundation of Canada.] 35

COURTNEY: "A few years later, when the money was raised my great-grandfather joined his Katie. John O'Sullivan started with Canadian Pacific while Katie worked as a domestic —"

GRANNY: Learning to cook more than just potatoes!

COURTNEY: When did they move to Winnipeg?

GRANNY: After their daughters married and settled in Quebec, John got a job in construction with Kelly Brothers and Company. Thomas Kelly was originally of Roscommon, Ireland.

COURTNEY: I read about him. He built St. Andrews Locks and the Free Press Building and wasn't there some scandal about "The Ledge"?36

GRANNY: There wasn't a really a scandal until the conviction. And he never did go to prison.

COURTNEY: Let's see, Thomas Kelly, Brian Mulroney. I heard the Irish also gave the word "whiskey" to the English language.

GRANNY: (brightly) We did surely!

(COURTNEY returns to her paper.)

COURTNEY: "In 1897, to mark the Fiftieth Anniversary of the events of Black '47, a group of the Ancient Irish Order of Hibernians visiting Grosse Ile were shocked by the sad neglect of the gravesites. They began a twelve year campaign which culminated in the unveiling of a monument to preserve the memory of those who were buried there.

(KATHLEEN and JOHN, now in their 90's slowly enter and stand gazing at the Celtic Cross. They are dressed in late 19th Century costumes.)

On August 15th, 1909, on the heighest point of Grosse Ile, they unveiled a 46 foot high, Celtic Cross made of granite. Inscriptions are written in three languages: English, French and Gaelic.

(Lights up on model of Celtic Cross, upstage centre.)

'Sacred to the memory of thousands of Irish emigrants, who, to preserve the faith, suffered hunger and exile in 1847-48, and stricken with fever, ended here their sorrowful pilgrimage ... Thousands of the children of the Gael were lost on this island while fleeing from foreign tyrannical laws and an artificial famine. GOD BLESS THEM. GOD SAVE IRELAND.'

GRANNY: God Bless Ireland.

COURTNEY: My great-grandparents joined this 1909 pilgrimage to Grosse Ile.

(JOHN steps to the edge of the stage.)

GRANNY: It was there, after the unveiling of that Stone Cross and a visit to the grave of their Thomas, that John O'Sullivan took a quiet walk to the water and hurled the cursing stone into the St. Lawrence.

(JOHN throws an imaginary stone into the audience. KATHLEEN looks on.

JOHN joins her at the foot of the Celtic Cross.)

COURTNEY: "Like a people reborn, the survivors of those lazarettos — like Lazarus himself — came back to life. And now the descendents of the Irish in Canada number 3.5 million. Like the sun, though hidden for a time, the Irish people rose again."

GRANNY: During the Famine, an Irish priest in America said that "Ireland had more lives than the blackest cat; she has been killed so many times that her enemies are tired of killing her, and there she is, as provoking as ever, ready to be killed again." Well, I may not wear the shamrock but I will wear this wee black cat and remember. They shall be remembered as long as love and music lasts.

COURTNEY: As long as love and music lasts.

(Lively jig music, as in the wedding scene. COURTNEY and GRANNY turn to the photo album. On the other side of the stage, JOHN, KATIE pose solemnly in front of the Celtic Cross. The other characters enter, THOMAS stands between his parents, the other characters behind. They all hold the pose. Lighting gives the look of a black and white photograph.

Fade to black.)

FIN

WORKS CONSULTED

Fallows, Marjorie R. *Irish Americans: Identity and Assimilation*. Prentice Hall, 1979.

"Great Disasters," pamphlet. Ed. Ron Watchorn. Readers' Digest.

Grosse Ile: Report on the Public consultation Program, Canadian Heritage/Parks Canada, March 1994.

Ideas: The Famine Irish in Canada. Transcript of Canadian Broadcasting Corporation radio program, first aired in 1994.

Kinealy, Christine. *This Great Calamity: The Irish Famine*. Dublin: Gill & MacMillan, 1994.

Nikiforuk, Andrew. *The Fourth Horseman*. Toronto: Viking, 1991.

O'Gallagher, Marianna. *Grosse Ile: Gateway to Canada, 1832-1937*. Quebec: Carraig Books, 1984.

Potter, George W. *To the Golden Door: the Story of the Irish in Ireland and America*. Boston: Little & Brown. c. 1960.

Public Consultation: Grosse Ile, National Historical Site, Development Concept. Environment Canada, March 1992.

Woodham-Smith, Cecil. *The Great Hunger*. New York: Harper and Row, 1962.

ENDNOTES

1 Traditional Irish or Gaelic greeting. Literally "God be with you," pronounced "Dia Guithe."
2 Potatoes were grown in "lazy beds"- a long row of earth in which seed potatoes were planted. "Lazy bed" potatoes required only a spade and a few days' work a year. A family, in a good potato year could live off "lazy bed" potatoes grown on as little as three acres of land.
3 Kindling or small firewood; pronounced "Kip-eens."
4 Potatoes, this staple in the diet of the Irish poor, had many names including: praties, or praithies, pratha, crokers, lumpers, spuds, taties or taters.
5 A church festival in honour of the archaengel Michael celebrated September 29th. Pronounced "Mickel-mas."
6 A common expression meaning: "will you join us for a bite to eat?" Originally referred to the standard meal of skim milk or buttermink, and salted potatoes.

7   Irish blessing; pronounced: "Gu Me-mid Beho Air An Amh Shu Arisch."

8   After 1815 Ireland underwent a transition period of some distress. Impersonal economics by landowners and proprieters created the decision to consolidate small farms into larger tillage holdings or into pastureland for grazing cattle. To the Irish Catholic "consolidation" was "extermination". It was also called "clearance" but rather than clearing the land to make wilderness suitable to human habitation as pioneers did in North America, in Ireland to "clear the land" was to throw off people, pull down their houses, and make a wilderness for grazing cows.

9   The Irish national sport using a small, hard leather ball, resembling lacrosse but played with a broad-bladed, netless stick.

10 Potato disease was unknown in Ireland. Prior to 1845, the potato crop was periodically attacked by two main diseases commonly referred to as "curl" and "dry rot." Neither of these had been as destructive as the blight. The unknown blight which was attacking the potato crop throughout Europe in the summer of 1845 was caused by the fungus "phytophthora infestans." The disease was thought to have originated in South America from where, facilitated by improvements in sea transport, it eventually made its way to Europe. The fungus initially attacked the potato leaves and then spread through the foliage to the actual potato. Some contemporary accounts described the blight on the potatoes as having the appearance of soot. The plant decomposed rapidly, the potatoes withering, turning black and finally rotting, emitting a putrid smell. (*The Great Calamity*, p. 33)

11 Traditional Irish Blessing.

12 *Great Disasters*, p.3. Based on a letter written by a Father Mathew in 1846.

13 *Great Disasters*, p.4. Based on letter by a relief official.

14 "Queen Victoria is often depicted as one of the villains of Famine mythology. A popular belief is that she gave a mere five pounds to help the starving people in Ireland but simultaneously donated a far larger amount to a dogs' home. In fact, the Queen donated over £2000 to Famine relief and, in the face of hostile British public opinion issued a Queen's letter asking for more public donations." (Kinealy, p.xviii.)

15 Peelers or bobbies were the police paid for by the English government.

16 Irish for "my sweet one"; pronounced "Ma-vorneen dee-lish."

17 Marianna O'Gallagher, *Grosse Ile: Gateway to Canada*, p. 56.

18 Irish for "son of my heart"; pronounced "vick-mah-cree."

19 George W. Potter, *To the Golden Door*, p. 93.

20 Refers to relatives. The pattern of Irish immigration was to travel from rural Ireland to their relatives in American cities thereby re-establishing a similar community in the new world.

21 Four pounds, fifteen shillings — a fair amount at the time. Probably just enough for ships passage for two.

22 Spalpeens were itinerant day labourers on farms.

23 Priest's blessing. Pronounced: "Slaan augus bean-nacht dia oriv gu lehir."

24 Based on quote by John Quincy Adams as quoted in Potter, p. 128.

25 Cecil Woodham-Smith, *The Great Hunger*, p. 71-72.

26 These ships were actually timber ships; they weren't meant for emigration at all. These were ancient vessels which had been turned into timber ships to bring out the great, rough timber, Canada's main trade export at the time, from Quebec City and New Brunswick. Once these were in Liverpool or the Irish ports, they were emptied of

timber (the weight or ballast), rough decks were put in down in the hold, and berths were made hardly bigger than dog kennels. There was evidence that once the ships had left Britain and were in the Irish Sea, they would knock down the bunks and add more space for people less than 18" and then pick up and cram in more "bootleg passengers" on the Irish coast. Families came aboard in a debilitated condition and at the slightest appearance of a storm, the hatches were battened down, leaving the space without air. In this same space people would relieve themselves, adding to the misery and threat of disease. (From *Ideas: The Famine Irish in Canada*, p. 6)

27   Sea Captain's Log based on two letters. One written by Dr. George Douglas, Medical Superintendent at Grosse Ile, taken from pamphlet "Grosse Il," (no date or page); the other written by Stephen De Vere, passenger on an Irish emigrant ship to Quebec in 1847 as quoted by Potter, p. 150-51.

28   The island is Grosse Ile which lies in the Upper St. Lawrence estuary, some 48 kilometres downstream from Quebec City. "Grosse Ile was declared of national historic significance due to its essential role as Canada's main quarantine station from 1832 to 1937, a period which saw European immigrants enter Canada in droves. The island holds the remains of thousands of victims of major epidemics who died during the huge waves of predominantly Irish immigration during the first half of the 19th century. Grosse Ile thus assumes particular significance for the Irish community." (*Grosse Ile: Report on the Public Consultation Program, March 1994*, p.8)

29   The blue flag was the flag of quarantine.

30   In 1832, the British government in Canada hastily set up Grosse Ile as a quarantine island. Cholera had hit Quebec City without warning on the heels of more than 100,000 immigrants from all parts of Europe. Because it was a British ship that had brought the deadly cholera epidemic, only ships from Irish ports and Liverpool were detained at Grosse Ile.

31   Based on letter by Medical Superintendent Dr. George Douglas, quoted in O'Gallagher *Grosse Ile: Gateway to Canada, 1832-1937*, p. 51-53.

32   One out of five Irish people who came to Canada that year died on Grosse Ile.

33   Based on keen of an illiterate Irish peasant woman. Found in Potter, p. 98.

34   Based on vow of Irish emigrant whose wife died on Grosse Ile: "By that cross, Mary, I swear to avenge your death. As soon as I earn the price of my passage home, I'll go back and shoot the man that murdered you, the landlord." Quoted in *The Fourth Horseman*, p. 123, by Andrew Nikoforuk.

35   Bracketed section not included in original production.

36   Manitoba Legislative Building. During its construction, Irish-born contractor, Thomas Kelly, was accused of misappropriating funds and using inferior construction material. He was convicted but never imprisoned and lived out his life a wealthy man in the United States.

Mom, Dad, I'm Living with a White Girl

by MARTY CHAN

PLAYRIGHT

Marty Chan is an Edmonton playwright whose shows have won hearts of audiences in Edmonton, Toronto and Vancouver. He is a main staple at the Edmonton Fringe Festival with hit plays including *Maggie's Last Dance, Something Dead and Evil Lurks in the Cemetery and It's My Dad,* and *Confessions of a Deli Boy.* In 1994, his play, *Polaroids of Don,* was nominated for best new work by the Edmonton Sterling Awards.

Marty contributes a humour commentary to CBC Radio in Edmonton. *The Dim Sum Diary* takes a quirky look at what it means to be Chinese and living in Canada. It has been airing weekly on CBC Radio Edmonton since August, 1995.

Marty also works in televison. He is an alumnus of the Canadian Film Centre. He played Henry Wong, a recurring role on the series *Jake and the Kid.* In 1996, he became a story intern for the same series. In 1996, he became story editor on *Subplot,* a series in development with Western International Communications. He adapted his short story *The Orange Seed Myth and Other Lies Mothers Tell* into a half hour television script, which was optioned by D. Day Film Productions.

In 1995, Marty married Michelle Vanderkeemel. They have three cats.

NOTE ABOUT THE PLAY

The reality-based part of the play is set in Vancouver, British Columbia in 1995. The fantasy story is set in the nightmares of the characters. The nightmares assume the metaphor of a fictional film noir movie in which two Canadian agents infiltrate the Yellow Claw's haven in a Chinatown.

The jump from reality to fantasy and back is heralded by the crash of a gong. When this sounds, the characters will switch to their other personae. The fantasy sequences are essentially metaphors of the reality-based play, revealing characters' inner thoughts and commenting on the action.

ORIGINAL PRODUCTION

"Mom, Dad, I'm Living with a White Girl", was workshopped in Cahoots Theatre Projects' new play development program, Lift-Off '94. The dramaturge was Sally Han.

The play was then produced by Cahoots Theatre Projects in association with

Theatre Passe Muraille. It premiered March 16, 1995 at the Theatre Passe Muraille Backspace with the following cast:

ORIGINAL CAST AND PRODUCTION TEAM

Mark Gee	Arthur Eng
Li Fen Gee	Brenda Kamino
Kim Gee	Paul Lee
Sally Davis	Linda Prystawska

Producer	Marion de Vries
Director	Sally Han
Stage Manager	Maria Costa
Set Design	Bill Rassmussen
Lighting Design	Aisling Sampson
Costume/Props	Mary Spyrakis
Sound Design	Victor Oland
Choreographer	Xing Bang Fu

The production was made possible with the generous help of the Ontario Arts Council, Laidlaw Foundation, Department of Canadian Heritage, The Alberta Foundation for the Arts, Air Canada, the Toronto Arts Council and the City of Toronto.

The Firehalls Arts Centre in Vancouver ran a second production of the play from February 1–24, 1996 with the following cast:

Mark Gee	Daniel Chen
Li Fen Gee	Donna Yamamoto
Kim Gee	John James Hong
Sally Davis	Kirsten Robek

Director	Donna Spencer
Stage Manager	Angela Kirk
Set and Lighting Design	Stephen Allen
Costume Design	Lana Krause
Sound Design	Stephen Bulat
Choreographer	JohnJames Hong

REVIEWS

"At its heart, Marty Chan's tidy, fast-paced comedy *"Mom, Dad, I'm Living with a White Girl"* is a blend of a couple of old stories: culture clash and generational conflict." (Globe and Mail) — March 18, 1996

"A truly engaging piece of theatre." (CBC Radio — Toronto) — March 17, 1995

"Edmonton playwright Marty Chan's, *"Mom, Dad, I'm Living with a White Girl"*, serves up a quirky, outrageously comic take on the familiar tension of inter-racial relationships." (Toronto Star) — March 19, 1995

"Marty Chan isn't afraid of racial stereotypes—as long as he can turn them upside down to make a point." (Vancouver Sun) — February 6, 1996

"The clever Edmonton-based playwright has actually written two plays—one, the sad tale of young momma's boy and wannabe auto mechanic Mark Gee ...The second play is a lively and campy satire of a Hollywood B-movie thriller." (Vancouver Province) — February 6, 1996

AUTHOR'S NOTE

The staging of this play seems complicated because of the shift from reality to fantasy, but it can be simple to execute. The set should be minimal, with props doubling as pieces that can be used in both worlds. For example, the acupuncture table doubles as the torture bench. The key to shifting realities is within the acting, not the technical aspects. This play challenges actors to take an audience on a journey into their characters' minds. Finding the right transitions will allow a fluid shift.

PERFORMANCE PERMISSION

For permission to produce *"Mom, Dad, I'm Living with a White Girl"* contact Marty Chan c/o the Playwrights Union of Canada, 54 Wolseley Street, 2nd Floor, Toronto, Ontario, M5T 1A5. Phone (416) 703-0201, Fax (416) 703-0059, Toll Free 1-800-561-3318, Internet cdplays@interlog.com.

"MOM, DAD, I'M LIVING WITH A WHITE GIRL"

CHARACTERS

MARK GEE (22) is an automotive mechanic who is caught between the world of his traditional Chinese parents and the values of Canadian society. He's worried about how to tell his parents he's living with a white girl. In the world of the Yellow Claw, Mark is a covert agent trying to infiltrate the Yellow Claw's domain.

KIM GEE (53) runs his own acupuncture clinic and practises the art of Chinese medicine that has been handed down to him from generations of Gees. He is a man with a big heart, a soft spot for family and a hole in his life that was supposed to be filled by his son Mark following in his footsteps. In the Yellow Claw fantasy story, Kim is lackey to his imperious mistress, the Yellow Claw.

LI FEN GEE (52) is Kim's very traditional Chinese wife. She isolates herself from her adopted country, choosing to stay in the sanctuary of her home and Chinatown. Her life revolves around family, in particular her son Mark. In the fantasy story, she is a conniving underlord, the Yellow Claw, who wants to destroy the western world.

SALLY DAVIS (24) is a reader for a film company who is infatuated with the Chinese culture—so much so that she becomes romantically involved with Mark Gee. In the Yellow Claw story, she is the patriotic Canadian agent who fights the evil Asian hordes from taking over the west.

ACT ONE, SCENE ONE

(At centre stage, a long bench stands for truth, justice and the Chinese-Canadian way. It represents an acupuncturist's clinic. On the wall behind it, two tasseled spears bracket a life-sized body chart. Behind the bench, KIM GEE holds an Earth-like balloon. Kim slides a long cruel needle across the balloon.)

KIM: The key is the entry point. Find the right one and we can reach the nerve centre. Strike where they are most vulnerable. Ah. The heart of decadence. Vancouver. We will infiltrate their society as a moth chews through silk. They will suspect nothing, Yellow Claw.

(Formality, lies and LI FEN GEE sit at a dining table stage left of the bench. She sits in shadows so that only her long cigarette holder is visible.)

(Li Fen flicks her cigarette. Kim inserts the needle. It pierces through the other side of the balloon. Lights down on Kim and Li Fen.)

(Lights up on stage right of the bench. There, a bed lays out intimacy and secrets. In front of it, MARK GEE stands back to back with SALLY DAVIES.)

SALLY: A little girl stole my ice cream cone.

MARK: The emperor has no pants.

SALLY: The lonely dog eats its young.

MARK: Clowns only smile when they grieve.

SALLY   I despise smokers.

(MARK lights a cigarette for SALLY.)

SALLY: Did you uncover the Yellow Claw's secret plot?

MARK: She has many secrets.

SALLY: Agent Banana, the freedom of the western world rests on your shoulders. If you can't learn her plans —

MARK: I know what's at stake, Snow Princess.

SALLY: Redouble your efforts. We're counting on you.

MARK: I won't let you down.

SALLY: Good luck and God speed, Agent Banana.

MARK: Save a drink for me Snow Princess. We'll toast an end to the Yellow Claw's tyranny.

SALLY: To the the unshakeable Rocky Mountains.

MARK: To the Can in Captain Canuck.

(She grabs him and plants a kiss. Lights down.)

(Lights up on KIM and LI FEN at the dining table [stage left].)

KIM: One of your minions no longer inhales the Opium of a Thousand Loyalties. What is your wish?

LI FEN: A lotus blossom plucked from the garden of obedience will wither and die.

KIM: I hear and obey, Yellow Claw.

LI FEN: Amuse me with the name of my betrayer.

KIM: He is no one of consequence.

LI FEN: Tell me.

KIM: His identity slips my mind.

LI FEN: His name!

KIM: Mark Gee.

LI FEN: Bring him to me.

KIM: I faithfully do your bidding, mistress of evil.

(Crash of gong.)

(Lights up on bed at stage right where MARK tries to sleep and SALLY flips through a script.)

SALLY: I can't believe the drivel some writers pass off as art. Listen to this title: *Wrath of the Yellow Claw.* Isn't that terrible?

MARK: Awful.

SALLY: Here's a good one. (reads) The Yellow Claw's influence undulated across the Pacific Ocean as a dolphin glides through the briny sea. But this was no playful fish. It was a dark porpoise.

MARK: Cheese deluxe. Can I read it after you're done?

SALLY: Why do you want to?

MARK: It's funny.

SALLY: Please.

MARK: I take it you're passing on it.

(A phone beside SALLY rings. She looks at it, but doesn't answer. MARK doesn't budge.)

MARK: Let it ring.

SALLY: It might be important.

MARK: Let the machine get it.

SALLY: Mark, answer the phone.

(MARK finally picks up the phone.)

MARK: Hello? It's midnight. Yes, I know about dinner. No, I don't need a reminder. Yes, I'll be there. Tomorrow night. Seven-thirty. Seven. Got it. You don't have to call again. I'll remember. Good night. Good night. Good bye.

SALLY: Your mom?

MARK: Who else? Man, I wish she'd stop doing this.

SALLY: It's the Dragon Boat Festival. It's important to her.

MARK: Yeah, this and a thousand other obscure Chinese festivals.

SALLY: Maybe we can watch the boat race this year.

MARK: Are you nuts? Mom would want to throw dumplings into the sea, and you know how dad can't stand to see food go to waste.

SALLY: Neither can you.

MARK: I wish she'd stop making excuses to get me to visit.

SALLY: She cares about her *sai j'i*[1].

MARK: I'm not her little boy.

SALLY: I love it when you try to be tough.

MARK: I am tough. Not an ounce of fat.

SALLY: Except right here.

(She tickles him.)

MARK: Cut it out, Sally. I mean it. Stop it.

SALLY: It's from all those years of eating war tips.

MARK: That's *w'aw teep*[2] You make it sound like I sucked on missiles.

SALLY: Okay, *w'aw teep*. Better?

MARK: Yeah.

SALLY: Are we going to tell them tomorrow?

MARK: It's too soon.

SALLY: That's what you said last time. Mark, they need to know about us.

MARK: Trust me, I'll know when to do it.

SALLY: We have to tell them some time.

MARK: Not yet.

SALLY: Why not?

MARK: It's my dad. He's got a weak heart.

SALLY: But he seems so healthy.

---

1   little boy
2   dumplings

MARK: It's in our genes. Grandpa Gee died of one.

SALLY: I thought you said he lived in Calgary.

MARK: He did, but now he's dead.

SALLY: When did it happen?

MARK: A while ago. Two, maybe three months. I'm not sure. Dad has the details.

SALLY: And we didn't attend the funeral?

MARK: (fumbling) Dad hasn't put the body into the ground yet. He and grandad never really got along.

SALLY: What are you scared of?

(Crash of gong.)

(MARK hands SALLY a cigarette.)

MARK: We shouldn't have succumbed to our primal desires.

SALLY: Sweet is the fruit that is forbidden.

MARK: Snow Princess, you are my queen.

SALLY: My little banana.

MARK: Um, maybe we should drop our code names.

SALLY: Call me Sally.

MARK: Mark.

SALLY: A strong name. Like Marc Antony. Slayer of Caesar. Ruler of Rome. Consort of Cleopatra.

MARK: Sally. Sally. Sally.

SALLY: No one must know of this. It could ruin us both.

MARK: Your secret is safe upon my lips. Let us seal them.

(They lean in to kiss.)

(KIM enters from centre.)

KIM: The Yellow Claw sends her greetings.

MARK: No.

(KIM flicks his hand. SALLY clutches her chest. She pulls out a throwing star.)

SALLY: Smells like highly concentrated opium. It will knock out an adult in three sec — unh!

MARK: Sally? Snow Princess? Wake up. (to Kim) What do you want?

KIM: You are guilty of consorting with the white devil. What have you told the infidel?

MARK: I won't talk.

KIM: You will break like so many Taiwanese toys.

(KIM throws a star at MARK. He falls. Crash of gong. KIM exits centre. SALLY and MARK sit up in bed.)

MARK: I just think we should wait.

SALLY: You have no idea how they'll accept the news. They might be fine with it.

MARK: Not mom.

SALLY: She is a reasonable woman.

MARK: Dream on. She's the original dragon lady.

SALLY: Don't say that. It's racist.

MARK: You don't know my mom.

SALLY: Mark, it'd be nice to get better acquainted with her. You know, invite her to visit *us* for a change.

MARK: How come you're so fired up to tell her?

SALLY: I'd like to answer the phone once in a while.

MARK: We'll get call display.

SALLY: Development likes their readers to be somewhat accessible.

MARK: We'll get a second phone.

SALLY: Mark, it's more than that. I'm still dressing out of my suitcases. I'm not paying rent so I can live out of boxes.

MARK: Give them a chance to get used to you. Just like your *opa* warmed up to me.

SALLY: He still calls you China Boy.

MARK: At least he doesn't ask me to break boards any more.

SALLY: That was uncle Wes.

MARK: Sorry, they all look alike to me.

SALLY: I was proud to tell my parents.

MARK: And they took it so well.

SALLY: Mark, what's the real reason you're lying to your parents?

MARK: It's mom. I wanted you to get on her good side before we said anything.

SALLY: You don't think I've been trying? I offer to help in the kitchen, she sends me away. I practise a few words of Cantonese, she laughs.

MARK: Compliment her food.

SALLY: She never accepts my praises.

MARK: It's just Chinese humbleness. Lay it on thick, no matter what she puts in front of you.

SALLY: Your mom's cooking is always delicious.

MARK: She's taken it easy on you. One day, she's going to cart out her mystery dish. Woof woof.

SALLY: Please stop that. You sound like my *opa*.

MARK: You'll try to get on my mom's good side?

SALLY: I can't earn her respect with this lie hanging over us. We have to be honest up front.

MARK: But you haven't given this lying thing a fair shake.

SALLY: Promise me. Tomorrow night.

MARK: Just remember to lay it on thick with the food.

SALLY: I'll insist everything's delicious.

MARK: Do it until she chokes on your compliments. Hmmm.

SALLY: Mark.

MARK: A boy can dream, can't he?

(Lights down.)

ACT ONE, SCENE TWO

(Lights up stage right. A fast-paced musical interlude as MARK and SALLY get dressed for dinner at bed. They exit stage right. Lights up on KIM and LI FEN at the dining table, stage left. They set the table. MARK and SALLY enter stage left. MARK hands his mother a basket of laundry and makes a beeline for the table.)

(Everyone sits. KIM sits in the stage left chair. SALLY and MARK sit together upstage and LI FEN takes the stage right chair. The GEES shovel food into their mouths, their arms and hands paddling wildly. SALLY nibbles.)

(KIM pats his belly and burps.)

KIM: Outdid yourself wife. Have to make room.

(KIM loosens belt.)

LI FEN: *Aiya*, don't do that.

SALLY: Do we have any dumplings to throw into the river?

KIM: Why should we do something so crazy?

SALLY: To protect the dead captain. Isn't this what you do at the Dragon Boat Festival?

LI FEN: How do you know?

SALLY: I took a course in Chinese folklore.

LI FEN: Very old tradition. Young people not respect it any more. They forget how important a simple act can mean. More dumplings?

SALLY: Mrs. Gee, this is the best Chinese meal I've ever eaten.

LI FEN: Shrimp too dry.

SALLY: They were perfectly moist.

LI FEN: *Aiya*, you just saying that.

SALLY: Moist like a Duncan Hines cake. No, moister. One bite of your shrimp sets my taste buds tingling with moistness. It's like a wet nap exploded in my mouth.

LI FEN: You are too kind.

MARK: She's too much.

LI FEN: Mark, ask your friend if she wants more rice.

SALLY: No thank you, Mrs. Gee. I'm full.

LI FEN: Oh.

MARK: She's a light eater.

SALLY: (to Mark) What did I do?

MARK: Always take seconds.

(Crash of gong.)

(LI FEN stands and lights a cigarette.)

LI FEN: At last I meet my enemy face to face. Have some rice.

SALLY: I don't think so.

LI FEN: I invite you to eat at my table. And you spurn my generous offer of hospitality. How rude.

MARK: She's not rude. She's Canadian.

KIM: Eat the rice.

SALLY: Don't touch it Mark.

MARK: What possible evil could she be up to?

(SALLY holds up a grain and sniffs it.)

SALLY: Truth serum. Slipped a few almonds so I couldn't detect the scent. Too bad you used West Indian instead of Hawaiian.

LI FEN: Curses!

MARK: Yellow Claw, you are devious.

KIM: Eat the rice.

MARK: Never.

KIM: Yellow Claw, they will not eat from the Rice Bowl of a Thousand Truths.

LI FEN: Your wills are strong, but I will break them.

(Crash of gong.)

KIM: Eat some more rice.

LI FEN: If she is full, she is full. No one can force *theg'why l'eur* to eat my food.

(Crash of gong.)

LI FEN: Take them to the Chamber of a Thousand Horrors.

KIM: I hear and obey, mistress of all things inscrutable.

(KIM shoves MARK and SALLY to the bench, centre stage.)

(Crash of gong.)

KIM: Here it is. My new acupuncture table. You like?

SALLY: It's impressive. Mark?

MARK: It's okay.

KIM: What does he know? Feel it Sally. Height can be adjusted. Treated leather.

SALLY: Looks great. Mark, you should get one for the apartment.

MARK: Must have been expensive.

KIM: Guess.

MARK: Three thousand.

KIM: Hmph! Sally, you guess.

SALLY: I don't know. Eight hun—

KIM: One thousand dollars. Don't tell Mrs. Gee. She thinks it only cost five hundred. I pay extra for the table, but they give me this chart. Rosewood frame. And Chinese chart. You like?

MARK: Whatever.

SALLY: The chart looks very nice, Mr. Gee.

KIM: I knew someone would appreciate it.

SALLY: I wish I could have something like this, but my apartment is so small.

MARK: Dad, did you read the Sun last week? The university is thinking of adding acupuncture.

KIM: Only a foolish man would give away his secrets. Acupuncture is a family art. My grandfathers passed down their secret techniques to us. It is a gift from ancient China. How could any one treat it with disrespect?

MARK: Maybe we should go upstairs. Mom probably thinks you've chained us to the table.

SALLY: Yes, Mark has something he wants to tell you.

KIM: Try the table, Sally. I will do acupressure. *Aiya*, you are tense.

MARK: It's from being hunched over scripts.

SALLY: Guess again.

KIM: Lie down. Treated leather. Comfortable.

MARK: We should get going.

KIM: You watch. Maybe you learn something.

(SALLY gets on the bench. MARK stands back.)

(Crash of gong.)

(KIM pushes her down.)

SALLY: Do your worst. Whatever instruments of torture you use. I can take it. Flogging. Burning cigarettes. Bamboo shoots.

KIM: Bamboo shoots? I like the sound of that.

MARK: Don't give him any more ideas.

(LI FEN enters from stage left.)

KIM: Yellow Claw, the girl is ready.

LI FEN: Good, very good. Prepare the Needle of a Thousand Perforations.

(KIM pulls out a long needle.)

LI FEN: What do you know of my plot to conquer the world? And who have you told?

MARK: Take me. She's knows nothing.

SALLY: Don't sacrifice yourself, Mark. The merest glance of you warms my icy tundra spirit.

LI FEN: Begin with her eyes.

KIM: You have an ironic sense of humour, imperious mistress.

(KIM holds SALLY's eye open. He starts to insert the needle.)

SALLY: Aiiieeeee!

MARK: Stop it. You should be interrogating me.

LI FEN: You do not understand. She is the instrument of torture and you are the victim. You will watch as she crumbles from a mighty mounted Canadian into a whimpering blind girl. This exquisite torture is for you.

MARK: Yellow Claw, you are evil.

(Crash of gong.)

LI FEN: *Aiya* Kim, stop that. That *g'why l'eur* is not one of your patients. Come eat dessert. I cut oranges. (to SALLY) Orange good for you. Clear up your face.

116

SALLY: Thanks, I'm certain they'll be moist.

KIM: Are you still working for the same company? Making movies?

SALLY: Yes.

KIM: Do you keep busy?

SALLY: It's been slow lately.

MARK: She's the best reader they have.

LI FEN: I never hear of people getting money to read.

SALLY: There's more to it. I also analyze and recommend scripts for production. I want to move up to development, but I can't get the calls I want for some reason.

MARK: Sally's got a real nose for finding produceable scripts. What was that one you recommended? *The Eagle's Last Cry.*

LI FEN: Is it about China?

SALLY: No, it's about the brutal murder of an environmentalist who tries to expose a greedy oilman but waits too long.

MARK: It's ironic, because they kill him before he gets a real chance to bond with the oilman's family.

LI FEN: Did not see it.

KIM: We only watch Chinese movies.

MARK: Sally and I have seen some pretty good ones.

LI FEN: (to SALLY) You?

SALLY: I became a huge fan in university. Took a film course. Wrote my essay on Chinese directors.

MARK: Every month now she drags me out to one.

LI FEN: How can she understand? They speak Chinese.

MARK: There are subtitles.

SALLY: Did you see Ang Lee's *Eat, Drink, Man, Woman?*

KIM: No.

SALLY: You should. It's excellent. Much tighter than *The Wedding Banquet.*

KIM: I never heard of these movies.

SALLY: You should rent *The Wedding Banquet.* It's in the stores.

LI FEN: What is it about?

SALLY: It's very funny. It's about a gay Chinese man who has to convince his parents he's straight.

(Uncomfortable pause.)

SALLY: Well, we liked it. You might prefer *Eat, Drink, Man, Woman.*

MARK: Guess what? The shop moved me up to lube jobs.

LI FEN: That is good for you. See Kim, he is doing well in his job.

KIM: (to MARK) When will you stop playing with cars?

SALLY: Mark's very good at it.

KIM: (to MARK) You work in clinic. It is much better for you.

SALLY: He loves what he does.

KIM: Mark, when will you grow up?

LI FEN: *Aiya* Kim, leave him alone. Mark, you don't have to work in the clinic if you do not want to.

KIM: How can he live on what he makes?

SALLY: As a matter of fact, Mark lives —

MARK: Great oranges mom. Really moist. Any more?

SALLY: Mark, answer your dad's question.

MARK: Oh, my chest. Can't breathe. Arm numb.

LI FEN: Eat too fast.

SALLY: Your dad is waiting.

MARK: Give me a couple of minutes.

SALLY: Why don't I tell him? I hope I get all the details right.

MARK: No, no. I'll do it. Mom, dad, I have an important announcement. It's actually quite funny … no, let me try that again. You know how you always worry about how I can make rent? I found a way to solve that problem. Uh no. Can I start over?

SALLY: Mr. and Mrs. Gee, what Mark is trying to —

MARK: I'm going into the family business.

KIM/LI FEN/SALLY: What!?

KIM: *Aiya*, did you hear that grandfather? Your dream is alive.

LI FEN: (overlapping) Is this what you really want?

SALLY: Mark?

(Crash of gong.)

(SALLY slumps into MARK's arms.)

SALLY: Agent Banana, what are you doing? I'm blind. I'm blind.

KIM: Foolish girl. He would never betray the Yellow Claw.

LI FEN: I am proud of you, son.

SALLY: Son?

MARK: She is a prime example of the gullible western race,mother.

SALLY: You're the Yellow Claw's heir?

MARK: You didn't know?

(MARK laughs. LI FEN and KIM join in.)

(Crash of gong.)

(Lights down.)

ACT ONE, SCENE THREE

(Stage left, LI FEN clears dishes from the table. KIM sits in the stage left chair reading a Chinese paper. He puts it down.)

KIM: Do you think he wants to come back to the clinic?

LI FEN: No. He just wants to come home.

KIM: More like he ran out of money.

LI FEN: You shouldn't push him so hard to work in the clinic. It is not right for him.

KIM: You mean like Sally is not right for him.

LI FEN: He knows that now. He is tired of playing with white girls.

KIM: How can you be so sure?

LI FEN: A mother can tell. He is unhappy. I see it tonight.

KIM: When?

LI FEN: At dinner. Did you not hear how he said pass the *w'aw teep?*

KIM: I think I missed it.

LI FEN: He was really saying get me out of this relationship. I'm suffocating. I'm dying. I need a nice Chinese girl.

120

KIM: *Aiya*, wife, you are blowing farts to beat the wind.

LI FEN: Maybe I could find one for him. I will talk to the girls at the mah jong club.

KIM: He does not need a matchmaker.

LI FEN: I know just the girl for him. You remember Lena Chow?

KIM: (shudders) Who could forget a face like that?

LI FEN: She has a sister in Gwandung. Her girl is same age as Mark. She is very traditional girl. She will know how to take care of Mark. I will talk to Lena.

KIM: Lena has a big mouth. By tomorrow night, all Chinatown will know you are hunting for a wife.

LI FEN: Better than him seeing the white girl.

KIM: It is his choice.

LI FEN: Not if I have anything to do with it.

KIM: Li Fen, I want to tell you a story. I never told you before, but now is a good time. It was when we were seeing each other. The clinic had money problems. Father worked day and night. Mother was sick so my sisters had to look after the house. Then my father learned the Kwans were looking for a husband for their oldest daughter. They were very wealthy. Father wanted me to marry her, but I loved you. I promised I would never marry any one other than you.

LI FEN: You only have one sister.

KIM: I had two, but dad was so poor he had to sell one of them. I've been searching ever since for my lost sister.

LI FEN: *Aiya*, what am I going to do with you?

KIM: You should get to know Sally better. She is a good kid.

LI FEN: What does Mark see in her?

KIM: She speaks her mind.

LI FEN: A good wife should be a silent one.

KIM: Counts you out.

LI FEN: Hmph!

KIM: You're turning out to be just like my mother.

LI FEN: I am not like her. She always tell me what to do. How to cook your favourite dishes. How to clean the house. Nothing I did was good enough for her.

KIM: Just like Sally?

LI FEN: That's different.

KIM: Li Fen, put on a few hundred pounds, put a drumstick in your hand and you'd be the spitting image of my mother.

LI FEN: Sally has no respect for our traditions.

KIM: She seemed to know them pretty good tonight.

LI FEN: Hmph! Learn from book.

KIM: She is trying to get to know us better.

LI FEN: You come to this country by yourself. Leave me and Mark in China while you save enough money to bring us here. We don't see each other for years. We make many sacrifices. There is no way she can know what we go through.

KIM: Her parents are immigrants too. Her father was a butcher in Holland. He come here to open his own shop. He had to work as a window washer to save enough money. They are just like us. Don't you see that?

LI FEN: Let me talk to Lena.

KIM: I forbid it.

LI FEN: This white girl is nothing but trouble.

KIM: They are happy together.

(Crash of gong.)

(Lights down on KIM and LI FEN. Lights up on stage right.)

(MARK leads SALLY on stage from stage right. They stand in front of the bed. Her eyes are bandaged.)

SALLY: Where are you taking me, traitor? To one of your torture chambers? What? Will you put me in a round room and tell me to stand in the corner? Will you show me —

MARK: Sally, listen to me.

SALLY: It's Snow Princess to you. Agent Banana, you've peeled away your thick yellow skin and revealed nothing but a rotting fruit inside. Oh, I was blind long before they gouged my eyes out.

MARK: I was pretending to be on her side. I couldn't let you die.

SALLY: Better dead than red.

MARK: But we're on the verge of uprooting her garden of evil. We can destroy the Yellow Claw, if we work together.

SALLY: I don't work with, for, or alongside traitors.

(Crash of gong.)

(SALLY gets into bed. MARK goes to stage left of the bed.)

ACT ONE, SCENE FOUR

(SALLY flips through the script. MARK folds laundry.)

MARK: How's the script? (pause) Maybe it'll get better. (pause) You shouldn't judge it until you read it all.

SALLY: Don't talk to me.

MARK: Maybe it's a diamond in the rough. (pause) This one might surprise you.

SALLY: It doesn't work that way.

MARK: It's so hard to change your mind once it's set.

SALLY: What do you know about screenplays?

MARK: That's not the point.

SALLY: About as much as acupuncture.

MARK: Look, I promised —

SALLY: How many scripts have I agonized over? How many scripts have I given my objective and fair attention to.

MARK: You're not listening to me.

SALLY: Over a hundred.

MARK: Maybe it's supposed to be funny.

SALLY: How would you know? You think everything's funny. This happens to be filled with cheap gags and Asian stereotypes.

MARK: It's a send up.

SALLY: It reinscribes offensive racial representations.

MARK: It's just a movie. It doesn't affect the way people see the Chinese.

SALLY: Pop culture has more influence than you think.

MARK: So you have to protect me? We Chinese do have a sense of humour. We might even be able to laugh at it.

SALLY: Oh, so now you presume to speak for a billion people?

MARK: And you know better because of a couple courses in Chinese folklore and a Chinese boyfriend?

SALLY: Ha! Some boyfriend.

MARK: What's that supposed to mean?

SALLY: What do you think "Mr. I'm-going-into-the-family-business"? When the hell do you plan to tell them? Ever? Do you expect me to live out of boxes forever? You broke your promise, dear, and if you're too ashamed to tell your mother, then maybe this relationship isn't worth it. If you didn't want to make a commitment, you didn't have to hide behind your mother.

MARK: I'm not hiding.

SALLY: Then why can't you tell them? Why didn't you—

MARK: I'm waiting for the festival of "Expose Living Arrangements to Parents."

SALLY: That's it. If you're not going to take this seriously, then forget it. I'm starting to think moving in together was a bad idea.

MARK: I'm sorry Sally. I panicked, that's all. I'll straighten everything out tomorrow. I promise.

SALLY: Forgive me if I don't unpack right away.

MARK: Then I'll do it.

(MARK reaches under the bed and slides out one of SALLY's boxes. He opens it and puts her books on the bed.)

(SALLY watches him for a moment and then helps him.)

(Lights down.)

ACT ONE SCENE FIVE

(Crash of gong.)

(MARK crosses from the stage right bed to the bench, centre stage. KIM enters from upstage centre and intercepts MARK.)

KIM: I heard everything you said in the Cell of a Thousand Silences.

MARK: You won't take me without a fight.

(MARK unleashes a few impressive kata moves, supplying his own sound effects.)

KIM: I see you have studied with Shaolin Master Way Wong. Well, here are a few tricks he did not teach you. Crane standing on one leg ready to swoop.

(MARK and KIM pose in various fighting stances, but never fight.)

MARK: I counter. Tiger with unsheathed claws.

KIM: Mongoose with buck teeth.

MARK: Owl with whiplash.

KIM: Snake with arthritis.

MARK: Dog about to pee. Ouch, cramp!

KIM: You fought well, betrayer. But none have bested me in hand to hand combat. To the Bench of a Thousand Confessions.

(KIM shoves MARK on the bench.)

MARK: You must tell me. Who was your kung fu master?

KIM: David Carradine.

(Crash of gong.)

MARK: Dad, there's a perfectly healthy practice dummy in the corner.

KIM: Don't worry. No needles yet. You are tense.

MARK: Had a rough night. And all that tranny work. You're not going to poke me, are you?

KIM: Relax.

MARK: I am relaxed.

KIM: Can you let your body know?

MARK: Okay, I'm relaxing now.

KIM: How is this?

MARK: Ouch, ow. Hey. How did you do that? My shoulders feel looser.

KIM: You will learn in good time. Now, the needles.

MARK: Dad, let's try something else.

KIM: Mark, it's acupuncture. There is nothing else.

MARK: Well, that's enough for one day.

KIM: Give it a chance, Mark. Lay back.

(As KIM talks, he sticks MARK with various needles.)

KIM: How is Sally?

MARK: She's fine. Great. Picture of health.

KIM: You made your mother very happy last night.

MARK: It's not permanent.

KIM: She never understood how you could waste your time working on machines.

MARK: Can we start the session?

KIM: The human body is an unlimited source of wonder. In total harmony. Everything has a place and a purpose. The key to acupuncture is to get the patient take his mind off what you are doing. Look.

MARK: Oh my god. This is amazing. I can't feel a thing.

KIM: Don't drink any water for the next hour.

MARK: Dad, come up with some new material.

KIM: Old acupuncturist. Old jokes. When you take over, you can make new jokes.

MARK: Uh, yeah. I'll think about that.

KIM: Yes. Good idea.

MARK: Won't your clients feel uncomfortable? I don't speak Cantonese very well.

KIM: Mark, I speak English to most of my patients.

MARK: You're kidding.

KIM: Too many dialects. It is easier to use English. You don't want to do this, do you?

MARK: Sure I do. Don't I look like I'm enjoying it.

KIM: How much money do you need?

MARK: I don't need any money.

KIM: Don't lie to me. I know why you are here.

(Crash of gong.)

KIM: You tell me what you know of the Yellow Claw's plans.

MARK: If these tiny pins are your idea of torture, we're going to be here a long time.

KIM: Actually, I had this in mind.

(KIM pulls out a giant needle and pushes it into MARK's stomach.)

MARK: Nooooo!!!

(Crash of gong.)

KIM: Sorry.

MARK: Painless acupuncture, huh?

KIM: You squirm too much.

MARK: Okay, that's enough, pull them out.

(LI FEN enters from stage left.)

LI FEN: What going on? I hear scream.

KIM: Needle slipped.

MARK: Dad's trying to kill me mom. Tell him to take the needles out.

LI FEN: *Aiya* Kim, take them out.

KIM: Only way for him to learn.

LI FEN: Enough work. Eat. I make dinner. Come upstairs.

MARK: Mom, I'm kind of indisposed right now.

KIM: Mark was going to tell us the real reason why he is here.

(Crash of gong.)

(LI FEN lights a cigarette.)

(MARK stands up and goes stage right of the bench. LI FEN and KIM stand together stage left of the bench.)

LI FEN: I am listening.

MARK: I am forever loyal to you Yellow Claw.

KIM: He lies Yellow Craw.

LI FEN: Amuse me, betrayer. How did you plan to uproot my garden of evil?

MARK: How did you know?

LI FEN: The Yellow Claw knows all.

(KIM pulls out a long needle.)

KIM: Shall I continue, Yellow Craw?

LI FEN: I have something better planned. But remain close by. I may need you.

KIM: I will stand over here and contemplate the number of angels that can dance on the head of this pin.

LI FEN: Twelve.

KIM: You are infinitely wise, Yellow Craw.

MARK: Claw not craw.

LI FEN: Silence.

MARK: You can't break me.

LI FEN: You will talk soon enough.

(Crash of gong.)

MARK: Mom, dad, there's something I haven't been telling you. It's about me and Sally.

(Crash of gong.)

LI FEN: Again with the girl.

KIM: His spirit cannot be broken as long as the girl is alive.

(Crash of gong.)

MARK: She wanted to tell you at first, but I was scared how you'd take it. Now, I have no choice.

KIM: Is everything okay?

MARK: We're in love.

LI FEN: *Aiya*, too young.

MARK: There's more.

(Crash of gong.)

LI FEN: What is this love?

KIM: A western concept.

LI FEN: Impractical.

KIM: You are right as always.

(Crash of gong.)

MARK: Please stop doing that. You know my Chinese sucks.

KIM: We are waiting.

MARK: I lied about wanting to work in the clinic.

LI FEN: *Aiya!*

KIM: I told you so.

MARK: Mom, dad, there's no easy way to say this.

KIM: Then say it.

MARK: Sally and I are living together.

(Crash of gong.)

LI FEN: This is most disturbing.

KIM: We have no other choice.

LI FEN: They both must die.

(Huge gong, vibrates to silence. Lights down.)

ACT TWO, SCENE ONE

(Lights up on MARK and SALLY, centre stage. They stand, back to back, in front of the bench.)

MARK: The spikes are closing in!

SALLY: It's a scare tactic!

MARK: It's working. What do we do?

SALLY: Put your back to mine. Make like a thin man.

MARK: We're going to be skewered.

SALLY: It'll take more than a brutal eye gouging and a thousand spikes to puncture my spirit.

MARK: I'm sorry I didn't tell you the truth. I'm the Yellow Claw's heir by blood, not by nature.

SALLY: I know now. Can you forgive my predilection to protect, serve and suspect?

MARK: I love — Oh, the spikes are pressing against me.

(SALLY and MARK try to hug each other backwards.)

(Crash of gong.)

(SALLY and MARK break away and survey the bedroom. They cross stage left to the dining table which is set for dinner.)

SALLY: Bed's made.

MARK: Table's set.

SALLY: Desk looks good.

MARK: Carpet is clean.

SALLY: I hope she likes the fish casserole. Mark, I know how hard it must have been to —

MARK: The important thing is that they know. Remember, stay on mom's good side.

SALLY: Well, duh.

MARK: Just don't start anything.

SALLY: I heard you the first twenty times.

MARK: She's still pretty leery —

SALLY: Mark, you're starting to sound like her.

MARK: Maybe we should have waited. Mom's only had a week to take it in. She still might be in shock.

SALLY: If she really cares about her *sai ji*, she'll be fine with it.

(Crash of gong.)

(Mark and Sally exit stage left.)

(KIM and LI FEN enter centre stage and meet at the bench. LI FEN slaps KIM.)

LI FEN: You let them escape?!

KIM: I beg your forgiveness, svelte and sinister mistress.

(LI FEN draws a huge needle from the folds of her sleeve. KIM backs away.)

KIM: The sting of your slap is retribution enough. I will wear it forever as a boutonniere of shame. Please let it also be a corsage of your tolerance.

(LI FEN retires the needle to her sleeve.)

LI FEN: Never fail me again. Bring me their heads.

KIM: I hear and obey, magnanimous mistress.

(Crash of gong.)

(KIM and LI FEN cross stage left to the dining table and survey the room.)

LI FEN: Not very clean.

KIM: This is a very bad part of town.

LI FEN: The bed is too small.

KIM: It is a small apartment.

LI FEN: Only pigs would live here.

(LI FEN runs her finger on the underside of the table.)

LI FEN: See? Very dirty.

KIM: Remember what you promised.

LI FEN: I said I would see their apartment. We see, we go.

KIM: You have to give them a chance.

LI FEN: I already did—

KIM: Li Fen! Try harder.

(From stage left, MARK and SALLY enter with food.)

MARK: Soup's on.

(Everyone sits at the dinner table. MARK and SALLY take the upstage seats, while KIM takes the stage right seat and LI FEN takes the stage left chair.)

LI FEN: You have … nice apartment.

SALLY: Sorry it's such a mess. It's tough when you work and live in the same place.

LI FEN: Get two bedroom. Much bigger.

MARK: We can't afford it.

SALLY: Work's been slow.

LI FEN: What you do then?

SALLY: I'm working on my own screenplay.

KIM: That sounds very interesting, eh wife? (to SALLY) What is it about?

SALLY: A Chinese man overcomes discrimination while working on the Canadian railway.

MARK: It's a very good script.

LI FEN: And you pay the bills while she does this?

MARK: Mom, we're not stupid.

SALLY: I do have my own savings.

KIM: (to MARK) What about you?

MARK: I'm making plenty of money.

LI FEN: You do what you want to do. I do not care.

KIM: Maybe we should eat supper before it gets cold. You outdid yourself Sally.

SALLY: Try the beef and greens. Mark made them.

MARK: Sally made the fish casserole.

SALLY: It's my mother's recipe.

LI FEN: You do a very good job, Mark.

MARK: Try the fish, mom.

LI FEN: *Koey yung tie d'aw schun t'ow.*[1]

SALLY: What did she say?

KIM: She likes the garlic smell.

LI FEN: Yes. A little bit is good for you.

SALLY: Go on try it, Mrs. Gee.

LI FEN: Maybe I try the beef first. What kind of vegetable is this?

SALLY: Diced asparagus.

MARK: It's Sally's favourite.

(LI FEN and KIM talk among themselves, while SALLY and MARK watch.)

LI FEN: *Na ging ying jeng di sic mut wun j'aw kay sut. Lay n'ying g'aw yung lo shun ga.*[2]

KIM: *Kay sut doo m'hi tie cha.*[3]

LI FEN: *G'um lan sic. Lay doo waa m'hi tie cha.*[4]

MARK: Mom, dad. One rule at our dinner table. We speak English or nothing at all.

(Dead silence.)

SALLY: Who wants wine?

MARK: Please.

KIM: Mrs. Gee does not drink.

LI FEN: If it not too much trouble, I will have tea.

---

1   She used too much garlic.
2   No way you should use asparagus. It's not right.
3   It's not that bad.
4   How can you say that. It is awful.

136

MARK: Earl Grey, okay with you?

LI FEN: No Chinese tea?

SALLY: We ran out.

LI FEN: That okay. Oh, that remind me. I have gift for you.

SALLY: You didn't have to.

(LI FEN gives SALLY a box of tea.)

SALLY: Oh how thoughtful. A box of Chinese tea leaves.

MARK: Mom, you're too kind.

SALLY: Thank you, Mrs. Gee. Here's a crazy thought. Why don't I brew some?

LI FEN: I will do it.

KIM: (to Sally) You must excuse my wife. She has been host for so long, she forget how to be a guest.

SALLY: I can make the tea, Mrs. Gee.

LI FEN: Only Chinese know how to make this kind of tea.

SALLY: Pour boiling water over tea leaves and wait. That about sum it up?

MARK: (to LI FEN) We're the hosts. Let us do it.

LI FEN: No trouble. Kim, give me your plate.

KIM: I'm not finished eating. I'm almost done. Very close. *Aiya*, take my plate.

MARK: All the more room for dessert.

SALLY: Yes, you'll like them. Orange slices.

LI FEN: Very sorry. We can not stay for dessert.

KIM: But they have oranges.

MARK: Why not?

LI FEN: Many plans to make for your wedding.

SALLY: Excuse me?

KIM: Li Fen, what are you doing?

MARK: We're not getting married.

LI FEN: Not to her.

SALLY: Someone want to fill me in.

MARK: Get in line.

KIM: What did you do?

LI FEN: Lena Chow's niece will be here next week. Mark will meet her and then we can make the wedding plans.

MARK: I can't believe you did this.

SALLY: She's out of her mind.

KIM: You can't do this, Li Fen.

LI FEN: So much to do. The bride's cookies. My cheong sam. The wedding banquet.

KIM: Li Fen, I told you not to do this.

LI FEN: He is my son. He will marry who I tell him to marry.

MARK: Forget it. I'm not doing it.

LI FEN: Come home Mark. You do not belong here.

MARK: I'm not your little boy.

(Crash of gong.)

(KIM exits stage left.)

(SALLY puts the bandage around her eyes.)

(LI FEN turns on MARK and SALLY. They all stand.)

LI FEN: How did you escape from the Chamber of a Thousand Bamboo Spikes?

SALLY: Amazing what you can do with long grain rice and ordinary saliva.

LI FEN: Curses!

MARK: It's over, Yellow Claw.

SALLY: Your scheme to conquer the world will never succeed.

LI FEN: You do not even have an inkling of my plot.

SALLY: What makes you so certain that we haven't uncovered it?

LI FEN: Believe me, I would know.

(LI FEN grabs a chopstick off the table.)

MARK: Stay back, Snow Princess. She has the Chopstick of a Thousand Acids.

(LI FEN and MARK circle each other around the table.)

SALLY: Be careful, Agent Banana.

LI FEN: Can you truly fight me, my son?

MARK: I'll do what it takes.

LI FEN: Even kill your own mother?

MARK: We were never close.

(LI FEN lunges at MARK. They struggle. LI FEN staggers back with the chopstick in her stomach.)

LI FEN: But you are yin to my yang. Ping to my pong. We are inseparable.

MARK: I have an adopted mother now, and her name is Canada.

(Upon hearing these patriotic words, LI FEN falls behind the table and dies, leaving us to wonder what really killed her. The chopstick or her son's rejection.)

SALLY: Agent Banana? Mark? Are you alright? What happened to the Yellow Claw.

(MARK walks behind the table and picks up LI FEN's empty dress. It is smoking.)

(Crash of gong.)

(Lights down.)

ACT TWO, SCENE TWO

(Lights up.)

(SALLY at the bed, stage right. She writes.)

SALLY: While the script delivers some comic moments, the offering is light, banal and without substance. Because of its heavy reliance on racial stereotypes, the screenplay may be construed as racist and outmoded for today's politically sensitive viewers. Close the fist on the Yellow Claw. Do not consider this fluff piece for further development.

(LI FEN enters from stage left and mimes knocking on the door. SALLY goes to meet LI FEN.)

SALLY: I'm out of tea.

LI FEN: You must stop seeing Mark. Lena Chow's niece is coming next week. He must meet his future wife.

SALLY: He's busy then.

LI FEN: You and Mark are not good together.

SALLY: What did I ever do to you?

LI FEN: Nothing.

SALLY: Come on, I'd like to have some context for your hostility.

LI FEN: You make him leave us.

SALLY: You drove him out. He couldn't stand being treated like a child.

LI FEN: Only Chinese would know how important this is.

SALLY: I know your traditions better than Mark does. He can't tell one festival from the next. And he can barely string together a Chinese sentence.

LI FEN: You make him forget who he is.

SALLY: He lost his culture long before I ever met him.

LI FEN: He needs a Chinese wife to take care of him.

SALLY: This isn't patriarchal China.

LI FEN: A wife who knows respect.

SALLY: You mean a domestic. Your entire culture is based on sexist underpinnings. I see how you act around your husband.

LI FEN: That is my choice.

SALLY: You mean your place. You can't really be satisfied being forced to stay in that house.

LI FEN: It is important Kim work so we have money. He must take care of his family.

SALLY: But he leaves you alone in the house.

LI FEN: That is how it is supposed to be.

SALLY: Now you're propagating a self-fulfilling cycle with this arranged marriage. You're looking for a servant to take your place.

LI FEN: You are so arrogant. You think we are wrong because we do not do what you believe is right. I am getting Mark a wife so he will not be alone.

SALLY: What am I?

LI FEN: You do not understand the Chinese way.

SALLY: I'm attending courses on China so I can find some common ground with you. I'm learning Cantonese so I can talk to you.

LI FEN: You cannot learn how to be Chinese.

SALLY: All I'm trying to do is show you I have respect for you.

LI FEN: *G'why l'eur.*

SALLY: Stop calling me white girl.

LI FEN: How did you know?

SALLY: *G'why l'eur* was the first thing I learned in my Chinese course.

LI FEN: Hmph, you take a course and you think you know everything about us.

SALLY: It's the only way I can get close to you.

LI FEN: Why do you want to?

SALLY: Because you see me as some white devil.

LI FEN: You do not know what it is like to be us. Soon you will get tired of playing with your China boy and then you will leave him.

SALLY: Mrs. Gee, I just want to find some middle ground.

LI FEN: And to Mark you are nothing more than a concubine. When he is tired of having sex with you, he will want a real wife.

SALLY: Get out. Now!

LI FEN: It is better you stay with your own kind.

(LI FEN exits stage left. SALLY exits stage right.)

(Crash of gong.)

(Lights up on bench.)

(KIM enters centre stage, holding LI FEN's empty dress.)

KIM: Cruel, cruel fate. You have snatched away my imperious mistress. You are an eagle swooping upon my heart. Clutching it in your talons and squeezing its bloody passion until it is a dry, lifeless organ. Do not stop. Peck out my eyes. I no longer need them. I have already gazed upon heaven. Scratch away my skin, for I have felt the caress of her supple skin as she struck me. Skin that surpasses even this fine silk dress. Oh, soft skin. Slap me once more.

(KIM pins dress to the chart behind the bench, upstage centre.)

KIM: Oh, empty dress. You will hang here to remind me of what I could never have. Now, my heart is as empty as your sleeve. Infidels, you have snatched away my only love and I swear on my ancestors' tomb, I will avenge her death.

(A mournful gong rings.)

(Lights down.)

ACT TWO, SCENE THREE

(Lights up on the bench, centre stage.)

(MARK and KIM are at the bench.)

MARK: She can't make me do it.

KIM: I agree.

MARK: I'm putting my foot down. I'm not doing it.

KIM: You should not have to.

MARK: Why can't she accept the fact that Sally and I are together. I mean, you're okay with it, aren't you?

KIM: Your mother worries about you.

MARK: I can take care of myself.

KIM: She wants you to make something of your life.

MARK: I have done something with my life.

KIM: You are wasting your talent on machines.

MARK: I like working on cars.

KIM: You have no future there.

MARK: They moved me up to lube jobs.

KIM: That pleases me to no end.

MARK: Dad, will you drop it? You know I was never good at it.

KIM: You never gave it a chance. You are the last Gee. It is your obligation.

MARK: You can't expect me to do everything you want just because you raised me.

KIM: We are family. My father look after me out of respect for his father looking after him. I do the same. I look after my father and I look after you.

MARK: But you came to Canada.

KIM: The clinic would not survive if we stayed in China. I could not let the family business die. I had to make sure it keep taking care of us.

MARK: You can't guilt me into the clinic.

KIM: I'm not making you do anything.

MARK: I'm happy working at the shop, and that's what's important.

KIM: What do you know about happiness? You are too young to know better. Some day, you will want a family. You will want to give your children the best things, because it makes them happy and that will make you happy. That is most important thing. To have family and be able to take care of them.

MARK: I don't need you to take care of me.

KIM: We worked hard for you. Sacrifice everything so you can have what you deserve. What you want.

MARK: You're only doing what your father expected of you. He pushed you into this just like you're pushing me into it.

KIM: He did not push me. I see for myself how much he do. I respect him by doing the same.

MARK: Can't you respect what I'm doing? Sure it's rough right now, but I'm paying my dues. I mean, the clinic didn't take off when you opened it, did it?

KIM: It is doing okay now.

MARK: But not at the start. I mean it must have been rough. You in the clinic. Mom and me in China.

KIM: My family helped. They take care of your mother and you in China. Let you live in their home. Your grandmother looked after your mother like she was her own daughter.

MARK: But you barely saw your own wife.

KIM: That is not important. Family must look after each other. There is no other choice.

MARK: This isn't China. I have the right to decide what I want to do. If I
          don't have that freedom, I won't be worth anything.

KIM: If you do not have family, you have nothing.

(Crash of gong.)

(SALLY enters from stage right with bandages around her eyes. MARK goes to her.)

(KIM grabs a spear from the upstage wall and brandishes it against her and MARK.)

KIM: You killed my malevolent mistress.

MARK: She brought it on herself.

KIM: You will suffer a thousand agonies for what you have done.

SALLY: What more can you do that you haven't already done?

KIM: See this? I suppose not. Suffice it to know that you will hear your
          own screams gurgle in your throat.

SALLY: Canadians don't scream.

KIM: You will when I am done. To the Slab of Sacrifice.

MARK: Not a thousand?

KIM: You will be the first.

(They exit upstage centre.)

(Crash of gong.)

(Lights down.)

ACT TWO, SCENE FOUR

(Lights up on bed, stage right.)

(MARK and SALLY are standing on opposite sides of the bed. SALLY is stage right and MARK is stage left.)

SALLY: I won't have anything to do with that woman.

MARK: Don't be like that. Come on, we have to work something out.

SALLY: Not with her.

MARK: Mom was desperate.

SALLY: I can't believe you're defending her. She dismissed me because I'm white. Because I'm sleeping with her little boy. And now she's trying to replace me with a little Chinese wife.

MARK: This whole thing with Lena Chow has gotten way out of control. Lena's got a big mouth and mom doesn't know how to get out of this mess.

SALLY: That's her problem.

MARK: If we give mom a chance to save face, I'm sure she'll take it. But I need your help.

SALLY: Forget it. I've done my share. I'm tired of setting myself up for her abuse.

MARK: If you would just talk —

SALLY: Why bother? She won't listen. All she does is treat me like a second-class citizen. Your mom's nothing more than a racist.

MARK: Sally, she's family. I put up with her just like you put up with your opa.

SALLY: I put up with him because all he does is talk.

MARK: Sometimes, that kind of talk hurts just as much.

SALLY: At least he doesn't try to set me up with Dutch husbands.

MARK: Give me a chance to straighten this mess out. Come with me. Please.

SALLY: Why do you need me there?

MARK: (Struggling to find words.) I don't know. It's easier. Dad likes you. You're my support.

SALLY: I'm also the *g'why leur*. Face facts. Your mom's not going to come around no matter what we do.

MARK: She has to. I won't be her little boy any more. Please, Sally.

SALLY: Why is it so hard for her to let go?

MARK: I'm the last of the line. I screw up, and that's it.

SALLY: I'm a mistake?

MARK: No. Of course not. You're my guide to Chinese culture. Festivals, food, traditions, language …

SALLY: Don't forget movies.

MARK: Exactly. Without you, I'd be lining up to see the next *Wrath of the Yellow Claw.*

SALLY: That script was bad, Mark. Definitely bad.

MARK: That's why I need you. You know, keep me away from schlock like that.

SALLY: Sometimes, you make me so …

MARK: Insane.

SALLY: Yes.

MARK: You'll come with me?

SALLY: This is it. If it doesn't work this time, I'm gone … for good.

(Lights down.)

ACT TWO, SCENE FIVE

(Lights up on centre stage.)

(Cymbal crashes and percussion sticks beat so that it sounds like a Peking Opera.)

(KIM pushes MARK and SALLY into the room from upstage centre. He carries the spear.)

(SALLY has bandages around her eyes. She stumbles to the floor stage right. KIM goes to her, giving MARK time to grab the other spear off the upstage wall.)

(KIM spots MARK and the two face off with spears ready to lance the other. SALLY staggers to far stage right.
The battle is fierce and fast, like a Peking Opera style fight. MARK spins around, throwing kicks and jabbing his spear at KIM, who deftly parries every attack.)

(The music builds to a crescendo as the two meet in front of the bench.)

(Suddenly the music stops. The left arm of the dress on the body chart pulls free of the chart. [Of course, if the budget is tight, the chart can just swivel open.])

(KIM and MARK back up to reveal what or who is coming through the acupuncture chart.)

(Crash of gong as LI FEN steps through the upstage chart.)

(KIM and MARK drop their spears. SALLY fumbles around stage right.)

MARK: It's impossible.

KIM: It's glorious.

SALLY: What's going on?

MARK: She's alive.

KIM: (to LI FEN) Can it be you? Are my eyes deceiving me? How can I truly know it is you?

(LI FEN slaps KIM.)

KIM: You have returned from the dead, my sweet villainous mistress.

MARK: But I saw you dissolve.

LI FEN: I am not without my resources.

SALLY: You are a woman of many mysteries, Yellow *Craw*.

LI FEN: And it appears another is about to be revealed. Kim, remove her bandages.

(KIM removes SALLY's bandages. SALLY has oriental eyes. [Production note: this is a mask painted with oriental eyes that is hidden under the bandage. In the reality scenes, the eye mask can slip under the bandage, which can then be turned up to double as a hairband.])

SALLY: Oh my god, I can see. What? Why are you looking at me like that?

(Crash of gong.)

(MARK joins SALLY stage right. SALLY flips her eye mask up.)

(KIM joins LI FEN stage left.)

LI FEN: This girl is no good for you.

MARK: Mom, Sally and I are living together. You can't change that.

LI FEN: She is nothing but trouble.

MARK: Mom, you barely know her.

LI FEN: I know her type.

KIM: Li Fen, you are not listening to Mark.

SALLY: I told you this wouldn't work.

MARK: Mom, you're making this harder than it has to be.

LI FEN: It can only be one way.

MARK: There has to be a way to work this out.

LI FEN: If she leave, everything will be okay.

MARK: At least give us a chance.

LI FEN: I already did.

MARK: If you won't even try, then maybe you should just stay out of our lives.

KIM: How can you say that? You have no respect.

SALLY: Respect. Familiar with that concept, Mrs. Gee?

MARK: Please Sally. Don't make it worse.

SALLY: She's the one who's making it worse.

LI FEN: A good Chinese wife would not talk back.

MARK: Mom, I'm not going to marry some complete stranger.

LI FEN: You're not going to stay with her either.

SALLY: What gives you the right to dictate who he sees?

LI FEN: Twenty years I am his mother. Mark, Lena's niece will move into our home and take care of you. She will be better for you. You will see when you meet her.

MARK: Didn't you hear anything I said? I'm not letting you arrange this marriage.

LI FEN: *Aiya*, you forget so much. You know nothing about your family any more. You lose traditions. Lose culture.

(Crash of gong.)

(SALLY pulls down her eye mask.)

LI FEN: Lose all vestiges of her western features. Sally's bandages were tainted with the Solution of a Thousand Assimilations. She will soon turn completely Chinese.

SALLY: I have to see myself. Agent Banana, hold your head still.

(SALLY grabs MARK's head and tries to see her own reflection.)

SALLY: Don't squint so much.

MARK: That's the way they normally are.

SALLY: Oh my god! Tell me there's an antidote.

LI FEN: What purpose would that serve? It would merely be an all too convenient solution for you.

SALLY: I'm doomed to be a freak. I look just like a minion of the Yellow Craw. Deformed. Grotesque. Hideous. (to Mark) Present company excepted, of course.

MARK: Is that how you see me?

SALLY: No. Of course not. Never. Maybe a little.

MARK: You used me all along. You just wanted to get close to the Yellow Claw.

SALLY: You got it all wrong Agent Banana. I never wanted to use you. They forced me to.

LI FEN: Ah so, the white devil reveals her true colours. (to Mark) She turned you from my path. She tinted your eyes with lenses of hate. She made you do this.

(Crash of gong.)

(SALLY puts her eye mask under her headband.)

LI FEN: She make you turn away from family. She drive you away from us.

SALLY: Mark makes his own decisions.

MARK: (to LI FEN) Stop blaming her. It's you. The way you treat me. You have to control every step of my life. Choose who I should be with. You even went to Sally behind my back.

KIM: Li Fen? Did you do that?

SALLY: She certainly did. She doesn't want her little boy messing with the white devil.

KIM: I forbid this, Li Fen.

LI FEN: He is my only son. He must obey me.

MARK: I'm not five years old any more.

LI FEN: You are still too young to know any better. I protect you.

SALLY: From what? Me? Real life? Growing up?

MARK: Mom, you expect me to do everything you want.

KIM: Mark, she's not making you do anything.

MARK: What do you call this arranged marriage?

KIM: You don't have to marry Lena Chow's niece.

LI FEN: *Aiya* Kim, what are you saying?

KIM: Li Fen, we can't make him do this.

SALLY: Finally, someone in this family is making sense.

LI FEN: Kim, I make the decisions about Mark. You run your clinic, but this family is my job. Mark is my responsibility.

KIM: He is our son.

LI FEN: Then let me do what is right for him. (to MARK) Will you meet her? Please. She will be coming all the way from China.

MARK: Forget it.

SALLY: Mark, let's go. There's no point in trying any more.

LI FEN: I can never face Lena Chow if you don't meet her niece.

KIM: Li Fen, stop this.

MARK: (to LI FEN) That's your problem. If you had trusted me to handle my own life, none of this would have happened.

LI FEN: You are my only son. I only do what is best for you.

MARK: No, you're trying to run my life.

LI FEN: How can I? You always shut me out. You get mad when I call. You never want to come home. You avoid us.

MARK: I've got a job. I can't spend all my time with you.

KIM: He is a man, Li Fen. He can make his own mind up.

LI FEN: Just because he is your son, you think he can do what he wants. I am your wife, but I have no say. You make me come here. You make me live in this strange country. You say you only want one child, I give him to you. But he is mine too. If he goes, I have nothing.

MARK: You're not considering what I want.

LI FEN: I come to Canada so you can have better life. You do things that make me crazy, but I don't say anything. You become mechanic, I tell your father it is what makes you happy. He is the one who wants you to work in clinic. Not me.

KIM: Li Fen, I thought it was what you wanted.

LI FEN: Don't lie, Kim. You always wanted him to be in the clinic. I don't care if he works in the clinic or not. I never stopped him from doing what he wanted. Anything he needs, I give it to him. I always let him do what he wants.

SALLY: Except for now.

LI FEN: One time, I want something for myself. Don't leave me alone Mark. I need you.

MARK: I didn't say I was leaving you. I just don't want any part of this arranged marriage.

LI FEN: I won't make you marry her. But just meet her. If you don't like her, I won't do anything else. All I ask is this one thing. Then you can do what you want. I promise.

SALLY: He doesn't want to meet her. Come on Mark.

MARK: No, wait.

(Crash of gong.)

(SALLY pulls down her eye mask.)

MARK: Snow Princess, you betrayed me.

LI FEN: (to MARK) There is a certain symmetry to it. All the times, she vowed to destroy the yellow horde. All the moments she expressed her hatred for the Yellow Claw. She meant you as well.

SALLY: All I wanted to do was put an end to the Yellow *Craw's* reign. I didn't mean to include you.

LI FEN: Know this, you will always be accepted here.

(KIM gives MARK a spear from the floor. Then KIM returns to LI FEN, stage left. MARK confronts SALLY stage right.)

KIM: The white devil has betrayed you. The Yellow Claw will embrace you.

SALLY: (Chinese accent) Mark, don't do it. The Yellow Claw doesn't care about you. To her, you're just another minion. If you let her succeed, you'll jeopardize the freedom of western world. You'll risk the royal Rockies. Can you do that? Can you turn your back on your adopted home?

LI FEN: A stirring speech. (to MARK) Kill her.

SALLY: (fights to keep normal accent) You can not do it, Agent Banana. Help me destroy the Yellow Claw.

(MARK drives the spear into SALLY. She staggers backwards toward stage right. MARK drops the spear and steps stage left, closer to his parents.)

SALLY: This is wrong. The collective powers of the west have always thwarted the corrupt east.

LI FEN: Why? Because we are weak? Because you are strong and powerful? Because you are young and I am older? Because you are white and I am yellow?

SALLY: Good always beats evil. It's written in all the history books.

LI FEN: Yes and in your history books, we Chinese all look alike. We run your laundromats. We hide in opium dens. We are shiftless, untrustworthy, evil. In your history books, we are easily beaten. Well, now you know that we are much more than you perceive. We are not evil. We are merely different.

SALLY: But you want to conquer the world.

LI FEN: A small character flaw.

SALLY: This isn't how it's supposed to end.

LI FEN: Tell me how should it end. You and Mark defeat us and then walk off into the sunset hand in hand? Is that your ending? Why must we always bow to your will. Why does white always beat yellow? That is such a cliche and in the world of the Yellow Claw, there is no room for cliches. Well, not many.

MARK: Sally, I'm sorry.

SALLY: Always know this. I never found you that repulsive. Ugh ...

(SALLY staggers stage right. MARK follows her.)

MARK: Snow Princess? Sally?

(Crash of gong.)

(SALLY slips her eye mask under her headband.)

(SALLY and MARK turn to LI FEN and KIM.)

MARK: I'm sorry, Sally, but I'm going to do this. It's important to my mom.

SALLY: Mark, you're caving in.

LI FEN: Quiet, Mark makes his own decisions.

SALLY: She's going to keep pushing you until you give in completely.

MARK: Sally, it's just one meeting.

SALLY: It's always just one thing. It'll never stop.

MARK: She's family. I can't turn my back on her.

SALLY: But you can ignore my feelings? Mark, your parents are running your life.

KIM: Mark does what is best for everyone.

SALLY: You mean what's best for you.

MARK: You're wrong. Just because I care about my parents, doesn't mean I have no control of my life. I'm making the decision to see this girl.

SALLY: Your mother's manipulating you. She's forcing you into this arranged marriage.

MARK: No one's forcing me to do anything.

SALLY: You have your own mind Mark. Use it.

MARK: I know what I'm doing. It's a compromise Sally.

SALLY: You're giving up everything, Mark. And for what? To make your mother happy?

MARK: I'm helping her save face.

SALLY: You mean you're giving in to her every whim. It's time to grow up Mark. Leave your parents. Don't wimp out.

MARK: What makes you think helping my mother is a wimp-out? I'm showing my respect for what she's done for me.

SALLY: If you go through with this, count me out.

MARK: I owe her this much. It's not going any further than that. I promise.

SALLY: Like you promised to tell them about us?

MARK: Can't you believe it's just going to be one meeting?

SALLY: I've heard that before. I'm not going to go through it again. Make your decision, Mark.

MARK: I'm sorry, Sally.

SALLY: No, I'm the one who's sorry.

MARK: Sally —

(SALLY exits stage right.)

(LI FEN joins her son at centre stage. KIM follows.)

LI FEN: You did the right thing.

KIM: Li Fen, you shouldn't say that.

LI FEN: She left him just like I said she would. You can never trust their kind.

MARK: (to the audience) A little girl stole my ice cream cone.

KIM: You drove her away.

MARK: (to the audience) The emperor has no pants.

LI FEN: You heard him, Kim. He makes his own mind up. I cannot stop him.

MARK: (to audience) The lonely dog eats its young.

KIM: You didn't even try.

LI FEN: I did not see you trying to make things right either.

MARK: (to audience) Clowns only smile when they grieve.

KIM: It is his business.

LI FEN: Then let him alone. (to MARK) This is for the best Mark. You will see.

(MARK forces a smile at his mother.)

(Lights fade out.)

THE END

GLOSSARY

Acupuncture: An ancient Chinese medicinal art which treats ailments by using needles in pressure points. Traditionally, it is an art that is passed down from family to family.

Aiya: A Chinese expression of exasperation. Similar to "darn," "damn" or "oh God."

Ang Lee: Taiwanese film director whose films include Jane Austen's *Sense and Sensibility; Eat, Drink, Man, Woman;* and *The Wedding Banquet.*

Arranged marriage: A custom where parents negotiate a fee to marry off their children. The go-between is a matchmaker. Usually, the bride and groom do not have a say in the matter.

Banana: Common slur for Chinese raised in Canada. They are considered to have lost their Chinese essence, so they look yellow on the outside, but are white on the inside.

Bride's cookies: A Chinese wedding token the groom gives to the bride's parents as compensation for taking their daughter. These cookies replace what would have been money.

Call Display: A function on phones that displays the phone number of the person calling you.

Cantonese: A Chinese dialect that is commonly used in the rural areas of China and in Hong Kong.

Captain Canuck: A Canadian comic book hero.

Cheong Sam: A Chinese dress worn by women for formal occasions.

David Carradine: A Caucasian actor who starred as a Chinese martial artist in the television series Kung Fu.

Development: In the film industry, the rewriting of scripts is referred to as development. A writer gets notes from various people to prepare the script for production.

Dragon Boat Festival: A Chinese festival to honour a dragon boat captain who died at sea. His crew threw dumplings in the water to keep fish from eating his body. The festival honours this custom and celebrates with boat races.

Dragon Lady: A woman who is conniving and manipulative.

Eat, Drink, Man, Woman: A Chinese film about an old cook who has lost his sense of taste and is losing his three daughters. Directed by Ang Lee.

Gwandung: A province in southern China.

G'why Leur: Cantonese for white girl.

Kata: A series of martial arts moves done without striking anyone.

Mah Jong: A Chinese game for four players that uses tiles. Similar to the card game rummy.

Opa: The Dutch name for grandfather.

Readers: People hired by film producers to analyze scripts and decide whether or not a script is worth investing in.

S'ai Ji: Cantonese for little boy.

Shaolin Master: A kung fu master.

Save Face: To prevent public embarrassment.

Screenplay: A script for a movie.

Taiwanese Toys: Similar to gadgets made in Japan in the 1950s, these toys are considered cheap and easily broken.

Tranny: Slang reference for transmission of a car.

Waw Teep: A Chinese dumpling that usually contains pork. It is cooked by frying and steaming.

Wedding Banquet: The Chinese equivalent of the wedding reception. However, instead of dancing, the wedding guests eat from a selection of at least ten Chinese dishes.

The Wedding Banquet: A film about a gay Chinese man who poses as a straight man when his parents visit. He pretends to be engaged to a woman, much to the chagrin of his gay lover.

Wet Naps: A brand name of moist tissues.

White Devil: Chinese slur for Caucasians.

Yellow Claw: A fictional character created by Sax Rohmer. It is a racist depiction of the Chinese as opium smoking, conniving evil underlords who want to take over the world.

Yin and Yang: The harmonius balance of good and evil.

PRONUNCIATION GUIDE

Cantonese: Aiya
Phonetically: *I yah*
Translation: Oh God, darn

Cantonese: Cheong Sam
Phonetically: *Chee-ong Sawm*
Translation: Formal Chinese dress

Cantonese: Gee
Phonetically: *Jee*
Translation: Proper name of Gee family

Cantonese: G'why Leur
Phonetically: *Guh why l'oi*
Translation: White girl

Cantonese: Li Fen
Phonetically: *Lie Fen*
Translation: First name of Mrs. Gee

Dutch: Opa
Phonetically: *Oh pa*
Translation: Grandpa

Cantonese: S'ai Ji
Phonetically: *Sigh Ji*
Translation: Little boy

Cantonese: Waw Teep
Phonetically: *W'aww Teep*
Translation: Chinese dumplings

Cantonese: Koey yung tie d'aw schun t'ow.
Phonetically: *K'oi yung tie d'awww sh'een t'ow.*
Translation: She used too much garlic.

Cantonese: Na ging ying jeng di sic mut wun j'aw kay sut.
Phonetically: *Na ging ying jeng dee sick mutt woon jaw kay sut.*
Translation: No way you should use asparagus.

Cantonese: Lay n'ying g'aw yung lo shun ga.
Phonetically: *Lay nuh ying guh aw yoong low shoon ga.*
Translation: It's not right.

Cantonese: Kay sut doo m'hi tie cha.
Phonetically: *Kay sut do my tie cha.*
Translation: It's not that bad.

Cantonese: G'um lan sic. Lay doo waa m'hi tie cha.
Phonetically: *Gum lawn sick. Lay do w'aww my tie cha.*
Translation: How can you say that. It is awful.

Gently Down the Stream

by AVIVA RAVEL

PLAYWRIGHT

Aviva Ravel's plays often reflect the experiences of Montreal's Jewish community where she was born and raised and continues to live. She holds a doctorate in Canadian Drama, directs the popular Performance Playreading Ensemble at the Côte St. Luc Library, and produces plays for adults and children for Cameo Production.

Ravel's stage plays include *Dispossessed*, published in *Major Plays of the Canadian Theatre* by Irwin, and *The Twisted Loaf*, which were both produced at the Saidye Bronfman Centre; *Moon People* published by Playwright's Press in *Six Canadian Plays*; and *Vengeance*, published by NuAge Press in *Escape Acts*. *Soft Voices* and *The Twisted Loaf* were published by Simon & Pierre in *A Collection of Canadian plays, Volume 3*. Ravel's plays have been broadcast by CBC, Israel Radio and produced in Montreal and by theatre groups across the country.

Aviva Ravel is the author of *Be My Friend*, a children's play published by Playwrights Press, and *The Sholom Aleichem Show*, published by Pioneer Drama Service. She is also co-editor of *A Point on a Sheet of Green Paper*, an anthology of Canadian poetry published with a Hebrew translation. *Separate Pieces*, a collection of monologues by Aviva Ravel was published in Israel. Her work has been the subject of a doctoral dissertation by Lucia D'Amato at the University of Rome.

The Courting of Sally Schwartz and *My Rumanian Cousin* ran for a year at La Diligence Dinner Theatre in Montreal. Another Ravel play, *Mother Variations*, was adapted for the screen under the title *Mothers and Daughters*; it was presented at the Montreal Film Festival in 1992. Ravel is the editor of *Canadian Mosaic*, the first anthology of Canadian plays published by Simon & Pierre in this series. *Dance Like a Butterfly*, which appeared in the first volume, has toured Canada extensively and is being produced as a film by Carol Campbell Productions, London, Ontario.

ORIGINAL CAST AND PRODUCTION TEAM

GENTLY DOWN THE STREAM was presented at the Quebec Drama Festival at Centaur Theatre in Montreal, April 26, 1990 with the following cast:

ALEX   David Raboy
MOISH   Herb Goldstein

166

Director	Aviva Ravel
Stage Manager	Thelma Perlman
Lighting Design	Simon Oliver

DEDICATION

GENTLY DOWN THE STREAM is dedicated to the memory of David Raboy, gifted actor, devoted colleague and good friend.

COPYRIGHT

GENTLY DOWN THE STREAM

CHARACTERS

2 characters

ALEX: Age 85

MOISH: Age 84

PLACE

A bench in a large park.

TIME

Mid-morning. The present.

MUSIC

Lively Yiddish melody.

ALEX enters slowly, walking with the help of an umbrella which serves as a cane. His clothes are clean, but his appearance is not too tidy. He approaches the bench. He taps the bench with his umbrella as though testing it. Looks to see if it's clean, sits down, leans the cane against the bench and stares around him, anticipating company. When he sees someone approaching, he quickly pulls a newspaper out of his pocket and buries his head in it as though very engrossed in the news and indifferent to the approaching person. MOISH arrives, he is spryer than Alex although he too suffers from assorted minor ailments. He dresses well, a hanky in his breast pocket, his suit pressed and clean. He stands at the bench and looks at Alex. MOISH carries a bag that contains a thermos and bag of cookies.

MOISH: Hello, Alex.

ALEX: Oh, it's you.

MOISH: Who were you expecting?

ALEX: Irving, Frank, Myer, Lou, Henry. What's the difference.

MOISH: If you'd like better company, I'll leave.

ALEX: It's all the same to me. Sit.

(MOISH dusts bench with handkerchief)

MOISH: It's a nice day.

ALEX: If you say so.

MOISH: I say so.

ALEX: You think you know everything.

MOISH: What's to know? I only said …

ALEX: I know what you said.

MOISH: (a beat) You sleep good last night?

ALEX: Who can sleep in that place? One snores, one cries, one coughs …

MOISH: I slept good.

ALEX: You always sleep good.

MOISH: But last night was special.

ALEX: You don't say.

MOISH: I had a young girl in my bed.

ALEX: What?

MOISH: My son, the lawyer, sent me a present.

ALEX: You don't say.

MOISH: It's true. Ah, I knew you wouldn't believe me.

ALEX: It's true? A young girl? You mean a …

MOISH: Who cares what she is? She was very nice, a little skinny, but she smelled good. A present for my birthday. 84 years old today.

ALEX: That's disgusting. Poo.

MOISH: She likes old men. I'll introduce you.

ALEX: You were always a degenerate — and a liar.

MOISH: Yeah, it's a nice day.

ALEX: It's true? About the girl?

MOISH: (laughs) No. But it was a nice dream. That's why I sleep so good.

ALEX: You and your lousy jokes. (a beat) Still, as a present, it's not a bad idea.

MOISH: So what's the news?

ALEX: What news?

MOISH: In the paper.

ALEX: The Orioles are playing the Red Sox in Boston.

MOISH: That's news?

ALEX: The Mets are playing the Expos in New York.

MOISH: I mean real news, in the world.

ALEX: I just told you. The Mets are playing …

MOISH: What's happening in England, France, Russia, Israel?

ALEX: The same.

MOISH: No news is good news.

ALEX: Moish, you were always an ignoramus. Why don't you buy your own paper and read for yourself?

MOISH: My eyes aren't so good anymore. I see good from far, but not from near.

ALEX: So get glasses.

MOISH: And spoil my good looks?

ALEX: You don't need glasses. You can't read.

MOISH: What do you mean I can't read. I went to night school in this country.

ALEX: So you can only read at night.

MOISH: (indignant) I ran a dry good business. I can also read Yiddish. I went to 'cheder'. I had a Bar Mitzvah.

ALEX: There's reading and reading. Some people read the words, but they don't understand the meaning. Some people read and they understand what's under the words. The hidden meaning, the depth.

MOISH: And you understand the depth.

ALEX: Yes I do.

MOISH: Well, don't let me disturb you. Here's a man who understands the deep and hidden meaning behind the Orioles, the Expos, the Mets. Huh. (laughs)

ALEX: Let me tell you something, Moish, and listen good, so even your weak brain will understand. If there was no sports, there would be fighting and killing right here in America. It's the sports that keeps the peace. The people watch the games, they shout "get him" "kill him" "steal" "knock him dead". It lets out all the aggressions. If there was no hockey, baseball, boxing, it wouldn't be safe to walk in the street.

MOISH: It's still not safe.

ALEX: But it would be worse.

MOISH: Last week I got mugged. A kid punched me and took my wallet.

ALEX: Did he break your head?

MOISH: No.

ALEX: Did you have to go to the hospital?

MOISH: No.

ALEX: You see, I told you it could be worse.

MOISH: It's a nice day.

ALEX: You already said that.

MOISH: I know, but it's still nice. Just a little black cloud in the distance, nothing special. And the sun to warm my old bones.

ALEX: Maybe it'll be a nice day after all. Maybe I'll get a letter from my daughter, my son, my grandchildren. Maybe today the pains in my legs will go away. Maybe today the "Meshiach" will come and I'll be a young man again. I'll be a union organizer. I'll make speeches. I'll shout: "Down with exploiters!!" "Down with the blood suckers." "Down with the capitalists!" Of course, I'm not referring to present company.

MOISH: I'm a capitalist?

ALEX: Sure, you used to exploit the public. You bought goods, sold for a profit, made a living on the backs of the workers.

MOISH: You're crazy.

ALEX: It's not your fault, Moish, it's the system. What could you do? You had to make a living. You bought cheap, sold dear, and now you're a rich old man.

MOISH: First of all, I'm not rich! (rises) Second of all, my prices were reasonable. That's why people bought at my store. I worked from seven in the morning to nine at night, like a "meshugener". And what do I have from all that? A few dollars in the bank. You know for what? For a private room in a hospital when you're old and sick. You work all your life, and in the end the hospital gets it all.

ALEX: Moish, why are you so depressed all of a sudden?

MOISH: You make me depressed.

ALEX: Me? What did I say?

MOISH: You pick on me. You insult me. I think I'll go. And you'll never see me on this bench again. (starts to move away)

ALEX: Don't be foolish. I was only joking. For a capitalist, you're a nice person.

MOISH: I'm not a capitalist.

ALEX: All right, I take it all back. Not an exploiter, not a capitalist, just a nice old man. (reads his paper)

MOISH: Huh. (sits, a beat) Alex, did you hear something?

ALEX: What?

MOISH: Somebody running behind us. Don't turn around.

ALEX: I don't hear nothing.

MOISH: Don't move. Now look straight ahead, a man running, over there.

ALEX: Yeah.

MOISH: He stumbles …

ALEX: Yeah.

MOISH: He fell. He's not moving.

ALEX: No.

MOISH: Alex, I think he's dead.

ALEX: No. (puts down his newspaper)

MOISH: Somebody shot him. Maybe a bullet in the chest.

ALEX: (rises) Then we have to do something.

MOISH: (rises) Do what?

ALEX: We can't let a dead man lie there and do nothing.

MOISH: If he's already dead we can't help him.

ALEX: That's true.

MOISH: If he's not dead yet, other people will see him. It's better for old people like us not to get involved with the police.

ALEX: Who's talking about police?

MOISH: For instance, if we tell a policeman, he starts asking questions, brings us to the station to be witnesses. If there's a trial we have to go to court, you have strength for all that?

ALEX: Frankly, no.

MOISH: It's enough to get up in the morning, get dressed, eat, go to the club, play cards ...

ALEX: You're right.

MOISH: So we do nothing. (sits) We sit here like two old men. Nobody pays attention to us. And everything will take care of itself.

ALEX: It's not moral. (sits) A human being should be responsible for all humanity.

MOISH: That's why I got mugged last week. Humanity, huh.

ALEX: But if you're old, you're exempt.

MOISH: Nobody expects anything from you.

ALEX: Like we don't count.

MOISH: We can't do any good.

ALEX: Nobody takes us seriously.

MOISH: So what difference can we make.

ALEX: We just sit back and observe the world from a distance.

MOISH: Anyhow I'm sure the man is dead. So much blood on his shirt. And the way he dropped …

ALEX: Look, I think someone's coming.

MOISH: Two someones. A boy and a girl. They'll see the body and do something.

ALEX: People see what they want to see.

MOISH: They're walking right by without looking down.

ALEX: They're looking only at each other.

MOISH: They're young. They have eyes for no one else.

ALEX: You remember what it was like?

MOISH: Sure. I tell you I dream about it.

ALEX: Me, I hardly remember.

MOISH: Look, they're stopping.

ALEX: They want to lie down on the grass.

MOISH: They'll see the body for sure.

ALEX: Yeah, I think they see it. She's screaming.

MOISH: He takes her hand and they run away.

ALEX: So death won't touch them.

MOISH: They're too young to think about that.

ALEX: They'll find another spot to lie down. And this time they'll examine the place real good.

MOISH: You think they'll tell someone about the body?

ALEX: No. They don't want trouble. They're too young.

MOISH: They'll lie down and kiss and touch and block out the whole world. (ALEX reads his newspaper) I tell you, Alex, it's the only thing that counts. Everything else is worth nothing.

ALEX: What are you talking about?

MOISH: Sex. It's the one thing that makes me mad to be old. Nobody can stand to look at you. The skin is all wrinkled, the bones are bent, the face — I won't even mention it. And you move like a tired, old horse. And who wants to mount a tired old horse? But inside I feel like that young man who takes his girl to a nice spot on the grass.

ALEX: All you talk about is sex.

MOISH: What else is there?

ALEX: Ah, let me read my paper in peace. Whenever you come around, there's trouble.

MOISH: What did I do?

ALEX: You sit there. You talk. You make me nervous.

MOISH: Can I help it if you're a nervous type? (takes thermos) You want tea?

ALEX: Yeah.

MOISH: Careful, it's hot.

ALEX: (tastes it) Hey, no sugar!

MOISH: So gimme back. (wipes rim and drinks) Look who's coming. Crazy Betsy!

ALEX: I hope she's in a good mood today. Last week she kicked me in the shin. I still got the bruise.

MOISH: There's not much garbage for her to look through. That's what puts her in a bad mood.

176

ALEX: Here's some change. Give it to her and maybe she'll leave us alone.

MOISH: She sees the body. Maybe she'll call the police.

ALEX: Fat chance.

MOISH: Why not?

ALEX: She knows people don't listen to crazies.

MOISH: That's when she tells made-up stories. But this is not made up.

ALEX: But only me and you know it.

MOISH: Look what she's doing.

ALEX: What's she doing?

MOISH: She's going through his pockets.

ALEX: I'm not surprised.

MOISH: She's taking everything out and putting it into plastic bags.

ALEX: I'm not surprised.

MOISH: Maybe we should do something.

ALEX: What for?

MOISH: They won't be able to identify the body.

ALEX: Do you know the body?

MOISH: Never saw him in my life.

ALEX: So what do you care?

MOISH: I don't believe it! She's taking off his shoes!

ALEX: A dead man don't need no shoes. He's not going nowhere.

MOISH: Also his socks. She's holding them up, examining them for holes!

ALEX: She's particular, yet.

MOISH: She's taking them too.

ALEX: She won't bother us now, that's for sure. Gimme back my quarter.

MOISH: She's putting his cap on her head.

ALEX: It's a nice cap?

MOISH: It's a cap. For the sun.

ALEX: Lucky Betsy made a good haul today. My quarter, Moish.

MOISH: (gives him his quarter) Ah.

ALEX: (calls) Hey, Betsy, what you got there?!

MOISH: Be quiet!

ALEX: Don't worry she won't bother us now.

MOISH: She's running away. You scared her.

ALEX: That was the idea. A corpse is bad enough. But a naked one is embarrassing. She would've stripped him clean.

MOISH: I gotta tell somebody. That nice lady over there.

ALEX: How do you know she's nice?

MOISH: She's dressed sensible. She's holding a little boy by the hand. So what's not to be nice?

ALEX: You wanna tell her, tell her. But if anyone questions me, I didn't see you or that body today.

MOISH: Alex, I don't believe you're so selfish.

ALEX: I didn't start off that way. I developed it. It kept me alive.

MOISH: The selfish socialist.

ALEX: I struggled plenty to help the working class. But I also learned to look after myself. Since I'm 13.

MOISH: I don't want to hear those stories.

ALEX: I won't tell you. I'm not in the mood today.

MOISH: We don't have to tell the lady anything. She sees the body by herself. She takes the little boy's hand and starts to pull him away. He doesn't want to go, she slaps him.

ALEX: Nice lady, uh?

MOISH: Poor little boy. He'll never know why his mother hit him.

ALEX: Stupid woman.

MOISH: How would *you* handle it?

ALEX: I'd say, the man is sleeping on the grass, we won't disturb him, so let's have our picnic somewhere else.

MOISH: What about the blood?

ALEX: What blood? The man's a painter. He was painting a red house, he got tired, so he came up here to rest.

MOISH: You're such a liar.

ALEX: Why destroy a child's innocence.

MOISH: You're really something, Alex.

ALEX: Is that a compliment?

MOISH: Take it any way you like.

ALEX: I once had a child like that. A beauty.

MOISH: So now he's grown up and not so beautiful.

ALEX: He never grew up.

MOISH: Ah.

ALEX: An accident. All of a sudden. And he was gone.

MOISH: Ah.

ALEX: At least fifteen children were walking on the sidewalk, coming home from school. Talking, running, laughing, you know children. All of a sudden a truck goes off the road and hits my Bennie. Fifteen children — and my Bennie gets hit. I never understood.

MOISH: What's there to understand.

ALEX: So many things happened in my life, but Bennie is still fresh in my mind. Like it was yesterday. I don't understand.

MOISH: What's there to understand?

ALEX: A minute before he was walking on the inside. Near the houses. Then he runs out to tell something to his friend. The friend's name is Abie. If he hadn't run out Abie would've been killed. I don't understand.

MOISH: "Ribono shel olam" what's there to understand?

ALEX: There's got to be reasons for things. Take that tree over there. The leaves are falling. The tree will soon be bare. Why will the tree soon be bare? Because the leaves fell down. A reason.

MOISH: Let's talk about something else.

ALEX: I wanna talk about my Bennie. You can talk about what you want and I can't?

MOISH: All right, talk. But I don't have to listen.

ALEX: I'll talk and you'll listen. Because that Abie is still alive, a man with a family, a judge, living the life he stole from my Bennie.

180

(takes his umbrella)

MOISH: It's not Abie's fault.

ALEX: I'm going to take a walk.

MOISH: No, sit here, sit. You're in no condition to walk.

ALEX: Let me tell you something interesting. Bennie was the best of all of them. A gentle child, a smart child. So tell me where's justice. Uh? I'll tell you. There is no justice. (exits)

MOISH: Come back! Alex, Come back! (a beat) What can I say to him. Who understands? Look at my hands, my feet, my head. Who put them there? Eyes, nose, mouth. We're funny creatures. And the animals, even funnier. Big tails, long ears, skinny necks, fat legs. God must've had a good time when he invented the animals. Ah, that's an artist with an imagination.

ALEX: (enters) Still talking to yourself like an old man.

MOISH: I was thinking about the animals.

ALEX: You got nothing better to think about.

MOISH: Alex, if you're going to be in a bad mood, I'll leave you right here and go to the club my myself.

ALEX: You wanna go, go.

MOISH: I don't wanna go. But I don't want to sit here and watch you cry.

ALEX: Just once a day I cry. Then it's finished.

MOISH: Me too I cry once a day.

ALEX: You? What for?

MOISH: You won't think it's serious.

ALEX: I bet it's about money.

MOISH: How did you guess?

ALEX: I know you, Moish. So how much did you lose?

MOISH: Five hundred thousand.

ALEX: That's a lot of money! How?

MOISH: I bought a ticket for the sweepstakes. One day I went to a restaurant and forgot my wallet. So I told the waiter I'd sell him the ticket to pay for the meal. I bought tickets before and never won a penny so I was sure I wouldn't win that time either. The rest you can guess.

ALEX: So the waiter bought the restaurant.

MOISH: That's right.

ALEX: He should've given you a present. After all, your ticket.

MOISH: As we said in the old country — he gave me "goornisht mit nisht".

ALEX: Nobody gets what he deserves.

MOISH: You can say that again …

ALEX: Nobody gets what he deserves …

MOISH: Okay, enough!

ALEX: So, where are they now, the lady and the boy?

MOISH: I don't see them anymore.

ALEX: She won't tell nobody. But one day he'll remind his mother and she'll say: "I don't know what you're talking about, it must've been a dream." But she's making a big mistake. Children see the ugly part of life very soon. They know and the parents don't know they know. When I was four a man exposed himself to me in the lane.

MOISH: Oh no.

ALEX: I never told nobody. I wasn't afraid, the man had a kind face. I knew he couldn't help himself. I was so young and I already knew.

MOISH: Alex, I was just thinking …

ALEX: That's a nice change.

MOISH: I wonder what the killer had against the dead man.

ALEX: Gangsters, bums. One owes money, one blackmails, one robs — to them life is cheap. After the bosses kicked me out of the factory for organizing the union, I drove a taxi. Thirty-five years I drove a taxi. I know all about it.

MOISH: Maybe he was a decent person. Maybe he just happened to be in the wrong place at the wrong time. He saw something, so they got rid of him.

ALEX: It's possible.

MOISH: Poor man. Lying there without shoes, without socks, without a cap. If that happened to me, I'd die.

ALEX: He did.

MOISH: Your heart is so hard, your arteries must be all blocked up. It's a wonder you're still alive.

ALEX: Moish, I come here to sit quietly on the bench and read my paper in peace and what do I get? A murder, a crazy bag lady, a mother who hits her child, and a "noodnick".

MOISH: Why do you blame me? I didn't have anything to do with all that.

ALEX: That's what *you* say.

MOISH: You think I know that man over there? I tell you I never saw him in my life.

ALEX: Go check it out.

MOISH: What for?

ALEX: To make sure.

MOISH: All right, I'll go, but keep your eyes on me all the time. If someone passes by, warn me. Whistle.

ALEX: I can't whistle.

MOISH: So sing *God Save the Queen*.

ALEX: Monarchist.

MOISH: So sing *The Star Spangled Banner*.

ALEX: Imperialist!

MOISH: So sing *Frère Jacques*.

ALEX: Separatist!

MOISH: Alex, I don't care *what* you sing, so long as you tell me what it is. So I won't think someone else is singing. Sing — *Bye Bye Blackbird*.

ALEX: I don't know that one.

MOISH: Alex, I'm not going over there unless you warn me if someone comes by.

ALEX: All right, I'll sing *Row Row Row Your Boat*.

MOISH: Practice it.

ALEX: (sings with flair) Row row row your boat,
Gently down the stream,
Merrily merrily merrily,
Life is just a dream.

MOISH: You sing like a frog with a sore throat.

ALEX: Get yourself another singer if you don't like it.

MOISH: Excuse me if I insulted your voice, Mr. Caruso. Now keep your eyes on me. Both of them.

ALEX: I told you I don't see too good from far.

MOISH: You can see if someone's coming.

ALEX: Yeah, *that* I can see.

(MOISH goes off. ALEX rises. Breathing deeply, tries to do some exercises. He is soon out of breath and sits. MOISH returns out of breath)

MOISH: That was some walk.

ALEX: So, do you know him?

MOISH: No.

ALEX: What does he look like?

MOISH: About 40-50, slim, black hair, little mustache, scar on the cheek …

ALEX: You made sure he's dead?

MOISH: I assumed …

ALEX: Never take anything for granted …

MOISH: So *you* go. And if someone comes *I'll* sing.

ALEX: (rises) All right, I want to settle this once and for all … (he moves toward exit and returns at once) I can't go. Hershel Caplansky is coming this way.

MOISH: Who?

ALEX: Hershel Caplansky, then Hershey Caplan, now Harvey Capp, the artist, if you'll excuse me.

MOISH: How do you know it's him?

ALEX: The red beret. He bought it in France fifty years ago and he still

185

wears it. With the red kerchief around his neck, so everyone will know he's an artist. I don't want him to see me. He'll ask me to sit for him. He tried to sketch me last year and I came out looking like a turtle.

MOISH: That's exactly what you look like — a turtle.

ALEX: You be quiet! (looks into his paper) Let me know when he goes away. Then I'll go look at the body. (a pause) So, he's gone?

MOISH: Remarkable.

ALEX: What's remarkable?

MOISH: He stopped by the body. Now he's putting his stool on the grass and sits down. He opens up a sketch book. He's drawing the body!

ALEX: A dead body is a good subject. Not that he'll do it justice.

MOISH: Maybe it'll be a masterpiece this time.

ALEX: Not in a million years. He draws, he paints, nobody bothers to look twice.

MOISH: He looks happy.

ALEX: He's probably singing Beethoven's Ninth. That's what he sings when he draws. The singing is also bad.

MOISH: Maybe he's a good artist and he'll be discovered in a hundred years.

ALEX: He's not even a "mensch".

MOISH: What does a "mensch" have to do with being a good artist?

ALEX: First and foremost a person has to be a "mensch". People are more important than paintings. Even dead people.

MOISH: That doesn't make the art any better.

ALEX: It's no use talking to you. (looks off) Is he still drawing?

MOISH: Yeah. How long does it take to draw a body?

ALEX: Dead or alive?

MOISH: Dead of course.

ALEX: The same as alive. Could be an hour. Could be five minutes. Hershel is pretty fast. A lousy artist but at least he's fast.

MOISH: He's touching the body now.

ALEX: For the texture.

MOISH: What do you mean?

ALEX: Is it hard, soft, smooth, rough — you know.

MOISH: You can't tell without touching?

ALEX: It's better if you touch.

MOISH: (laugh) You're telling me!

ALEX: You're such a sleeze.

MOISH: Look, someone else is coming. He's carrying an easel and setting it up beside Hershel Caplansky.

ALEX: So now there'll be two versions of a body under a bush.

MOISH: And he's painting like crazy. They're both painting like crazy.

ALEX: As if the model will run away.

MOISH: They want to see who'll finish first.

ALEX: Everything's a race. Even art.

MOISH: Maybe when they finish they'll go tell a policeman.

ALEX: Never. Artists don't like to get involved.

MOISH: Why not?

ALEX: It might interfere with their art.

MOISH: I see what you mean. They mustn't see anything but their subject, so they don't get distracted.

ALEX: I see a cloud in the sky, a gray cloud.

MOISH: Maybe it'll rain.

ALEX: And you said it's a nice day. A lot you know.

MOISH: It *was* a nice day.

ALEX: It's going to pour.

MOISH: Should we go?

ALEX: And leave the body lying in the rain?

MOISH: (Putting out his hand) Yeah, I felt a drop. And another!

ALEX: Not to worry. I have an umbrella. (Picks up his umbrella, opens it up) Let it pour.

MOISH: The artists are going away.

(ALEX sits under umbrella beside MOISH)

ALEX: Sure, when things get rough, artists go away.

MOISH: The poor body is gonna get soaked.

ALEX: Don't worry, it can't feel a thing.

MOISH: What if he's not entirely dead. You said you'd go and check.

ALEX: I might slip on the wet grass.

MOISH: That's true.

ALEX: And if I take the umbrella, *you'll* get all wet.

MOISH: That's true.

ALEX: And the bench will get all wet.

MOISH: That's true.

ALEX: Unless you want to go to the Club now and play cards.

MOISH: We can't leave until something is done about the poor man lying under the bush.

ALEX: So we'll wait here. Lucky I have an umbrella. I always carry one. It helps me walk, it's a good weapon, it keeps me dry, and when it's hot it keeps the sun off. (smiles) Because of an umbrella, I met my wife, Gittel.

MOISH: Is that so?

ALEX: In 1934 I was standing in line in front of the Palace. It was playing a Ginger Rogers movie. *Forty-Second Street* (sings) "Hear the beat of dancing feet …" In front of me stood a pretty girl. Right away I like her. Suddenly it begins to rain. Everybody runs away, so they lose their place in the line. But me, I just open my umbrella and I say to the girl: "Would you like to stand under my umbrella, Miss?" She gives me a smile that could melt a heart of stone and says: "A person with an umbrella is reliable. Such a person will protect you in all kinds of weather." So we went in to see the movie and four months later we married. It was a good life with Gittel. Three children, never a bad word in the house, she was always singing even in the hardest times. She gave me lots of happiness. So I never complain when it rains.

MOISH: For me too the rain is special.

ALEX: Is that so?

MOISH: When I was coming over on the boat, a trip of four weeks, it rained almost every day. It was terrible. People couldn't go up on deck for fresh air. And down below we were packed like sardines. That's how I met my darling Masha. That was some story.

ALEX: (indifferent) Hmm …

MOISH: If you don't want to hear, I won't tell you.

ALEX: What else do I have to do?

MOISH: When I left Odessa I was going with Faygeh Soreh, a nice girl, lived next door. Our parents said, this is a match, so it was a match. In those days children listened to parents not like now.

ALEX: You're telling *me*.

MOISH: Anyhow, she got a ticket from her uncle to come to Canada. He lived in Cornwall, a rich family, in furs. I tell her I'll join her as soon as I can and we'll be together in the new country. Three months go by, I don't hear from her. Then my brother sends me a ticket. I write her that I'm arriving on such and such a date with God's help. But on the boat I meet my beautiful Masha, and we fall in love. Such passion it was like Paradise. So, we decide to get married right away. In Montreal I go to work in the Dry Goods business with my brother, she goes to work in the factory and everything is hunky-dory. But at night I dream about Faygeh Soreh, I'm feeling guilty, I never told Masha about her, I never even call Faygeh Soreh in Cornwall. One day I'm walking down Park Avenue and I see a woman, dressed beautiful and we look at each other and who do you think it is?

ALEX: (pretends to guess) Faygeh Soreh …

MOISH: That's right! She asks why I never wrote her when I arrived and I ask her why she never wrote me. So she tells me that on the boat she met a Chaim Sokoloff and they fell in love and she married him. So she's now a mother of twins and could I forgive her. So I tell her I'm married too and we fall into each other's arms and kiss — and I never saw her again. Last month I read in the paper that she died. Five years after my Masha.

ALEX: Look, it stopped.

MOISH: What?

ALEX: The rain.

MOISH: Oh. So now you can go look.

ALEX: I'm going, I'm going. And if someone comes, sing loud. (rises) Don't move from here. Keep your eyes on me all the time.

MOISH: Walk careful.

ALEX: (ALEX closes umbrella and using it as a cane, goes off) Yeh, yeh, yeh.

MOISH: So what would be if I married Faygeh Soreh? Nothing. Probably the same like with Masha. It all ends the same anyhow. (sings) "Row row row the boat/gently down the stream/Merrily merrily merrily/Life is but a ..."

ALEX: (enters) Moish, what is it?

MOISH: A boy is chasing a baseball. It's flying over there. It fell.

ALEX: By the body?

MOISH: Yeah. He looks scared. He picks up the ball and he's running back to the game.

ALEX: He won't tell nobody.

MOISH: No. He's telling the coach. The coach is laughing at him. Now he's telling the other boys. They're laughing at him too. I think he's crying. Poor boy. He's running away.

ALEX: You see, even if you tell the truth nobody believes you.

MOISH: He won't tell nobody else. He learned his lesson.

ALEX: But he'll dream about it.

MOISH: When I was a little boy I once told the truth about something I saw. Everybody laughed at me. So I never told anything again.

ALEX: What did you see?

MOISH: My uncle beating his wife.

ALEX: No!

MOISH: Everyone said he's such a nice man, wouldn't hurt a fly, but I knew better.

ALEX: It's a terrible world. You should only know how we suffered in the old country.

MOISH: I also suffered. And I don't want to talk about it. And I don't want to hear.

ALEX: People don't want to hear, to see, to know. Who reads? Nobody. Who listens? Nobody. Even you, you don't want to hear.

MOISH: You're not the only one who suffered. (Moves away.)

ALEX: You want to measure?

MOISH: How do you measure suffering?

ALEX: For example, my father lost a leg in the Russian army and couldn't work no more. My mother had to take care of eight small children. Days we didn't have a piece of bread in the house. There was no workmen's compensation in those days.

MOISH: So, *my* father was *killed* by pogromnicks. Then my mother got sick. So me and my brothers had to support the family. There were no antibiotics in those days.

ALEX: There was typhus in our town.

MOISH: By us people dropped like flies from a flu epidemic.

ALEX: We had no plumbing, no water …

MOISH: No flour, no sugar, no tea …

ALEX: I had no shoes. I wore rags around my feet.

MOISH: I had no rags. I wore paper.

ALEX: I had lice in my hair.

MOISH: *We* had rats. Big ones.

ALEX: I slept with six brothers in one bed.

MOISH: We *had* no bed. I slept on the floor.

ALEX: Moish, enough. It's not a joke.

MOISH: So why does it sound so funny?

ALEX: I don't know.

MOISH: After we left, it got a lot worse.

ALEX: We got out in time.

MOISH: Who could imagine such a monumental tragedy?

ALEX: I want to tell you a secret, Moish, if you promise you won't tell nobody.

MOISH: Sure. I promise.

ALEX: Sometimes I wish I was there when it happened.

MOISH: No!

ALEX: I'm no better than them. Why was I spared?

MOISH: You mustn't ask such questions.

ALEX: Wrong. A person must ask. There may be no answers but you have to ask.

MOISH: I never ask.

ALEX: Sure, because you don't want to know.

MOISH: That's right.

ALEX: Tell me something, are you so special that you were spared?

MOISH: I never said I was.

ALEX: Neither am I. So that's the big puzzle. It's not because my children would make a big contribution to society. Or I would bring the world a great poem, a piece of music, an invention that saves lives. But nothing. My children are ordinary, my grandchildren are ordinary. I'm ordinary. So it doesn't make sense.

MOISH: Most people are ordinary.

ALEX: That's not the point.

MOISH: Do you believe in God?

ALEX: Only on Monday, Thursday, and Saturday.

MOISH: What kind of answer is that?

ALEX: Sometimes on Sunday, Tuesday and Friday.

MOISH: Alex, you're giving me a headache. Either you believe or you don't.

ALEX: Sometimes I do, sometimes I don't.

MOISH: If you believed all the time you wouldn't ask questions. Me, I always believe.

ALEX: (Points to off.) You believe *that* man's soul is in Heaven now?

MOISH: If he's dead, that's where it is.

ALEX: How long does it take for a soul to get to Heaven?

MOISH: How should I know?

ALEX: Take a guess — an hour, a day, a million light years.

MOISH: I said I don't know.

ALEX: Think of all those souls flying around in Heaven, saying hello, how are you, bumping into each other, looking down on the earth, having a good laugh. Pink souls, blue souls, white souls, black souls.

MOISH: I thought you didn't believe in all that.

ALEX: I don't. I want to point out how foolish you are for believing that nonsense.

MOISH: I'd rather believe in God and be foolish, than not believe and be smart like you.

ALEX: If you think that man's soul is happily flying around in the sky, what are you so concerned about his body?

MOISH: It's out of respect for a human being that is made in God's image.

ALEX: Are you made in God's image?

MOISH: Sure.

ALEX: You're not only a fool, you're a conceited fool. Men are men and God is God. That's two separate things.

MOISH: It's the goodness in man I'm talking about.

ALEX: There's no goodness.

MOISH: There's plenty of goodness. People give to charity, they visit the sick in the hospital, they take old people across the road.

ALEX: Only when there's something in it for them …

MOISH: Like what?

ALEX: A person is good because he thinks he'll go to Heaven, because someone will make a dinner in his honour, give him a medal, and everyone will say what a nice man he is. Or to make a profit.

MOISH: How can you make a profit from helping an old lady across the street?

ALEX: For instance, you help Mrs. Miller across the street. She remembers you, she tells her son and daughter to buy dry goods from you because you're such a nice man, so you make a profit.

MOISH: You're a cynic.

ALEX: Cynics never get hurt. They don't expect nothing so they're never disappointed.

MOISH: You think you know everything, uh?

ALEX: Ah, Moish, I don't know everything. But there was a time when I did.

MOISH: When was that?

ALEX: I was a little boy. Maybe six or seven. Everything was as clear as the day. When I got older, it got all mixed up.

MOISH: That's a fact.

ALEX: I thought a person understands more when he gets old, but the truth is, you understand less.

MOISH: Why is that?

ALEX: I don't know. Maybe it's because when you're young all you have to think about is the mystery of life. When you're old, there are other things to occupy you. Like eating, sleeping, the pains in your joints.

MOISH: Alex, I never understood the mystery of life. And now all I care about is to live one more day, one more day. I can't understand why a person wants to live so much even though it's such a rotten world and sometimes the pain is so sharp.

ALEX: It's nature. An animal is caught in a trap. He struggles to get out, and leaves half his foot in the trap. Just to stay alive.

MOISH: One more day, one more day.

ALEX: Still it's enough to breathe the fresh air and look round at the grass and you say, everything is worth it.

MOISH: Are you going to look at the body or not!

ALEX: Don't get so excited, I'm going.

MOISH: Watch your step.

ALEX: I always watch, that's why I managed to live so long. (exit)

(ALEX stares off at the body.)

MOISH: (looks at his pocket watch, takes a cookie out of bag and bites into it) It's 11:15. Another half hour to kill then we'll play cards at the club, have a bowl of soup, go home for a nap, and the day is practically gone. Then a little walk before supper, television, and it's all over. Funny, when I was a young man, I would've given anything for all this free time. Even a minute I couldn't spare to sit outside and relax a little. Now I have all the time in the world, but nothing to do except make sure I live one more day, one more day. Some joke.

(ALEX returns)

MOISH: So you saw?

ALEX: You're talking to yourself like an old man. You're giving old men a bad reputation.

MOISH: I asked you a question.

ALEX: (sits) Dead.

MOISH: I told you.

ALEX: All the usual signs. No heart beat, no pulse, and he's wet and blue.

MOISH: You want a cookie?

ALEX: Sure, why not. (fishes into MOISH's bag for cookie)

MOISH: My landlady packs me a snack every day. Like I was a little boy.

ALEX: (eats) At some point in our lives we all become little boys and girls. But we're not so cute.

MOISH: Look! Another visitor. A lady.

ALEX: I bet the dead man never had so much company in his life.

MOISH: She sees him all right. She's calling her husband to come have a look.

ALEX: Her lover.

MOISH: Why her lover?

ALEX: In the middle of the day it has to be a lover. The husband's at work, earning a living for her.

MOISH: And where is *his* wife?

ALEX: How do you know he has a wife?

MOISH: A man like that, looks so settled, so neat, he has to have a wife.

ALEX: She's looking after the children.

MOISH: Ah, they're discussing the situation. They're going to do something. No, she's running away.

ALEX: I know why.

MOISH: Why?

ALEX: How would it look if they report the body to the police? What would his wife say? What would her husband say? "What were you two doing in the park at 11:15 in the morning? Where were you going?" And you know what that would lead to?

MOISH: Two divorces.

ALEX: So they won't tell.

MOISH: He's still standing by the body.

ALEX: So he has a conscience after all.

MOISH: No, he's leaving, slowly. Now he runs to her and takes her in his arms. They're going away. No, they won't tell.

ALEX: You can't blame them. The dead are dead, they can't be helped. But those two still have a few more months, maybe a few years together before anyone finds out.

MOISH: You ever have a lover?

ALEX: Never you mind.

MOISH: Tell me. What difference does it make now?

ALEX: Yeah … for maybe six months. There was a strike in the factory, no work anywhere, so I drove a taxi. One day I picked up a lady. A beautiful lady. You could tell by the clothes she was rich. She was crying. She tells me an address in Westmount I should take her there. When we got there she asks me to come in, she can't be alone now. So I went in. I was hungry, I figure she'd make me a nice cup of tea. She made me tea, then a meal, dessert. I can still taste it. You don't know how good food is when you're hungry. And she watches me eat. It gives her pleasure to watch. Then she takes my hand and brings me to her bedroom with a satin bedspread and beautiful pictures on the walls and all kinds of little figurines from glass and china everywhere. She strokes my hair and tells me how handsome I am. In those days I was.

MOISH: Huh. (smiles and waves his arm dreamily)

ALEX: Then one things leads to another. And to make a long wonderful story short, I am her lover for maybe six months. Every day I visit her in the afternoon. We talk and laugh — it was wonderful.

MOISH: Why only six months?

ALEX: The husband who left her came back.

MOISH: She used you to pass the time.

ALEX: But I used her too. She gave me presents for my children. I told my Gittel I got them from passengers, I don't remember what I told her, but she was too smart to ask questions. Those were hard times. I brought home a cake, a doll, even a nice dress for Gittel — and always she knew I loved her and wouldn't leave her.

MOISH: I hate to say this, but you behaved like a common you know what.

ALEX: I know. And to tell you the truth I'd do it all over again. She was beautiful — her eyes, her hair …

MOISH: I don't want to hear.

ALEX: Your loss. (a beat) So, did *you* ever have a lover?

MOISH: With me it was different. Not a nice story. I don't want to talk about it.

ALEX: You ever think about it?

MOISH: Not if I can help it.

ALEX: I guarantee you tell me and you'll never think about it again.

MOISH: It's too terrible.

ALEX: Suit yourself. I'm not interested anyhow.

MOISH: I was 37 years old and there came to work for me in the store a very young girl, only 16. Straight off the boat. A pretty little thing with big black eyes. I showed her how to measure the cloth, serve the customers. She was smart, learned fast, worked hard.

ALEX: So?

MOISH: She was an orphan, lived by an aunt who was sick to whom she gave every cent she earned. Very poor.

ALEX: So you did it to her in the store.

MOISH: I went crazy. I don't know what happened to me. I didn't force her, I swear. She just let me, like you take a sheep to the slaughterhouse. I know why. She was afraid if she didn't let me I'd fire her.

ALEX: Sure. The bosses control the workers for a piece of bread. It's an old story.

MOISH: I was always ashamed after, but I couldn't help myself. In the end, she got pregnant.

ALEX: No!

MOISH: I went crazy. I didn't know what to do. I was already married. So I gave her money to get rid of it. She came back to work afterwards looking like a ghost. I couldn't stand to look at her. So I asked a friend to give her a job. I never saw her again.

ALEX: Some story.

MOISH: I'm sure she still curses me.

ALEX: Probably.

MOISH: My poor Masha, may she rest in peace, never knew.

ALEX: Sure she did.

MOISH: What makes you say that?

ALEX: Women know, but they don't say.

MOISH: Sometimes I wonder what became of Chana'le. That was her
          name.

ALEX: Nothing much happened. The same like everyone else.

MOISH: We should tell that couple over there, warn them. It doesn't pay.
          You have bad dreams all your life.

ALEX: Don't waste your breath. Nobody listens anyhow.

MOISH: God has a way of getting even. My children never call me, never
          visit …

ALEX: You believe God is responsible?

MOISH: Sure. Especially on Tuesdays and Thursdays. (laughs)

ALEX: (laughing with MOISH). This is turning out to be some
          morning.

MOISH: Yeah.

ALEX: So much excitement.

MOISH: Yeah.

ALEX: When I sit with someone else, nothing much happens.

MOISH: Admit it, Alex, you like me.

ALEX: Sure I like you. I like fools.

MOISH: Alex if you're going to insult me again …

ALEX: Don't be so sensitive. You're not the only fool.

MOISH: That man coming this way, he's no fool. He looks smart. He's
            wearing a fedora, a nice suit, eyeglasses.

ALEX: Does he have a briefcase?

MOISH: Yeah.

ALEX: Then he must be respectable. And the shoes?

MOISH: Polished.

ALEX: A good sign. A man who takes care of himself, he has self-respect.
            Must be a distinguished gentleman.

MOISH: I wanted to be a man just like that.

ALEX: With a nice big office.

MOISH: Carpet on the floor.

ALEX: A big desk.

MOISH: Lots of windows. You got to have big windows ...

ALEX: A few secretaries.

MOISH: Pretty ones.

ALEX: Two telephones on the desk.

MOISH: Three.

ALEX: Let it be three.

MOISH: And lots of appointments.

ALEX: I can't see you for two weeks.

MOISH: Make that three weeks.

ALEX: Let it be three.

MOISH: I have an appointment book as big as an encyclopedia.

ALEX: Lots of mail.

MOISH: I don't have time to open my letters.

ALEX: So ask the secretary.

MOISH: Wait. (looks to off) He's bending over the body, looking around, from left to right, right to left.

ALEX: And?

MOISH: He's getting up and walking away.

ALEX: I can see that.

MOISH: He's going to tell a policeman.

ALEX: You're sure?

MOISH: (walking like a businessman in thought) He's walking like a man who has made a decision.

ALEX: (Pacing like MOISH.) Such men always make decisions.

MOISH: I'm sure he'll do the right thing. Oh no! There's crazy Betsy again with a big shopping cart. She's come to collect more stuff from the body.

ALEX: We shouldn't let her.

MOISH: What can we do? She's strong like a horse and carries a big stick. I don' t want to spend the rest of my life in a hospital.

ALEX: What's left to take?

MOISH: A ring, a gold chain around the neck.

ALEX: Tickets to the opera.

MOISH: Men like that don't go to the opera.

ALEX: Oh, you think only nice people enjoy music?

MOISH: I never saw her work so fast in my life. Thank God she's going.

ALEX: Some business.

MOISH: A terrible business.

ALEX: Well, she needs the property and the dead man doesn't. So it's only fair.

MOISH: It's still stealing. The property belongs to the man's heirs.

ALEX: Who said he has heirs?

MOISH: A mother, a wife, a child.

ALEX: At least he was robbed after he died. Some people are robbed while they're still alive. The heirs, if he has any, can look out for themselves.

MOISH: This is a moral question.

ALEX: Look who's talking about morality.

MOISH: The morality of property. Property is holy. A man works hard all his life for what he has. It belongs to his loved ones after he's gone.

ALEX: It belongs to whoever gets there first.

MOISH: I hope you're robbed after you're dead. Then we'll see how you'll feel.

(ALEX looks at him, laughs. MOISH realizing what he said, laughs too.)

ALEX: Oh Moish, Moish, Moish ... Well, our distinguished gentleman isn't back. Can't say I'm surprised. He has to protect his reputation. How would it look if they said on the T.V. tonight: "Mr James so-and-so, the renowned so-and-so, came upon a body yesterday morning while strolling in the park. The aforementioned so-and-so denies all connection to the dead man,

... who has not yet been identified, but in view of recent developments in Rio de Janeiro it is rumoured that so-and-so and so-and-so ... ". And in one blow his career is ruined.

MOISH: Yeah, you're right.

ALEX: So it looks like he's going to lie there for a long time.

MOISH: I was thinking — you know the man who picks up the papers and the garbage?

ALEX: The park attendant.

MOISH: Yeah. We'll go look for him. Tell him there's something suspicious under the bush, so he'll report it. Nobody will blame him, after all, it's his job. You see what I mean?

ALEX: Yeah, I see.

MOISH: We'll wait until noon. We'll go for lunch as usual. On the way we'll tell the park attendant.

ALEX: Look how the time passes and I didn't finish the paper yet.

MOISH: There's nothing to read in the paper.

ALEX: You don't read, that's why you're ignorant.

MOISH: Every day the same old thing.

ALEX: But not tomorrow.

MOISH: What's tomorrow?

ALEX: Tomorrow they'll write on the front page. Body of the famous criminal Al Capone discovered in the park. And there'll be a whole story about him.

MOISH: Al Capone's been dead for years. (a beat) Wait, wait, look there. No don't look. Give me a piece of the paper. Hurry. Cover your face.

(They cover their faces except for the eyes that peer over the papers.)

ALEX: I don't believe it.

MOISH: Two men are coming to take away the body.

ALEX: Policemen?

MOISH: No. Men in striped gray suits.

ALEX: Who are they?

MOISH: I think one is the killer.

ALEX: They must be part of a gang.

MOISH: Yeah. Don't move. They mustn't see us. Pretend you don't hear, you don't see, you don't know nothing.

ALEX: Like everybody else.

MOISH: They're picking him up by the head and the feet.

ALEX: Where are they taking him?

MOISH: Toward the road. There's a car waiting.

ALEX: They'll be mad about the missing wallet, the shoes, the gold ring.

MOISH: They're putting the body in the trunk of the car.

ALEX: What kind of car?

MOISH: Blue. I can't tell what kind.

ALEX: Must be a Cadillac. People like that ...

MOISH: Maybe a Rolls.

ALEX: A Mercedes.

MOISH: Yeah.

ALEX: Air conditioned.

MOISH: Yeah … And now the car is moving … moving … and they're gone.

ALEX: And that's that.

MOISH: It's been some morning.

ALEX: Yeah.

MOISH: I'm totally exhausted.

ALEX: Yeah.

MOISH: A good thing no one noticed us.

ALEX: No one notices old men.

MOISH: Lucky for us, or we'd be in trouble.

ALEX: We didn't do nothing.

MOISH: We're witnesses.

ALEX: Well, it's all over now. I hope from now on things will be quiet here. I can't take such excitement anymore. When I sit with Irving or Frank, there's never any trouble.

MOISH: When I sit with Myer I'm so bored I fall asleep. And then I can't sleep all night.

ALEX: It's time to go.

MOISH: You have to admit we had a good time.

ALEX: Sure, a very good time.

MOISH: So, now we'll go.

ALEX: Yeah. We'll have some lunch and play cards.

MOISH: Good.

ALEX: Maybe Irving and Myer will play too.

MOISH: We'll ask them.

ALEX: Myer cheats you know.

MOISH: Who cares, it's only a game.

ALEX: Moish, I was just thinking.

MOISH: What?

ALEX: Maybe there was no body after all.

MOISH: But we saw it, we both saw it.

ALEX: Maybe it was a dream. Like everything that happened long ago is like a dream now.

MOISH: It happened this morning. Just now!

ALEX: It could be in our heads, the whole thing.

MOISH: No!

ALEX: Like when I worked in the factory and drove a taxi and met the lady who lived on the hill.

MOISH: The girl in my store.

ALEX: Our children.

MOISH: Our wives.

ALEX: Even coming over on the boat.

MOISH: When I was a little boy and went to "cheder".

ALEX: The only thing that counts is now, this minute when we walk slowly, carefully to the club and we make sure we get there safe and nobody bothers us on the way. That's all that's important. (Takes umbrella.)

MOISH: Alex, you're right. It's just that sometimes in my head I have so much energy. So much desire to live active like I used to. I think

I can work and run to the ends of the world.

ALEX: Like you said, in your head.

MOISH: Yeah, yeah.

ALEX: I suggest we don't tell nobody what we saw today.

MOISH: Why not?

ALEX: They'll think we're crazy old men. And maybe put us away.

MOISH: We won't say a word.

ALEX: Nobody has to know. It's better that way.

MOISH: But the two of us, we can talk about it.

ALEX: Sure, whenever you like. Give me your arm, Moish. I have a pain in my leg.

MOISH: You want your paper?

ALEX: I'm finished with it.

MOISH: Let's pass by the place where the body was.

ALEX: Sure.

MOISH: Maybe we'll find a sign, a souvenir.

ALEX: Sure.

MOISH: We'll frame it. (laughs)

ALEX: Sure. (laughs) Ah, Moish, you're some character.

MOISH: You too, Alex, some character!

(MOISH and ALEX exit.)
(Music)

THE END

GLOSSARY

Bar Mitzvah: confirmation ceremony of thirteen-year-old Jewish Boy

Capone, Al: (1899-1947) American gangster

Caruso, Enrico: (1873-1921) Italian operatic tenor

cheder: old style orthodox Hebrew school

goornisht mit nisht: nothing plus nothing

Meshiach: Messiah

meshugener: a mad person

noodnick: a nag, a pest

ribono shel olam: Lord of the Universe

The House on Hermitage Road

(a play for radio)

by DIRK MCLEAN

PLAYWRIGHT

Dirk McLean was born in Trinidad. At the age of thirteen he came to Canada to join his mother and attend Riverdale Collegiate. During his five years at Riverdale, he developed an interest in theatre and writing.

Dirk is now an actor and a writer. In 1991, the CBC produced *The House on Hermitage Road* which Dirk adapted from his autobiographical novel of the same title. His plays for young audiences include *Shall We Call a Teacher?* and *The Real McCoy* (with Amah Harris and Itah Sadu). His first children's book, *Steel Drums and Ice Skates,* is published by Groundwood Books. A recipient of numerous grant awards, Dirk is a member of Playwrights Union of Canada, CAW:BAIA, ACTRA, Canadian Actors Equity Association, Writers Guild of Canada, Black Film and Video Network, and The Academy of Canadian Cinema and Television. He has written a feature-length romantic comedy screenplay, *Encore!* Dirk lives in Toronto.

ORIGINAL CAST AND PRODUCTION TEAM

THE HOUSE ON HERMITAGE ROAD was produced by CBC Morningside Drama as a radio play in the Fall of 1991 with the following cast:

DIRK (narrator)	Dirk McLean
DIRK	Max Beckford
MR. O'REILLY	John Bayliss
JACQUELINE	Monique Seheult
AUNTY LAURA	Denise Jones
NURSEY	Amah Harris
VOICE/FISHMAN	Henry Gomez
LADY	Hope Sealy
BBC ANNOUNCER	Graham Haley
LORRAINE	Sabine Reinch
ELSA	Karen Burthwright

RADIO ANNOUNCER/REV. CUTHBERT   Ralf Joneikies

DR. TOBY/IMMIGRATION OFFICER   Marvin L. Ishmael

VOICE/STEWARDESS   Helen-Claire Tingling

The Story Editor was Dave Carley.

The Producer was James Roy

Note: In the text, DIRK refers to child, while DIRK (narrator) is the adult.

REVIEWS AND COMMENTS

"The listener hears of a country new to independence, of the change-over from British to Trinidadian control in the 60's. Religion, education, calypso, steel-band music, carnival and other factors influence the central character's life while he's waiting for his mother to return."

Jon Kaplan, *NOW*. Toronto, 1991

"The author has mined his bittersweet memories of his youth in Trinidad, and the result is a radio treasure."

CBC, Toronto, 1991

"*The House on Hermitage Road* ... is only 'five percent fiction and error'. The rest draws on powerful memories. There was his grandmother's funeral in 1969, for instance, when, watching her lying in her coffin, the 13-year-old Dirk prayed to see some sign of life. Yet for all his grief, he knew his grandmother's death would finally bring about his reunion with his mother."

Judy Raymond. *The Sunday Express*. Trinidad, 1991

PERFORMANCE PERMISSION

For permission to perform *The House on Hermitage Road* please contact Dirk McLean, P.O. Box 1358, Station F, Toronto, Ontario, M4Y 2V9, (416) 656-9365 (416) 469-0936

DEDICATION

To my mother, Jacqueline.
And to the memory of Nursey and Aunty Laura.

THE HOUSE ON HERMITAGE ROAD

SEGMENT ONE: "IN SAFE KEEPING"

MUSIC: *Soft instrumental "God Save the Queen".*

DIRK: (NARR) Port of Spain. Trinidad. The Union Jack battles with the ever-changing Caribbean wind on a sunny day in 1961. I had just turned 5 and was still attending O'Reilly Private school, higher up on Hermitage Road. I lived at number 77 with my mother, my grandmother, Nursey, and my great-aunt, Aunty Laura.

SOUND: *Music fades to children playing in a yard, laughter. Fade under:*

DIRK: (NARR) Ernest, my god-father's brother, lifts me off the handle-bar of his bicycle, after the two-minute ride from home, places me in front of the open gate. Mr. O'Reilly, the headmaster with a military moustache, peers over the top of his lowered glasses at me. He taps his baggy pant leg with a thin silver-headed cane — used sparingly for floggings. I don't think I'm late from lunch.

DIRK: Good-afternoon, Sir.

SOUND: *A wooden gate closing.*

DIRK: (NARR) The school rooms are an extension of his own house, plus two rooms inside the house itself.

DIRK: Good-afternoon, Miss Gordon.

DIRK: (NARR) My teacher, brown-skinned, like me. But she wears glasses, like Mr. O'Reilly, with a chain around her neck. Her hair is pulled back in a relaxed bun and she carries a ruler for pointing … and for our knuckles. I have seen her laugh and giggle when she's not being serious. Today, they both look serious.

SOUND: *An army whistle blows. Silence.*

Mr. O'REILLY: Children, you are all aware that Andrew Peter Innocent has been sick in hospital for the past few days. I am sad to say that he won't be coming back to school. He died this morning.

SOUND: *Children whispering, mumbling.*

MR. O'REILLY: Let us all observe a minute of silence for Andrew Peter Innocent.

DIRK: (NARR) I walked home thinking about Andrew and how we played together just last week. Then I told Nursey and Aunty Laura. And my Mum.

SOUND: *A woman's coughing.*

J'LINE: Dirk's too young to go to a funeral.

AUNTY: It's the boy's friend.

NURSEY: Jacqueline, Laura is right. Unfortunately, I have to nurse Mr. Metevier in D'Abadie for the next two days.

AUNTY: He was too young to attend your father's funeral, God rest his soul. So when he'll be old enough? (coughs) He needs to know about these things. If I wasn't suffering from this cold, I'd take him, myself.

J'LINE: Aunty Laura, don't fret yourself. He's not going any place.

NURSEY: Who else from the school is going?

J'LINE: Ask him. Where is he anyway?

NURSEY: In the yard, I'm sure.

SOUND: *Aunty Laura's cough under.*

J'LINE: (shouts) Dirk! Always playing. (sharply) Dirk!!

NURSEY: Easy, Jacqueline. Don't shout at him like you're angry. I know you won't have time to take him.

J'LINE: I'm afraid, Nursey. I don't know how to tell Dirk.

NURSEY: Jacqueline, my daughter! It's not an easy thing, but only you can do it.

J'LINE: It's all so sudden. Only two weeks. Why couldn't they give me two months?

NURSEY: Listen. You have a God-sent opportunity. You applied and were fortunate enough to be chosen. Children adapt to news better than us grown-ups.

J'LINE: You really think Dirk will understand?

NURSEY: Be direct, Jacqueline. If you can't face him, how will you face dying patients when they ask you if they're dying?

SOUND: *Door closing.*

DIRK: You call me, Mum?

J'LINE: Yes, darling.

AUNTY: Dirk, I'm taking you to the funeral.

DIRK: Thanks, Aunty Laura.

J'LINE: What about your cold?

AUNTY: The dead won't catch it.

(Laughter)

J'LINE: What are we going to do with you, Aunty Laura?

NURSEY: You know Laura when she sets her mind to something.

J'LINE: Yes. Now, don't catch pneumonia and die on us or I'll be very cross with you.

DIRK: You vex, Mum?

J'LINE: No, son. Come into the living-room with me.

SOUND: *A curtain being drawn.*

216

DIRK: (NARR) My mother puts me to sit on her lap. She hugs me with young shaking arms. I know she's thinking. We sit quietly and I can smell my afternoon cream custard pudding coming from the kitchen. Finally, she speaks.

J'LINE: I have to leave. I'll be going to England. And I don't want you to cry, because if you cry I'll be very sad. And I won't go. I need to go to make a better life for us.

DIRK: Alright. I promise I won't cry.

DIRK: (NARR) All I know is that England is very far. Nursey's son, Uncle Roderick and Aunty Laura's daughter, Aunty Marjorie live there. But at least, Nursey and Aunty Laura won't be going with her. They're staying right here with me.

MUSIC: *Latin organ pipe piece up then continues low under.*

DIRK: (NARR) The small white coffin enters Holy Rosary Catholic Church ahead of us. Mum brings me to Mass here on Sundays. A silver cross on top sparkles in the afternoon sun. Andrew Peter Innocent sleeps beneath the round glass. The priest swings incense around the coffin. Mr. O'Reilly removes his glasses, wiping tears, heightening my sadness. Is this what Nursey means by "The best of friends must part"? Outside, Aunty Laura nudges me forward.

DIRK: Please accept my sympathies, Mrs. Innocent.

DIRK: (NARR) She nods, tears flowing below her dark sunglasses as the coffin is lifted into the hearse. I will not see where they bury my friend.

SOUND: *Camera clicking, Flash popping.*

DIRK: (NARR) In the week and a half my mother has before leaving, we pose for a picture together. She says goodbye to my God-mother, Yvonne, and a few friends.

MUSIC: *1961 Hit — "Every Beat of My Heart" by Gladys Knight and the Pips. (or, "You Must Have Been a Beautiful Baby" by Bobby Darin) Fade Under.*

NURSEY: (calling) Jacqueline … food's getting cold.

J'LINE: (distantly) I'll be there right away, Nursey.

AUNTY: I don't know what she went back in that suitcase for. Everything was packed so neat.

NURSEY: She just wanted to add some more.

AUNTY: More? Jacqueline taking the whole of Trinidad with her?

NURSEY: Only the Christmas cakes for Roderick and Marjorie.

AUNTY: Can't she carry them in her hand?

NURSEY: For three long weeks on that boat? Be sensible Laura. They'll steal it. You know how nice they're smelling already.

AUNTY: I'm going to miss her, Nursey.

NURSEY: Yes, me too.

AUNTY: I was watching Dirk; he looked so sad, poor thing. Why can't Jacqueline train to be a nurse here like you did? Why does she have to go off and leave the boy?

NURSEY: You know she can't take him. And she'll be sending money every month. Besides it won't be for too long.

AUNTY: My Marjorie went there and still hasn't come back. Roderick. People leave this place and don't return.

NURSEY: (whispering) Keep your voice down.

AUNTY: I'm afraid she'll go and …

NURSEY: (whispering) Be brave, Laura, we can't go to pieces and make her miserable. Jacqueline's doing a good thing. Be happy for her.

AUNTY: I am. Just feeling sorry for myself because I never had any opportunities. I, too, would have left this land. (normal voice)

But, we're too old to go any place now.

NURSEY: I didn't know you felt that way.

SOUND: *High-heeled shoes across the floor.*

J'LINE: I finally got that suitcase closed. You both look so wonderful. Where's Dirk?

DIRK: Coming, Mum.

J'LINE: You washed your hands?

DIRK: Yes, Mum.

J'LINE: Nursey and Aunty Laura, this is splendid. I'll miss this food. Especially the ochroe and rice. After this meal, all I'll probably eat until I come back is fish'n'chips, and cake with tea. Dirk, come and stand beside me. Nursey, please say grace today.

NURSEY: Lord, forgive us for not going to church today. But you know why. Lord, we thank thee for this meal we're about to partake of. We thank you for our lives and we ask you to look upon Jacqueline and guide, guard and protect her on her journey. Help her to study hard to be a good nurse. And when she's done, send her back safely to us, Lord. Amen.

EVERYONE: Amen.

SOUND: *Wooden chairs being pulled out.*

MUSIC: *1961 Top Ten hit up, then low under.*

DIRK: (NARR) The food was, as you can well imagine, sweet, sweet, sweet. Lots of silences. Everyone trying not to think about the next hour. My mother saying how cold it's going to be in England. Somebody told her it's like living in a fridge — only colder. And fog. So dark you can't see your hands in front of your face, much less your neighbour's house.

SOUND: *Brushing of teeth, swishing of water, spitting of water, running water, under.*

DIRK: (NARR) I watch my mother brush her teeth. I turn away to walk in the yard.

SOUND: *A van's horn.*

DIRK: They come!

J'LINE: Nursey and Aunty Laura, there's only room for me and Dirk. The van will come right back for both of you. I'll see you on the dock.

NURSEY: Alright.

J'LINE: Here's the chicken I baked for you to eat on the boat.

NURSEY: We'll see you down there.

SOUND: *Van pulling out and fade up with boat's fog-horn blowing twice.*

DIRK: (NARR) My God-father, Kelvin, hugs me. He's off to study engineering. My mother will have a travelling companion; along with her friend, Iris, who will also be a nurse. She hugs me again, kisses me.

SOUND: *Boat's horn, twice.*

DIRK: I kept my promise, I didn't cry.

J'LINE: Yes, son. I love you and I'll miss you and I'll write soon.

DIRK: I love you, too, Mum, and I'll miss you and write back soon.

DIRK: (NARR) There are no visible tears. My mother says goodbye to Aunty Yvonne, Uncle Mervyn and my cousins Wade, Kurt and Karen. She walks up the gang-plank, waving; still hoping to say farewell to Nursey and Aunty Laura who have been forgotten at home. The *Ascania* pulls away from the dock.

SOUND: *A long boat's horn. Then silence.*

DIRK: (NARR) It's almost a week now since my mother left. She's somewhere out on the sea. I know she's thinking about me, as I'm thinking about her. I wonder how long she'll be away for.

(pause) I awake suddenly.

DIRK: Huh, huh. Huh, huh. Huh, Huh. Huh, Huh. (Coughs) Huh, huh. Huh, Huh. Huhhhh …

DIRK: (NARR) Nursey rushes to my bedside.

DIRK: My … chhhest … hurts. Huh, huh. Huh, huh. (Continues Under)

DIRK: (NARR) I feel like I'm going to die. Each breath is a painful effort. She rubs my chest with Vicks, places a flannel cloth on my chest, buttons my pajama top. Holds me.

NURSEY: Easy. There, there. Everything will be alright, my darling.

DIRK: Huuuuuh, huuuuh, huuuuuuh, huuuuuuuuuuuuh …

DIRK: (NARR) This asthma attack was short. Sometimes it's so bad I get delirious. Always in the middle of the night. I hate this.

DIRK: I miss … my … mummy.

NURSEY: I'm here. We all miss her. Remember she loves you. Close your eyes. The pain will ease up soon.

DIRK: (NARR) Eventually, the pain eases. I breathe easier. Nursey stays with me until I fall asleep.

MUSIC: *Up.*

SEGMENT TWO: "THE MARBLE CAKE"

MUSIC: *Instrumental "God Save The Queen" — last two bars up, with instrumental "Trinidad National Anthem", continue to the end , under.*

DIRK: (NARR) Independence at last! A new beginning for our nation, August 1962. All Trinidadians fetting tonight, spending new currency. Some start since last week. I wish my mother was here for this. "Let every creed and race find an equal place, and may God bless our nation". As schoolchildren, we're given a small new flag for waving during the parade. Red — the blood of the people. White — the pure hope of the people. Black — the earth of the people. A large chocolate bar wrapped in the flag's colours also mark this event. But what will outlast them all is a brass medal. "Together We Aspire, Together We Achieve". A motto to impassion us with brotherly and sisterly love, as we charge into the future; leaving all laziness, all recklessness, all don't care attitudes behind.

SOUND: *21 Gun Salute fired three times.*

DIRK: (NARR) My mother has been in England for almost a year now, training to be a good nurse. We write to each other on Air Letter Forms, already stamped. She writes more than I do and her letters are longer. Maybe it's because her hand-writing is smaller than mine. I miss my mother very, very much. My birthday is this weekend. I'm going to be six. My first birthday without my mother. Since Independence Day, a few weeks ago, Nursey promised me a marble cake, if I am good. I've been trying to be good by helping out and by coming home straight from school without playing along the way. (PAUSE) A decree has been issued today.

SOUND: *Police siren, fade.*

VOICE: (Through megaphone) Tie up your dogs! Tie up your dogs. Any dogs found in the streets after 8 o'clock at night will be taken to the pound. Tie up your dogs! Tie up your dogs! Any dogs found … (Fades under Narration)

SOUND: *Dog barking, heavy boots on concrete, dog growling. A thud —under.*

DIRK: (NARR) I watch from the window as policeman chase and catch a dog with a net, throw him in the caged van. This is done to get rid of stray dogs and to decrease disease. Some are beautiful, healthy dogs. The owners were warned. The law must be taken seriously — we're independent now. Ignorance won't be bliss.

SOUND: *Silence. A cock crows. Up with market sounds, then fade under.*

DIRK: (NARR) Early Saturday morning in the market on Charlotte Street. Smells of vegetables, ground provisions, nutmeg, Spanish thyme and cinnamon sticks. Of beef and pork weighed for

Sunday dinner. Of fresh fish lying in mounds on concrete slabs.

AUNTY: You see the gills on this fish, Dirk, how washed out the colour is — that means the fish lying here for days.

DIRK: What about this one, Aunty Laura?

AUNTY: Now, this is good. The gills bright red. But this one over here, (Pressing it) the flesh soft. That means it rotten. It should be firm.

FISHMAN: Madam, stop feelin' up mih fish.

AUNTY: Mister, you should take out the rotten fish from the good fish.

FISHMAN: Madam, you come here to give me a religious sermon? Look, buy or don't buy before ah lose customers an' chop off yuh hand.

DIRK: (Panicking) Aunty Laura, he have a cutlass.

AUNTY: And what he going to do with it? I know him since he was small wearing short pants and now he old, he still wearing short pants.

FISHMAN: Look, ah warnin' yuh.

SOUND: *Cutlass clinking against concrete. Under Fishman's speech.*

DIRK: Le' we gooo!

AUNTY: (Going) For your sake. If I ever send you to buy fish, don't buy from that no-teeth, short pants ole man.

SOUND: *A large penny falls and rolls, stopped flat by a shoe.*

DIRK: Miss Lady, you dropped this penny.

LADY: (Laughs) Keep it, sonny boy, is no longer mine. God bless!

DIRK: Thank you. Thanks, Miss Lady.

AUNTY: You want to spend it or put it in your piggy bank?

DIRK: Piggy bank.

AUNTY: Good, Now, let's get some crab for the calaloo. And some ripe plantains.

DIRK: (NARR) Women sell currant rolls, coconut rolls, sugar cake, cassava plone. Women cuss and complain about some man, or their boy-child or girl-child. I enjoy this time with Aunty Laura; learning how to shop.

SOUND: *Police siren, fade.*

VOICE: Tie up your dogs! Tie up your dogs! (Fades under narration)

DIRK: (NARR) The sun is bright now as Aunty Laura and I return home with hungry bellies. And all the while I'm thinking that she didn't buy flour or eggs or butter or colouring. Maybe I don't deserve a marble cake.

SOUND: *A tap running. Dishes clinking. Fade.*

DIRK: (NARR) After breakfast of fried blood pudding and hops bread, I clean the yard with a cocoyea broom.

SOUND: *Broom sweeping and chickens clucking, slow fade under.*

DIRK: (NARR) And help check the chickens for pips.

DIRK: Nursey, can I go next door and pitch marbles?

NURSEY: You did your homework?

DIRK: Yes, Nursey, yesterday evening.

NURSEY: All of it?

DIRK: Almost all.

NURSEY: Almost all is not all.

DIRK: (Yelling) But Nursey, I can't do the sums right!

NURSEY: Don't you raise your voice to me!

DIRK: I didn't mean to. I beg your pardon.

NURSEY: I'm too old to put up with this sort of behaviour.

DIRK: (Pleading) I need your help, Nursey, with one of the problems …
            when you're finished cooking and everything, tonight.

NURSEY: I will make sure I'm not too tired to look over all of your
            homework. If it's one thing you bound to have, it's an education.
            And not liming and skylarking on Belmont street corners. You
            dust the furniture, yet?

DIRK: Yes, Nursey. I'm ready to help you change the sheets.

DIRK: (NARR) Well, I think it's going to be a no-cake birthday
            tomorrow. I didn't mean to raise my voice, as Nursey put it. But I
            need help with my homework. (*Pause*) I am allowed to play for
            an hour or so. I go next door and pitch with the boys — winning
            and losing and winning and losing …

SOUND: *Bage of marbles shaken.*

AUNTY: (Calling) Dirk! Dirk!

DIRK: (NARR) Aunty Laura calls me for a customary errand.
            Somewhere, sometime, years ago — it was arranged that Mrs
            Roberts would cook a big pot of soup on Saturdays and share it
            with our household. I prepare for the ten minute walk to collect
            a powdered milk tin three-quarters full of hot split pea soup, with
            cornmeal dumplings, green figs, potatoes, pumpkin, and
            sometimes cassava or eddoes.

MUSIC: *Nat King Cole's "Ramblin' Rose" ends. Static sound under.*

BBC ANNOUNCER: This is the BBC with the news at noon. Prime Minister
            Harold Wilson met today with U.S. President Kennedy at 10
            Downing Street to discuss … (*Fade under next speech*)

NURSEY: Don't stay too long this time. And when you come back I want
            you to sit down and write a proper letter to your mother.
            Otherwise, I won't go through the trouble of baking any cake.

DIRK: I wrote her yesterday, remember?

NURSEY: You call that a letter? A proper letter, Master Dirk, your mother deserves that much, for all her hard work. And I'll even draw the lines on the Air Letter form so your poor mother won't have to turn her head from side to side as she reads your slanty handwriting.

DIRK: (NARR) While I'm away, Nursey and Aunty Laura continue preparations for Sunday dinner and readying their appetites. Most times the trip takes half-an-hour, an hour. I have "hot feet" like my mother. I pitch marbles with any willing boy along the way. I even try to convince the unwilling. Not today. I'm going straight there and back in 10 minutes. I want to be eating cake all day tomorrow. (Pause) Well, when I get there the soup isn't quite ready. Mrs Roberts has me go around to the back to pick up some limes for her. Elsa, her niece, fills the tin up because I tell her I'm strong enough. With both hands I struggle and I'm already late. Halfway home the bag bursts.

SOUND: *Full tin of soup hitting concrete pavement.*

DIRK: (NARR) The tin hits the pavement but nothing spills. I stand there crying because I'm later than late, my birthday cake is in jeopardy and I don't know how to get home with a tin too hot to carry. Fortunately, one of our neighbours, a big strapping Guyanese man saw my dilemma and carried me and the soup home. Nursey and Aunty Laura didn't make a fuss.

SOUND: *Police siren fades.*

VOICE: Tie up your dogs! Tie up your dogs! (Fade)

DIRK: "Dear Mummy. Sorry to keep you so long. But Nursey was very busy helping Aunty Laura at home. I went to spend a few days with Aunty Yvonne during the holidays."

DIRK: (NARR) My cousins miss you. And I miss you, too.

DIRK: "I went with Aunty Laura to see the decorations and everything was grand and I saw the Princess Royal. Please send me some lead pencils and rubbers."

DIRK: (NARR) When are you coming back?

DIRK: "I go to church every Sunday at Blessed Martin and wear the pants that you sent me. I like them very much. I hope you are quite better now."

DIRK: (NARR) If you were in Trinidad you wouldn't be sick.

DIRK: "But Christmas will soon be here and I am still giving Nursey trouble but I promise to behave myself better. Make haste, pass your exam to come back to me."

DIRK: (NARR) When are you coming home?

DIRK: "I send all my love. (Kiss, kiss, kiss, kiss) From your darling Dirk (kiss, kiss, kiss)"

NURSEY: This is much better, dear. Time for bed.

DIRK: (NARR) Seems like I did something right today!

SOUND: *Silence. Bells tolling. Fade.*

DIRK: (NARR) Nursey and Aunty Laura are Moravians. They used to be Anglicans, but started attending Services at Rose Hill Moravian Church in Laventille because of the Roberts family. Women wear white; carry hankies or fans or both. Everything is white, except purses or hairnets or bibles. Cream and beige are silently accepted. The first Sunday of every month — white. Men wear suits — all colours; mostly black. All sing.

MUSIC: *Voices sing "How Great Thou Art", fade under.*

DIRK: (NARR) No shyness in worship here. All praise and glory is to God alone. We listen from an adjacent room during Sunday School. At seven this morning I went to Mass with my neighbours at Blessed Martin Catholic Church. It was short. Nursey and Aunty Laura kissed me happy birthday and made me a nice breakfast. But I still didn't smell any cake baking. This singing and preaching will go on for two or three hours. I am already thirsty. The new pastor will stop only when tired, or when two or more women faint. Reverend Cuthbert is younger than last pastor. Full of energy, showing his love of Christ and making a good impression on the people. Mrs. Cuthbert is pretty and wears white shoes and white stockings. High heels on uneven Laventille hills will require good practice. Car or no car. If she doesn't have strong ankles, she'll get them. A small son and a baby. Kind folks from Canada. How far is that from England?

MUSIC: *Hymn then comes up to a close.*

DIRK: (NARR) Reverend Cuthbert is tall and has short wavery hair, rosy cheeks, spectacles. His white collar is always choking him. They quarrel like us. Maybe it's our Trinidad heat. I guess they're showig they're mortal after all. New blood is pumped into this church. (Pause) Only illness and hurricane floodings prevent Nursey and Aunty Laura from Services. On such days they sit with their Bible nourishing mind and soul. Contact with God is an everyday commitment. Practical Christians. My models.

MUSIC: Up and fade.

DIRK: (NARR) Back at home I have my afternoon nap and wake up to Nursey and Aunty Laura.

NURSEY & AUNTY LAURA: (Singing) Happy Birthday dear Dirkie, Happy Birthday to you.

NURSEY: Blow out your candles.

SOUND: *Blowing out candles.*

DIRK: Thank you, Nursey (Kiss). Thank you, Aunty Laura (Kiss).

AUNTY: We baked it yesterday. I had asked Mrs. Roberts to keep you a little longer. We didn't count on the bag bursting as well.

NURSEY: This is from your mother.

SOUND: *Paper tearing. Unwrapping.*

DIRK: My own knife, fork and spoon. I wish Mum was here for this.

AUNTY: And we have this.

DIRK: Coconut ice-cream, my favourite! Nursey?

NURSEY: Yes, love.

DIRK: Do I have to write another whole letter to thank my Mum for the gift?

NURSEY: (Laughs) No, you can add a line on the same letter. I haven't sealed it yet.

DIRK: (NARR) Cake. Ice-cream. Love. Happiness. Nursey cuts the marble cake. Inside is cream, pink, chocolate and green. It is perfect. Just what I wanted for this birthday. And more!

MUSIC: *Up.*

SEGMENT THREE: "LESSONS TO LEARN"

MUSIC: *1968 Steelband Music up; continue under.*

DIRK: It's Carnival time, 1968. I'm now 11 years old and preparing to sit my Common Entrance Exams in a month. By passing, I will get into a Secondary School like St. Mary's or Queen's Royal College. By failing … well, nobody thinks or talks about that. My mother is still in England, working as a nurse. She was here for last Carnival and we had lots of fun. But she had to go back to finish more special exams. The new plan is that she'll send for me as soon as she can and I will go to school there. In the meantime, it's Carnival, four days off from school and there's something I have to talk to Nursey about.

MUSIC: *Steelband music fades.*

NURSEY: You think, young man, you deserve to play Mas'? Jumping up in a band, parading the streets of Port-of-Spain?

DIRK: Yes, Nursey, I've been good.

SOUND: *Paper unfolding, shaken.*

DIRK: Here's my last test marks.

NURSEY: You passed. But these marks would be higher if only you listened to me and stopped playing marbles. You want to pitch your life away?

DIRK: No, Nursey. I'll study harder, I promise.

NURSEY: You need higher marks for Common Entrance, my boy. I have to think seriously about this. And if anything went wrong on those streets your poor mother would never forgive us. God knows, we're trying our best ... (Fade)

MUSIC: *Steelband music up, continue under.*

DIRK: (NARR) Carnival Tuesday morning. For the first time Nursey and Aunty Laura allow me to join in Carnival by playing Mas'. Their last reason was that since my mother might send for me at any time, this could be my first and last chance to fully experience Carnival. Solo Harmonites are now the Panorama steelband champions, for the first time in Trinidad. Parnell, my neighbour, and I pay $7.00 each to play "Sailors" with a band from up Quarry Street. White bell-bottom pants, white tee-shirt, white canvas shoes and socks. And, of course, white sailor hats. Wait! One more thing: white sweet-smelling powder.

MUSIC: *Calypso tune, fade.*

NURSEY: I want you to be very careful out there.

DIRK: I will, Nursey.

AUNTY: (Sings) Social Bacchanal! (Pause) Enjoy yourself. And if any fighting breaks out, come straight home.

DIRK: Don't worry Aunty Laura, nothing will happen to me.

NURSEY: Regardless, be home by six, dear. I must say you do look nice. Your mother, Jacqueline, should see you now.

AUNTY: You're in my prayers.

DIRK: Lucky for me, Aunty Laura was in a great mood. She loves Carnival; though she's too old these days to play. Her favourite Calypsonian, the Mighty Duke, was crowned Calypso

Monarch for the year, with "What Is Calypso" and "Social Bacchanal".

MUSIC: *Calypso "Miss Tourist". Fade under.*

DIRK: (NARR) Pernell and I jump up in the band to Lord Kitchener's "Miss Tourist".

MUSIC: *Steelband, "Miss Tourist", under.*

DIRK: (NARR) We dance through the streets and through the Savannah onto the largest open-aired stage in the world; linking shoulders — swaying from side to side in drunken fashion, in alternating rows ... raining powder upon each other. The music sweet. The feeling is jubilation beyond my wildest imagination. From the Grand Stand the band looks like a ship tossing on the ocean with white clouds, from the powder, floating above. (Pause)

SOUND: *A shower running.*

DIRK: (NARR) I get home, scrub most of the powder from my hair, change and head out again by four o'clock for more jumping up.

MUSIC: *Steelband up, then low, very distant under.*

DIRK: (NARR) At night, long after everything is over and I'm dead-tired, I still hear the stellband ringing in my ears. Rubber on steel, producing the most heavenly music to bear me off to sleep. (Pause)

MUSIC: *Fades. School bell ringing — distantly, then louder.*

DIRK: (NARR) With Carnival behind us we continue to prepare for Common Entrance Exams at Tranquility Boy's school. Dwight, Keith R., Keith B., who is very smart, and I go for extra, paid, private lessons from Mr. Roberts — after school and Saturday mornings. Lorraine, from Tranqulity Girl's attends also. Pretty for days, slender, long dark braided hair, part-Chinese with smooth brown skin and serious-looking. (Sigh) Last Saturday while playing monopoly at Keith B.'s, I admitted my crush on Lorraine. He dialled her number for me.

SOUND: *Phone rings, click, line dead under.*

LORRAINE: Hello. Helloooo …

DIRK: (NARR) I hang up, not knowing what to say. Today, Wednesday, I wait outside of Mr. Roberts' gate after sending both Keith's home.

SOUND: *Bicycle wheeled.*

DIRK: (NARR) Lorraine comes out with her bicycle; head bowed in Carmelite contemplation.

DIRK: Excuse me, Lorraine, can I talk to you?

LORRAINE: (Mildly) Yes. Go on.

DIRK: Last Saturday, it was me on the phone who didn't answer.

LORRAINE: (Surprised) You? What make you do a thing like that?

DIRK: I wanted to talk to you. Keith B. dialled, then I didn't know what to say. I thought you'd be angry that I called.

LORRAINE: I was angry.

DIRK: You sound like you're still angry.

LORRAINE: Shouldn't I be? You have a nerve!

DIRK: Please accept my apology.

LORRAINE: Just don't do it again or you'll get me vex and you won't ever want to see me vex, boy.

DIRK: I won't. I'm sorry.

LORRAINE: Alright. I'm surprised at you. You always look so quiet. What's your name, again?

DIRK: Dirk.

LORRAINE: Dirt?? What kind of name is that? (Giggles)

DIRK: No, *Dirk*.

LORRAINE: That sound better.

DIRK: (NARR) She is standing next to flowers which don't begin to compare with her fiery beauty. We have spoken. We are going to be friends.

SOUND: *Catholic altar bells sound three times.*

DIRK: (NARR) I attend Mass and receive Holy Communion this morning of my Common Entrance Exams. I pray to God and to all the saints to help me. The priest blesses my sharpened pencils, erases, religious medals and good-luck charm: a rabbit's paw. I'm wearing new Marks & Spencer socks my mother sent me in a package, for extra luck; along with my freshly-ironed school uniform. I wish my mother was here to walk me to school. (Pause) I attempt to answer all three hundred multiple-choice questions on English, Arithmetic and General Knowledge in two hours. It is my first try. My cousins Wade, Kurt and Karen passed their first time for good schools. I must also pass or I'll be a dunce.

SOUND: *Phone ringing. Click. Occasional traffic sounds, under.*

LORRAINE: Hellooo!

DIRK: Lorraine, Dirk here.

LORRAINE: Where you calling from?

DIRK: The phone booth on Norfolk Street.

LORRAINE: You lucky it working. (Laughter) Boy, those exams were hard.

DIRK: Nah. Easy. I finished in one hour flat. Then I slept for the next hour.

LORRAINE: What? Yuh lie. Nobody, not even the Prime Minister, Doctor Eric Williams himself could do it in an hour.

DIRK: As a matter of fact I didn't get to answer everything.

LORRAINE: Me neither. You think you passed?

DIRK: I have to pass. With all the prayers and novenas, even from my mother up in England, I bound to pass. (laughs) Seriously, I don't know. The arithmetic was hard like a iron pot. The English was hard like cassava. And General Knowledge was hard like ...

LORRAINE: (Cutting in) Like the principal's eye balls.

DIRK & LORRAINE: *Both laugh.*

DIRK: (NARR) Now came the period of waiting. And classes as usual. And marbles to pitch. And mangoes to stone. And ...

SOUND: *Intermittent traffic, bicycle, bell on bicycle under.*

DIRK: (NARR) Robinsonville. A cul-de-sac off Norfolk Street, close to where Lorraine lives. It is four o'clock on a sunny school afternoon. I climb onto a bike and stay on for the first time in my life. I ride, not ever wanting to stop. I am Gary Sobers and Rohan Kanhai flying between wickets. I am Solo Harmonites beating pan with white clouds on a stick. Smooth. Musical. Destined. From this moment all I want for passing is a bi-cy-cle ... so I can ride to Secondary School. (Pause) Finally the day came and the results were announced.

SOUND: *Tropical birds fade.*

DIRK: (Reading) "Dear Mum, I did not get through with my exams. I will work had to pass next year. School has closed and I am now on vacation for eight weeks. Next week I will be going to Aunty Yvonne for a month's holiday". (Fade)

DIRK: (NARR) Well, it's not the kind of letter I was hoping to write. And it's not the kind of letter my mother was hoping to receive. If only the letter would take 6 months to reach England. By fishing boat! Nursey also wrote at the same time.

SOUND: *Thunder and lightning. Rain up, continues low under.*

NURSEY: "Dear Jacqueline, sorry to have kept you so long. As you will see your son did not pass his C.E. in which he did not work hard enough/ too much play and too little study/ as you know I am not in a position to help him out in certain subjects which he can't understand. You must when you write to him give him a stern warning that he must put down marbles and T.V. when school reopens and stick to his books a lot more/ he is still a bit stiff and stubborn as you know and so I am trying my best. Are you still trying to get him up to you as you said? If so let us know early so that we may be able to start looking after that as soon as we can. I'm glad you are making yourself happier and less worried about him/ and I think too it is best to have him with you/ I just can't stand the environment any more/ I am praying to get away from the locality and with this rainy season it is just worse/ otherwise all remains the same/ hope you are getting on fine at hospital. Love from all of us. Sincerely yours. Nursey & Aunty Laura. Write soon.

DIRK: For days I walk around, hanging my head with shame. To some it's no surprise, they didn't think I'd pass anyway. They don't think I'll amount to anything.

SOUND: *Marbles thrown onto gravel, then continue until empty under.*

DIRK: (NARR) I take a handful of marbles from my tin and pelt them under the house and I keep doing so letting out all of my frustration, anger and disappointment until there are none left. This doesn't mean I have given up marbles for good. Only until I pass, next year. Because come hell or high water I must pass that exam. Unless my mother sends for me first.

DIRK: I wish it could be tomorrow. I'm always doing something to make Nursey and Aunty Laura cross with me. Maybe they'd be happier if I wasn't around. I want to be with my mother and go to school in England. Everybody had their parents. Maybe my mother doesn't want me with her. I'd be more trouble for her, too.

SOUND: *Empty tin hitting ground and rolling.*

DIRK: (NARR) I smash the tin on the ground, and kick it. Sitting on the back steps, I think about my mother and I think about Nursey and Aunty Laura. I love them all. And I think if my mother really sent for me tomorrow I'm not sure what I would do. Because it would be very, very hard for me to leave Nursey and Aunty Laura. And the more I think about it, the more I wonder how my mother could tear me away from them. If I had a choice — if they gave me a choice … I don't know what I would do. (*Pause*) Until that time comes, I'm going to study hard to pass that blasted exam. I don't like this feeling of failure. It's new to me. And I don't like it one bit.

MUSIC: *Up.*

SEGMENT FOUR: "A SINGLE WHITE ROSE"

SOUND: *Skinned drums beating, fade under.*

DIRK: (NARR) Saturday April 18th, 1969. A single white rose/ blooms on a tree/ in the front garden. It is a sign. (*Pause*) I'm now 12 and a 1/2 years old, still in Trinidad, and all dreams of life in England are dashed forever — because my mother moved to Toronto, Canada, last month. I am not pleased! In her letter she said the money is going to be better, which means when she does send for me we'll have a more comfortable life. I've sat my Common Entrance Exams for the second and last time. I'm bound to pass or my life is ruined. My friend, Lorraine, feels the same way.

SOUND: *Nursey humming a hymn — "When I Survey the Wondrous Cross", under.*

DIRK: (NARR) Nursey washes in the backyard at 33 Norfolk Street in Belmont — Mrs. Roberts' home. Mrs. Roberts passed away last November. We've been here for a couple of months. 77 Hermitage Road is being re-built to a two -storey house. We had been promised the downstairs half. But now that does not seem likely. Being uprooted here has not been easy on us. Mrs. Robert's sister lied on me, but Nursey knew the truth and stood up for me. But sometimes I've been short- tempered with Nursey.

SOUND: *Water wrung from clothes and fade.*

DIRK: (NARR) However, Nursey is happy this afternoon.

NURSEY: Tomorrow, all I plan to do is rest. I'm tired. One last pillow slip. (Hums)

SOUND: *Clothing being shaken out.*

DIRK: (NARR) Nursey goes into her bedroom for a nap before supper. She lies on the edge of the bed, not wishing to wrinkle newly-spread sheets. Sleep descends and is welcomed. She turns and falls to the ...

SOUND: *A loud thud. Footsteps running.*

ELSA: (Calling) Nursey!! (Panicked) Oh, my Lord! Don't move. Help!! Aunty Laura!!

AUNTY: (Distantly) Coming!

DIRK: (NARR) Nursey is placed on the bed, covered with sheets and a blanket to her neck. Elsa phones for Dr. Toby. She is a very efficient and controlled woman. Her love for Nursey, her God-mother, is deep. Despite her nearing 21, illness still comes as a shook to her. (Pause) Aunty Laura rests a damp wash cloth on Nursey's forehead. I'm scared, worried. My mind races.

DIRK: Nursey? Nursey?

DIRK: (NARR) I stay there not knowing what else to say. Dr. Toby arrives. It is a stroke. Nursey's left side is numb.

DIRK: Nursey?

NURSEY: (Pause) Y-e-sss.

AUNTY: At least she hears, thank God.

DIRK: (NARR) Nursey manages to say a word or two. Then rests. She is watched throughout the night.

SOUND: *Drums beating. Fade under.*

DIRK: (NARR) Sunday April 19th. I go to Mass and pray for Nursey. Everything remains the same.

SOUND: *Drums beating. Fade under.*

DIRK: (NARR) Monday April 20th. The same. At night I stand at
              Nursey's side, alone.

DIRK: Nursey?

NURSEY: (Pause) Yes?

DIRK: Nursey?

NURSEY: Yes.

DIRK: (NARR) I can thing of nothing else, so I pray silently for God to
              bless her and help her recover soon.

SOUND: *Drums beating. Fade under.*

DIRK: (NARR) Tuesday April 21st. The same. Morning. I make the
              effort to go to school. In the middle of a lesson I put my head on
              my desk and cry. Miss Barrow sends me home. I enter the quiet
              house.

ELSA: We've notified God-father Roderick, but there's no reason for
              alarm. You should try and go back to school this afternoon.

DIRK: No, I don't have to go.

ELSA: Look, boy, go to school.

DIRK: I said I'm not going and that's that.

ELSA: You think you're a big man! Well, anyway, I'm not your mother.

DIRK: (Shouting) No, you're not. (Pause) I really don't feel up to it,
              Elsa. Besides we're only killing time until Common Entrance
              results come out. I'm sorry I shouted at you. (Pause) So what you
              really think about Nursey?

ELSA: Hard to say. Her condition is stable. Doctor looked in on her this
              morning. At least we don't have to take her to hospital.

DIRK: I don't want Nursey to die.

ELSA: (Warmly) Go in and keep her company.

DIRK: (NARR) Aunty Yvonne in San Fernando is kept informed. Nursey slips in and out of consciousness through the afternoon. What is she thinking at this time? What bargain is she making with God? Yes, she has attained three score and ten, plus four. Surely there's more life in her. A few ailments, Trinidad bush tea and rest, and people carry on until their nineties. That's her future after this recovery.

SOUND: *Full teacup rattling in soucer.*

ELSA: Here, have some tea, Dirk.

DIRK: Thanks, Elsa.

ELSA: Nursey is restless this evening.

DIRK: Look, her feet moving under the sheets.

ELSA: That means she's travelling. I saw this before.

DIRK: With Mrs Roberts?

ELSA: I'm going to try Dr. Toby again.

DIRK: Does this mean she's dying?

ELSA: No. It's the restlessmess. But he should know her condition anyway.

DIRK: (NARR) Elsa is so kind. I hope she gets married to a nice fella. (Pause) Nursey's breathing changes constantly. More compresses are applied to her forehead. She settles down. That's good! I lie in bed, not even changing my clothes. I doze off.

SOUND: *Footsteps on a creaky wooden floor.*

ELSA: (Low voice) Dirk … get up.

DIRK: Hummmm …

ELSA: Come.

SOUND: *Nursey's breathing is loud, raspy. Three long throaty breaths. Silence.*

DIRK: (NARR) Nursey closes her eyes. Then she opens them, quickly. They remain open, fixed. She has seen God. We pray for her soul. There is a calm amidst tears. We close her eyes. Cover her face.

ELSA: At least she didn't suffer long. (Sniffing)

DIRK: (NARR) Elsa ties Nursey's big toes together with a piece of string.

SOUND: *Heavy footsteps.*

DIRK: (NARR) The men from Clark & Battoo Funeral Home arrive. They are not very gentle. I touch Nursey's forehead. Her cool body leaves the house for the last time. I feel empty. I feel a loss so deep, yet I am dazed by this. If I could have her back, tell her how sorry I am for giving her so much trouble over the past few months. I never got to tell her. I did get to tell her. Why couldn't I say so when she laid there, still breathing, still able to hear my voice, still able to respond; to pardon?

SOUND: *Drums beating. Fade under.*

DIRK: (NARR) Wednesday April 22nd. Phone calls this morning. A cold brisk shower. A light breakfast. I stare at the empty stripped bed. Arrangements. Tomorrow is the funeral.

DIRK: Is Mum coming? Is Uncle Roderick coming?

DIRK: (NARR) Aunty Laura comes in from her night job, where she looks after Mrs. Blizzard. I try to be brave as I hug her.

AUNTY: (Sobbing) What am I going to do without her?

DIRK: (NARR) Aunty Laura sits on the bed her sister left only hours before. (Pause) I make the rounds in Belmont, Gonzales, Laventille.

SOUND: *A car screeches to a halt.*

DIRK: (NARR) I reach the sidewalk, safely. No, it's not time for me yet. I must walk more carefully. My feet never tire as I go, briefly, from face to face bearing the saddest news of my life.

MUSIC: *Drums beating. Fade. Up with solemn organ music and contine under.*

RADIO ANNOUNCER: We regret to announce the death of Mary Adelaide Barde, better known as Nursey. Beloved sister of Laura. Mother of Roderick in England, Jacqueline in Canada, Yvonne in San Fernando. Grandmother of Pat and Dirk ...

SOUND: *Glass with ice and liquid shaken.*

DIRK: (NARR) Thursday April 23rd. I drink a glass of maube with plenty ice. The death announcement played at 5 past 6, 5 past 9 and 5 past 12 today. I hope my mother and Uncle Roderick reach in time for the service or make it to the cemetery. I'm anxious to see my mother again. It's been 2 years. I have the feeling that I passed my Exams. God can't take Nursey and have me fail, all in the same year. Not the God I know. (Pause) Today, I am looking my best for Nursey in my English wool suit.

SOUND: *A car's horn. Four doors shut under.*

DIRK: (NARR) A long black private taxi arrives and we climb in. As the taxi swings up Rose Hill, I see, ahead, for the first time, Nursey's blue-grey casket in the hearse. Since Tuesday night, this is the first realization of the finality of her death. Tears flow quietly down my cheeks.

SOUND: *A car door opens. Traffic passes. Footsteps on concrete under.*

DIRK: (NARR) I rush out of the taxi, leaving the others behind. I walk past the hearse, staring and staring. I fly up the steps of the Moravian church.

DIRK: Uncle Mervyn ...

MUSIC: *Church organ continues until minister speaks, low under.*

DIRK: (NARR) We stand aside, permitting the casket to enter before us, though others are already seated in the packed church. Inside, I look at her face, her hair, her sealed eyes, her newly-made pink shroud. I pray silently while Nursey sleeps. I look to see if she is breathing; any sign of life. Mistakes have been made before, and the dead woken up. (Pause) I take my place beside Aunty Laura. (Nest speech will continue under Dirk's monologue.)

REV. CUTHBERT: Brothers and Sisters in Christ, I greet you in the name of the Father and the Son and of the Holy Spirit, Amen. We are assembled here in sorrow and in faith to commend the spirit of Sister Laura Barde into the hands of Our Lord Jesus, the risen Christ. Sister Laura was known to many as a generous and warm spirited woman who ... (Fades)

DIRK: (Whispering) Nursey! Not Aunty Laura. Aunty Laura, why doesn't someone correct him?

AUNTY: Nevermind, son.

DIRK: Didn't he see her body?

AUNTY: He must have. Funny, our whole lives, nobody ever mixed us up.

DIRK: Somebody should just whisper to him.

AUNTY: It's alright. We know who the Service is for. And Nursey knows, too. (Pause)

MUSIC: *A hymn comes to a close. People murmur. Numerous footsteps along a paved road. Ocasional traffic sounds cintinue under.*

DIRK: (NARR) The procession begin outside the church. I walk ahead of the hearse, dabbing my eyes and face with my handkerchief. Sometimes, I am beside the hearse, holding on for comfort. I speak to no one. I experience this alone — this marching to Calvary, as it were, with my dead. After 2 miles, we enter Lapeyreuse Cemetery in Woodbrook.

REV. CUTHBERT: "Surely goodness and mercy shall follow me all the days of my life, and I will dwell in the house of the Lord forever. Amen."

MUSIC: *Choral " Abide With Me" under.*

DIRK: (NARR) A last look at Nursey's peaceful face, reflecting the nature of her personality. I stand alone. They point her head to the east.

SOUND: *Above "Choral", casket lowered mechanically.*

DIRK: (NARR) A grave digger shows us a skull, belonging to Nursey's sister, Teacher, who was last buried here, nine feet deep, before I was born.

SOUND: *Earth thrown onto casket in hole. Heavey thuds. Earth softer. Shovels patting earth.*

DIRK: (NARR) I place the first wreath. A woman adjusts it. I COULD SCREAM!!! I wanted it there, why move it, she's not your grandmother. Why the hell can't adults respect the wishes of children? I keep looking in the distance for Mum and Uncle Roderick. It's not too late right now. (Pause)

DIRK: (Inner voice) I regret my rebellious behaviour. Oh, Nursey, I regret not finding the strength to tell you how sorry I am for causing you heartache, when all you needed was understanding. I don't understand how people can be asked to move with the promise of a new home, then be betrayed after more than thirty years — plunging them into despair and endless worry. Why should I understand that?? NO!!!!!

DIRK: (NARR) We say good-bye to Nursey. We return home. My mother arrives half-an-hour later from Toronto. Then Uncle Roderick arrives a few hours later from London. Delayed flights. It is too late and too costly to dig up the grave for one final look.

SOUND: *Drums beat ferociously. Silence. Drums beat.*

SEGMENT FIVE: "AT LONG LAST"

MUSIC: *1969 top hit "Time is Tight" by Booker T. & The MG's, up, then fade.*

DIRK: (NARR) It's December, 1969. I finally passed my Common Entrance Exams and got into Tranquility Secondary School. By the time I started in September, my papers were already being processed for Canada. Aunty Laura and I are now staying in Belmont Valley Road with Terris St. Bernard, my mother's long-time friend, and her children. I sleep on a cot which I fold up every morning. At night, Aunty Laura continues to keep watch over the ailing Mrs. Blizzard, up Hermitage Road. We're very happy here. I turned thirteen in September. My first birthday without Nursey's marble cake. I still miss her so much. Sometimes I go by the grave after school and say a short prayer. (Pause) I'm anxious to be with my mother in Toronto. Today, I visit Dr. Toby.

SOUND: *An air conditioner, continues under.*

DR. TOBY: Your smallpox vaccination has healed very well. Your urine and stool samples were healthy. Keep this International Certificate of Vaccination with you. Have you received your passport yet?

DIRK: Yes, Dr. Toby. But I don't like my picture.

DR. TOBY: (Laughs) I didn't like mine either. Your passport number goes here on the cover. Any problems?

DIRK: No, Dr. Toby. Everything's fine.

DR. TOBY: I like to hear that. So, when you're leaving?

DIRK: Next Thursday morning.

DR. TOBY: Well, enjoy your first flight. And give your mother my regards. I know you're not coming back in a hurry, but whenever you do, don't forget to look me up.

DIRK: I'll do that. Thanks for everything, Dr. Toby.

DIRK: (NARR) After 24 hours I've finally told somebody outside of the household that I'm leaving the land of the humming bird. Except for my Aunt Yvonne, who told me. Now, I have the task, like my mother before me, of telling a million people. Feels like a million. That's the whole population. I might as well go on TV. But I'm not that brave. Besides, even if I went on and said, "Hi everybody, ah going to Canada next week", they'll all say, "Well, if yuh goin'go!". I really had half of Belmont to say good-bye to. But where to start?

SOUND: *Dog barking.*

MR. O'REILLY: Stay, Daisy, stay. Who is it? (Dog stops)

DIRK: It's me, Mr. O'Reilly, Dirk.

Mr. O'REILLY: Who?

DIRK: Dirk McLean.

MR. O'REILLY: Ohhh. I don't have my specs on. Come in, McLean.

SOUND: *Creaky wooden gate is opened. Shuts. Is bolted.*

DIRK: I'm leaving for Canada next week to join my mother. So, I came to say good-bye and to ask you for a letter of recommendation to transfer to a Secondary School in Toronto. I'm at Tranquility now.

MR. O'REILLY: Gladly, my boy. Now what do you want me to say? (Laughs)

MUSIC: *Near the end of the speech, "Something" by the Beatles begins and continues under.*

DIRK: (NARR) Mr. O'Reilly was a gem. On the other hand, my Principal only promised that he would send it, along with my first term marks. He was bogged down with exams and the up-coming Christmas party. (Pause) I resigned in writing from the Cadets. I heard myself saying the words leaving and going so many times I wish I was gone already. And people wanted me to come back again. It proved fruitful because Mr. & Mrs. Choy Sing gave me a set of hand-kerchiefs from their store. There was sugar cake and tamarind balls and tulum to collect. My God-mother, Yvonne, gave me a silver I.D. bracelet and some money. Keith R. bought me a snowcone with plenty syrup. I didn't know how to say good-bye to him, or to some people. I pretended I was going on a vacation or so and I'd see them next year. It was difficult. One person I delayed, then summed up the courage to face was Lorraine.

MUSIC: *Fades under.*

LORRAINE: You look like you have something else to say. (Pause) Well, say it.

DIRK: I was wondering if you'd like to go steady with me.

LORRAINE: Is now you come to ask me this? You had all the time in the world.

DIRK: I know.

LORRAINE: But look at my crosses! I have seen shy before, but Dirk you beat back all. What kind of relationship you expect us to have?

DIRK: I'll write to you. You can write back.

LORRAINE: And then what?

DIRK: We'll see each other again. I like you, Lorraine.

LORRAINE: Nah, nah, nah. That too complicated.

DIRK: Ahm, let's just write to each other, then.

LORRAINE: That sound better.

DIRK: We're still friends?

LORRAINE: (Laughing) Of course. Are you scared to be leaving Trinidad?

DIRK: A little. I've been thinking about it for years. I'm ready enough.

LORRAINE: Your mother must be excited.

DIRK: She'd better be.

LORRAINE: You're right. She'd better be. Good-luck up there.

DIRK: Bye, then. (Kiss)

LORRAINE: Bye, Dirk.

DIRK: (NARR) A kiss on the check. And a vow of friendship was greater than empty speculation. I had to say something or I'd never know what was in her heart. I felt relieved. Toronto must have a few thousand girls, pretty like Lorraine, just waiting for a fella like me! (*Pause*) My friend Elsa was getting ready to go to New York to stay with an aunt. Our farewell was brief and light-hearted. When I got home, Aunty Laura was sitting in the verandah.

MUSIC: *Up and fade.*

DIRK: Don't be sad, Aunty Laura.

AUNTY: (Crying) I can't help it. I've watched you grow up, helped raise you, and now you're leaving.

DIRK: You won't be alone for long. Aunty Marjorie is sending for you to be in England with her. Uncle Roderick is there. I'll write. And phone.

AUNTY: (Sobbing) I know that. I miss Nursey so much. She was a good soul. Sometimes, I don't know what to do. I depended on her a whole lot.

DIRK: I think Nursey died so that I could be with my mother. And she knew Aunty Marjorie would take care of you.

AUNTY: You may be right, there. It would have broken her heart to see you go.

DIRK: I might not have gone.

AUNTY: Your mother needs you. It's been long enough without her.

DIRK: Aunty Marjorie needs you. Your daughter needs you, so be strong, Aunty Laura. I love you very much. Remember that.

AUNTY: I'm glad you turned out so well. You weren't that much trouble, for a boy. Your mother, Jacqueline, must be proud. (*Pause*) When are you heading to San Fernando?

MUSIC: *Up and fade under.*

DIRK: (NARR) In San Fernando, Aunty Yvonne and Uncle Mervyn help me pack. I've promised so many people to write, I won't have time to do any homework in Toronto.

SOUND: *Crickets. A car passing, under.*

DIRK: (NARR) A final stroll at night. I look up at the stars. It's clear. I wonder if the sky looks like this in Canada. And I wonder how many Trinidadians I'll find there. I leave the home of my friends, the Smarts, not promising to write. I'm ready for the change, knowing Aunty Laura will be fine. I'll save up my money and visit her. I've longed to see England. I don't know much about Canada except that it's a whole lot bigger and not as cold. Perhaps I should have asked Rev. Cuthbert. Too late now. (*Pause*)

SOUND: *Airport noises, under.*

VOICE: Final Boarding for BOAC Flight 538 to New York.

DIRK: (NARR) Damn!! No more time. I can't miss the plane. From New York I take another plane to Toronto. Where is Aunty Laura? Did Mr. Rouse not pick her up? Did she have a heart attack or something? I have no choice.

DIRK: Bye, Aunty Yvonne (Kiss). Bye, Uncle Mervyn (Kiss). Please go to Belmont and see if Aunty Laura is alright.

DIRK: (NARR) I rush through with my passport and papers, paying the $2.00 Government Service Charge and Emigration Tax, grabbing the receipt, and dash out into the windy, glaring heat.

SOUND: *Airport grounds. Engines under.*

DIRK: (NARR) I look back, hoping to spot Aunty Laura in the crowd, but she is not there. A last look at the mountain ranges which protect this blessed land. I must not cry.

SOUND: *In addition to engines, shoes on metal stairs under.*

DIRK: (NARR) I run up the steps to the plane, look back. A sea of faces, multicolored clothing, through waves of heat. Even if she is there, I don't know if I'm seeing her. I'm the last one on.

STEWARDESS: Good morning, welcome aboard.

DIRK: (Panting) Good morning, Miss.

STEWARDESS: I guess you're the young chap who's travelling alone. I'll escort you to your seat.

SOUND: *Interior plane, noises under.*

DIRK: (NARR) In a daze I follow her. The plane is less than half-full. A window seat where I can still see the terminal.

SOUND: *Seat belt buckling.*

STEWARDESS: There. Is that too tight?

DIRK: No, it's fine.

STEWARDESS: If you need any assistance, just ask. I'll come back after we take off.

SOUND: *Plane starting up, moving, under.*

DIRK: (NARR) I stare out of the window, after watching the emergency life-saving demonstration, which I could care less about. I don't have time or energy to waste on being scared if this plane crashes. I rest my head against the window as the plane begins to move, still wishing I could see Aunty Laura. My vision is blurred by tears. I cry for Nursey who is with God. I cry for all that I'm leaving — thirteen years of mixed memories. I understand now how my mother felt eight years ago when she left without being able to say farewell to Nursey and Aunty Laura. Like her, I know that I will see Aunty Laura alive again. It is a small consolation as I cry for Aunty Laura and how lonely she must be feeling right now.

SOUND: *Plane lifting off. Silence. Interior hum of plane under.*

DIRK: (NARR) I wake up and remember that I'm on a plane and not on a chair in Trinidad. I remove the pillow, placed there by the stewardess. She's very pretty.

STEWARDESS: Would you like some dinner now, sir, I saved it for you?

DIRK: Yes, thanks.

SOUND: *Tray sliding onto surface — cutlery jingling.*

STEWARDESS: And this is for you. A Flight Club membership.

SOUND: *Pages turning.*

STEWARDESS: The Captain has logged your mileage and signed it, himself. And a pin to wear when you travel with us again. Do you know what BOAC stands for?

DIRK: British Overseas Airway Corporation.

DIRK: (NARR) She was impressed. I'll bet she doesn't know that TTT stands for Trinidad & Tobago Television. But I didn't ask her. I think she knew that I had been crying, but she didn't ask me about it. She pointed out the lights below. New York. So many. And different colours outside the house and buildings. Christmas lights. (Pause) We shook hands and I boarded Air Canada flight 793 at JFK Airport. This was short trip. (Pause) White below. Snow. My watch says 10:30.

SOUND: *A plane landing. Wind howling under.*

DIRK: (NARR) A bumpy landing. I step off the plane into the cold, windy night. A stewardess holds my hand. We walk across the white carpet of snow laid down just for me — by God.

SOUND: *Footsteps echo along a corridor.*

IMMIGRATION OFICER: Next.

DIRK: Good evening.

IMMIGRATION OFFICER: Your ticket and passport please.

SOUND: *Papers shuffling.*

IMMIGRATION OFFICER: Who's meeting you, sir?

DIRK: My mother.

IMMIGRATION OFFICER: Is she outside?

DIRK: I hope so. Yes.

IMMIGRATION OFFICER: Any alcohol or plants?

DIRK: A bottle of Trinidad Rum. For my mother.

SOUND: *Stamping into passport. Sounds of tearing form. Stapling.*

IMMIGRATION OFFICER: This is your Canadian Immigration Identification Card, eh? Sign here. Keep this attached to your passport at all times. You are now a Landed Immigrant. Welcome to Canada, son. Go through those doors there.

DIRK: Thanks very much.

DIRK: (NARR) December 11th, 1969. A date stamped in my passport. A date stamped in memory.

SOUND: *Automatic doors opening under.*

DIRK: (NARR) I reach for the doors, but they open before me. Like magic. My mother stands beaming. I rush into her welcoming arms, at long last.

MUSIC: *Up.*

THE END

GLOSSARY

Blessed Martin:	St. Martin de Porres Catholic Church
Blood Pudding:	A highly seasoned cow's blood mixture stuffed into cow's intestines as a sausage
Bush tea:	Herbal tea
Calaloo:	A thick sauce made from dasheen leaves, ochroes, coconut milk and spices. Crab is often added.
Carmelite:	A religious order of nuns.
Cassava pone:	A pastry made from grated cassava and coconut.
Common Entrance :	An exam for 11 and 12 year old students Examination for placement in secondary schools. Failure led to trade school or work force.
Cul-de-sac:	A short, dead-end street.
Green figs:	Green bananas — vegetable
Ground provisions :	Vegetables grown to maturity in the earth, for example: eddoes, dasheen, potatoes, yam, cassava
Hops Bread:	Large buns made from flour, hops and yeast.
Iron pot:	A cast iron pot for cooking.
Liming:	Hanging out with friends
"Looking at my crosses":	Expression: "Look at my troubles" or "What a burden!"
Moravians:	Christians from the Protestant denomination
Ochroe and rice:	A popular dish of ochroes and rice with cod fish
Plantains:	Large vegetable from the banana family. Ripened, they are boiled or fried.

Pips:	A growth on the tip of a chicken's tongue which has to be removed.
Play Mas':	Masqueraders in a parade of bands, like Toronto's Caribana or Montreal's Carnival.
Skylarking:	Hanging out with friends
Spanish thyme:	An aromatic seasoning
Sugar cake:	A sweet made from grated coconut, boiled in sugar, with added food colouring.
Tamarind balls:	A sweet made from the tamarind fruit sugar, and hot pepper.
Tulum:	A sweet made from coconut, molasses, and spices, rolled in small balls.
Snowcone:	Shaved ice with syrup on top, in a large paper cone; sometimes condensed milk is added.

The Golden Door

by W. Ray Towle

PLAYWRIGHT

Ray Towle holds a Doctorate from the University of London, England and was employed as an economic consultant and senior economist in the energy industry before embarking on a career as a freelance writer. He writes plays, screenplays and children's books, and edits a newsletter for the Genesis International Research Association.

The Golden Door is the author's first play. It was conceived during Bill Somers' playwriting class in the Faculty of Continuing Education at the University of Calgary. Subsequently, it was developed with the support of the Alberta Playwrights' Network.

The author lives with his wife and four daughters on an acreage near Calgary, Alberta where he raises Norwegian Fjord Horses and is the Canadian representative for Öllöv Original Horseshoes from Sweden.

ORIGINAL PRODUCTION

A public reading of *The Golden Door* was presented at the 1989 Alberta Book Festival under the auspices of the Alberta Playwrights' Network. It was directed by James Dugan, head of the Drama Department of the University of Calgary, with the following cast:

Toshio Tanaka	Knobby Sato
Tom Tanaka	Al Tsuji
Aiko Tanaka	Akemo Sato
Mae Tanaka	Katherine Nishimura-Yasui
June Tanaka	Tomoko Sato
Ken Tanaka	Taiji Sato
Tadashi Sakamoto	Teak Sato
Jim Johnson	Kevin Rothery
Mr. Jones	Chuck Rose

Setsuko, George Kato and the RCMP Officers were doubled by the cast.

The play was workshopped by the All Nations Theatre Company in Calgary, Alberta under the direction of Yvette Dudley and produced in the fall of 1996.

GRANTS, AWARDS

The play received a grant from the Alberta Playwrights' Network as a winner in its New Play Development Program competition. It was a finalist in the Full-

Length Discovery Category and Full-Length Any Subject Category in Alberta Culture and Multiculturalism's 22nd Annual Playwriting Competition in 1989.

PLAYWRIGHT'S NOTE

The Golden Door is an historical play about a Japanese Canadian family in British Columbia during the Second World War. It focuses on the Tanaka family's struggle against racial discrimination, unjust government policies, and internment in light of their birthright and identity as Canadian citizens.

Although the Tanaka family is a fictitious one, their story incapsulates actual events outlined in a number of historical accounts by such authors as Ken Adachi, Muriel Kitagawa, Takeo Ujo Nakano, and Barry Broadfoot. Their plight documents one of the most dramatic incidents in Canadian history and the lessons we learn from their story should not be forgotten.

This play is dedicated to the Japanese Canadian people in Taber, Alberta who gave me many fond childhood memories and who were instrumental in my growth and maturity. More specifically, to my good friends, Albert Tsuji and Roger Teshima, who sat in front and back of me throughout high school as a result of our school's commitment to alphabetical seating; and to Jim Oshiro, my home room teacher in Grades 8 and 9, whom I admired and who taught me how to play golf.

PERFORMANCE PERMISSION

For permission to perform *The Golden Door*, please contact RAY TOWLE, Box 2, Site 26, R.R.8; Calgary, Alberta T2J 2T9. (403) 256-6410.

NOTES

B.C. Security Commission — Established by the Federal Government by Order-in-Council P.C. 1665 on March 4, 1942. The Commission planned, supervised, and directed the evacuation of all persons of Japanese "race" from the designated "Protected Area" which included all lands within 100 miles of the West Coast.

Custodian of Enemy Alien Property — All properties owned by Japanese Canadians were placed in trust. The Custodian had the power to sell this property without the consent of the owners.

Hastings Park — The Exhibition grounds in Vancouver. Former stables and cattle stalls of the Livestock Building were transformed into detention housing for Japanese Canadians on their way to being interned in the interior of British Columbia.

King — Mackenzie King, the Prime Minister of Canada.

Mackenzie, Ian — Liberal Member of Parliament from Vancouver Centre in Mackenzie King's cabinet.

Morii, Etsuji — Selected as the head of the liaison committee between the B.C. Security Commission and the Japanese community. Given preferential treatment by the RCMP, but was considered unrepresentative, patronizing and dictatorial by many of the Japanese Canadians.

Nisei Mass Evacuation Group — Resisted the breakup of families during the evacuation of Japanese Canadians.

Order-in-Council P.C. 1486 (Feb.24, 1942) — Directive from Louis St. Laurent, Minister of Justice, erasing the distinction of Japanese Canadians from Japanese Nationals by controlling the movements of all persons of Japanese origin in certain "protected areas."

Petawawa — Prisoner-of-war camp in Ontario.

Taylor, Austin — Vancouver businessman. Chairman of the B.C. Security Commission.

War Measures Act — Unlimited powers given to the Federal Cabinet in the event of war.

Wilson, Harold — Notorious anti-Japanese Canadian politician in Vancouver.

THE GOLDEN DOOR

LIST OF CHARACTERS

TOSHIO TANAKA: fisherman, about 60 years old
TOM TANAKA: son of Toshio, about 25 years old
AIKO TANAKA: wife of Toshio
MAE TANAKA: wife of TOM
JUNE TANAKA: daughter of Toshio, 16-18 years old
KEN TANAKA: Son of Toshio, 12-14 years old
TADASHI SAKAMOTO: boyfriend of June, 18 years old
SETSUKO: mother of Mae
JIM JOHNSON: employee of B.C. Security Commission
MR. JONES: senior supervisor of Jim
RCMP OFFICER
GEORGE KATO: neighbour, about 30 years old

TIME AND PLACE

The play opens in the first week of December, 1941 in the fishing village of Steveston on the outskirts of Vancouver. It concludes in the spring of 1945 in the Slocan Valley in the interior of British Columbia.

MUSIC

The big band 'swing era' jazz sounds of Benny Goodman open the play. A Japanese lullaby, *Nen-nen-koro-ri*, is sung in the Second Act.

ACT ONE, SCENE ONE

(The fishing village of Steveston near Vancouver, British Columbia. The first week of December, 1941. Afternoon. The Tanaka living room. The stage setting shows a simply furnished but very tidy room. Two women, MAE and AIKO, are setting a table for dinner near a door leading to a kitchen stage right. A teenage girl, JUNE, is reading a book while lounging on a sofa and listening to Benny Goodman on the radio [stage left]. A couple of chairs and a coat rack are located near the front door entrance [stage centre]. A sewing machine is set in a corner behind the kitchen table. A Buddhist shrine is located near a door leading to the bedrooms and a back entrance stage left.)

(MAE smiles and speaks softly to AIKO after glancing at JUNE to make sure she is not listening to them.)

MAE: Oka-a-san, wa Oba-a-san ni naru no yo.

AIKO: Watakushi shi-te imashita.

MAE: Doshite shite ta no?

(AIKO, smiling, turns and goes back into the kitchen. MAE continues to set the table and smiles bemusedly to herself. She looks over at JUNE whose body is swaying to the beat of the music on the radio.)

MAE: June, will you bring the chairs over to the table for me, please?

(JUNE gets up and dances to the music as she makes her way over to the front door. She lifts and dances with each chair as if they were make-believe partners.)

MAE: Don't let Mama-san see you.

JUNE: I can't help it ... it's in my bones.

MAE: It couldn't have been inherited.

JUNE: You've got to move with the music.

MAE: Then try moving gracefully ... like Madame Butterfly.

JUNE: Madame Butterfly and Benny Goodman don't mix.

MAE: I didn't dare move with the music when I lived at home.

JUNE: I'm glad I'm part of the younger generation.

MAE: You're not that much younger.

JUNE: Let me teach you how to dance.

MAE: No ... I can't.

(JUNE grabs MAE's hand and pulls her to the centre of the room.)

JUNE: Come on ... it's easy ... now listen to the music and feel it in your
            bones.

MAE: I can't ... really.

JUNE: Watch my feet and follow me. That's it.

(MAE awkwardly starts to dance with JUNE. AIKO enters and stares at them. MAE and JUNE stop dancing abruptly when they notice AIKO. AIKO shakes her head and goes back into the kitchen.)

JUNE: I thought she'd scold us for sure.

MAE: She has something else on her mind.

JUNE: What's that?

MAE: I shouldn't say anything ... not yet anyway.

JUNE: Why not?

MAE: It's a secret ... between her and Papa-san.

JUNE: But she told you.

MAE: She couldn't contain herself.

JUNE: What is it?

MAE: I shouldn't have mentioned anything in the first place.

JUNE: You didn't promise not to tell, did you?

MAE: Well ... no ...

JUNE: I'll tell you my secret if you'll tell me yours.

MAE: You have a secret?

JUNE: Yes.

MAE: You're not making it up just to get me to ...

JUNE: No. I promise.

MAE: Well ...

JUNE: Mae ... come on ... this is agony.

MAE: All right. Papa-san told Mama-san that they may be able to visit their family in Nagasaki next year.

JUNE: Really? That's great.

MAE: Auntie's letters were really beginning to make Mama-san homesick.

JUNE: She's dreamed of going home for over 30 years.

MAE: She used to talk alot about her family in Nagasaki but now I think it's too painful for her.

JUNE: She sure seems happy ... compared to yesterday.

MAE: She hasn't stopped working all day. She was even at the market buying vegetables before we were up this morning.

JUNE: If Mama-san had to wait much longer I'd hate to think what might happen to her.

MAE: Now it's your turn. What's your secret?

JUNE: Do you promise to keep it a secret?

MAE: I promise.

JUNE: I've got a date Saturday night.

MAE: A date?! (JUNE nods her head.) I thought you were in love.

JUNE: (blushing) Love?

MAE: Yes, love. I know the symptoms.

JUNE: He's very nice ... and handsome.

MAE: He?

JUNE: Tad ... Tad Sakamoto. He's meeting me at the movies. Don't tell

Tom ... he might tell Papa-san.

MAE: A secret's a secret. I won't even tell Tom. (laughing) I remember when Tom first took me to the movies. My Father was most upset that I may bring dishonour to our family. He said it would be difficult to arrange a suitable marriage if my reputation was in question.

JUNE: From going to the movies?

MAE: No, from what might happen after the movies.

JUNE: On your first date?

MAE: You know how people talk.

JUNE: Well, what happened?

MAE: When?

JUNE: After the movies.

MAE: Oh, I let Tom hold my hand when we walked down some side streets on the way home.

JUNE: Is that all?

MAE: That's all.

JUNE: I don't think I'll even be able to hold hands with Tad. I'm going with Kumi and Evelyn.

MAE: They'll keep you honest.

JUNE: Did your Father really think he'd arrange your marriage?

MAE: He not only thought it ... he was already in the process of communicating with my prospective family.

JUNE: Who did he want you to marry?

MAE: The son of a successful businessman in Victoria.

JUNE: What was he like?

MAE: He was okay I guess … but I wanted to make up my own mind. Then I met Tom … then the fireworks started.

JUNE: But you got your own way.

MAE: It was a delicate matter. My Father didn't want to lose face. He had to quietly explain through a go-between that the union wouldn't take place.

JUNE: How embarrassing!

MAE: I don't know exactly what he said, but … yes … it was rather embarrassing.

JUNE: Papa-san is beginning to act like your Father. When he sees me he gets that look in his eye and says, "Pretty soon we find you good boy".

MAE: He only wants what's best for you.

JUNE: I don't want an arranged marriage. If you and Tom got to decide for yourself I should too.

MAE: We still had to make the arrangements through a go-between. It wasn't exactly traditional but it appeared that way.

JUNE: Pretences … I hate pretences.

MAE: It's only a matter of respecting the old ways.

JUNE: Well, the old ways wouldn't have any rules about dating at the movies … would they?

MAE: (smiling) Not specifically perhaps, but protocol should still be followed … don't you think?

JUNE: Well, maybe … Do you need any more help?

MAE: Later, after Papa-san and Tom get home.

(MAE exits to the kitchen. JUNE returns to the sofa and her book.) (Lights dim)

SCENE TWO

(Lights rise down left on two men, TOSHIO and TOM. TOSHIO is gutting some fish while TOM is mending some fish nets.)

TOSHIO: Not much fish in ocean.

TOM: We already caught them all.

TOSHIO: (jokingly) Too many hole in net.

TOM: I fixed them all yesterday ... you didn't sail where the salmon were running.

TOSHIO: Running? I think salmon swimming.

TOM: Just a figure of speech Papa ... the salmon run.

TOSHIO: Salmon swim.

TOM: It's just an expression.

TOSHIO: You miss hole.

TOM: Where?

TOSHIO: (pointing) There.

TOM: I don't see it.

TOSHIO: (gets up) There. I tell you ... too many hole in net.

TOM: Yes Papa.

TOSHIO: I fix. You gut. (TOSHIO and TOM trade places.)(pause) Tom, you gut funny. Don't cut head first.

TOM: I've been doing this as long as I remember.

TOSHIO: Gut first ... then cut head.

TOM: (irritated) What difference does it make?

TOSHIO: Easy my way. I show you. (TOSHIO and TOM trade places.)Hold head. Slit. Gut. Chop head. See ... faster.

TOM: (hanging up the nets) That's the last fish. I don't think speed is important today.

TOSHIO: Speed important. We go home early. I drive new car. Speed now ... speed later. (laughs)

(TOSHIO completes the fish cleaning and he and TOM begin to walk from stage left to stage right.)

TOSHIO: Tom ... when I have grandson?

TOM: I don't know Papa.

TOSHIO: You keep tail between legs I never have grandson.

VOICE: Here come some Japs.

(TOSHIO and TOM stop walking abruptly and look in the direction of the VOICE.)

TOM: Look at those guys glaring at us.

TOSHIO: Don't look. (TOSHIO continues to walk.)

VOICES: The Japs are ruining the fishing industry.

(TOM looks back.)

TOSHIO: Don't hear.

TOM: We're not ruining the fishing industry!

TOSHIO: Don't worry.

TOM: They're just too damn lazy.

VOICES: Go home Japs ... Nips.

TOSHIO: (chuckling) We are going home.

TOM: Papa, when is it going to change?

TOSHIO: In time, people change.

TOM: How can you say that?

TOSHIO: It was bad when I come here forty year ago.

TOM: They haven't changed. I'd like to give them all a black eye.

TOSHIO: Then they look like us (laughs). Tom, you have hot head. Better to keep hot in, not let it out.

TOM: We've got to do something.

TOSHIO: Shikata-ga-nai. Shikata-ga-nai.

(TOSHIO and TOM exit stage right.)

SCENE THREE

(Lights rise on JUNE who continues to read on the sofa. The front door opens and a young teenage boy, KEN, enters with books under his arm and slams the door. He kicks off his shoes, hangs up his coat, and stomps into the living room.)

KEN: (mumbling) What a waste of time.

JUNE: Ken, did you say something?

KEN: Yeah. What a waste of time.

JUNE: What?

KEN: Japanese language school.

JUNE: If we go to Japan, we'll have to speak Japanese.

KEN: Go to Japan? We can't afford to go to Stanley Park!

JUNE: That's not true. We just bought a new '41 Ford, didn't we?

KEN: Yeah, that's why we can't afford to go to Stanley Park.

JUNE: Well, I lived through it. So can you.

KEN: I have to go to Japanese school, after school, every day of the week. I don't have time to play baseball and the teachers are so dumb. They can hardly speak a word of English.

JUNE: They're supposed to teach Japanese, not English.

KEN: Then they should teach us something about Japanese baseball.

JUNE: They don't play baseball in Japan, silly.

KEN: Well, I'm going out to play some Canadian baseball.

JUNE: Dinner's at six o'clock.

KEN: Six o'clock?! There's no time to play baseball. I hate Japanese language school!

JUNE: Don't let Papa-san hear you.

KEN: Guess what I'm doing on Saturday.

JUNE: Playing baseball?

KEN: I'm going swimming with Tak and Roger.

JUNE: Swimming, in December?

KEN: We're going to the Crystal Pool near English Bay.

JUNE: What! You can't swim there. They won't let you in.

KEN: Yes they will. The pool supervisor said we can swim between 7:30 and 9:30, but we have to leave before 10:00 when it's open to the public. (pause) You know what we did last Saturday before we left? (chuckling) We all peed in the pool.

JUNE: Ken, that's disgusting! (she stifles a laugh)

KEN: Tak and Roger said they saw you with somebody after school.

JUNE: It was only Kumi.

KEN: It wasn't a girl ... it was a boy ... and you were holding hands.

JUNE: A boy?

KEN: They said his name was Tad.

JUNE: I don't know anyone by the name of Tad.

KEN: Try Tadashi Sakamoto. Son of Takeo Sakamoto.

JUNE: Don't tell Papa-san.

KEN: What's it worth to you?

JUNE: If you tell, I'll tell him you peed in the Crystal Pool.

KEN: I was just kidding.

JUNE: No you weren't. I heard you. (A door shuts stage left.) They're home early. Now don't tell ... or else.

(TOSHIO and TOM enter stage left. Coats and boots have been left by the back door.)

KEN: Catch any fish?

TOSHIO: Not much fish in ocean.

TOM: The salmon run is over.

TOSHIO: Salmon swim.

TOM: Smells like my favorite sushi. Is it?

KEN: I don't know. I just got home myself. I go to Japanese language school, remember?

TOSHIO: Ken, kyo gakko de otonashiku shite itaka?

KEN: (wryly) Yes, I was a good boy in school, Papa.

TOSHIO: Good. Then we go for drive in new car.

KEN: Yippee! Can Tak and Roger come?

TOSHIO: Sure.

KEN: Oh boy! Wait 'til they ride in our brand new '41 Ford. I'll be the most popular kid in school.

TOM: (teasingly) Is that English or Japanese school?

KEN: Both. I'll get Tak and Roger.

(KEN throws on his coat and shoes and runs out the front door.)

JUNE: I'd better go and help in the kitchen.

TOSHIO: (eyeing JUNE) Pretty soon ... pretty soon.

(JUNE exits as MAE enters from the kitchen.)

MAE: Hello, Papa. Would you like some tea before dinner?

TOSHIO: No, thanks. I drive Ken and friend around block. I go and polish car. Ken very happy, very happy.

(TOSHIO exits stage left.)

MAE: (laughing) How many times has he polished it today?

TOM: Only twice. Is Mama-san making my favorite sushi?

MAE: Yes, she's cooking everyone's favorite dish tonight. Would you like some tea?

TOM: Yes, thanks.

(MAE serves TOM some tea as he sits on the sofa with his newspaper.)

MAE: What a good year this has been. Plenty of fish, a new car ... (TOM nods and becomes engrossed in his newspaper.) ...

270

something to look forward to.

TOM: What's that?

MAE: Mama-san and Papa-san may go to Japan next year.

TOM: Papa-san told me.

MAE: I'm really happy for Mama-san. She's often talked about the lovely gardens in Nagasaki, the cherry blossoms in spring, how she and her sister would play in the park and watch the boats sail in and out of the harbour, not knowing that one day she would sail away to a husband and a new home. Tom?

TOM: Hmmmm.

MAE: That's what I want to talk about.

TOM: What?

MAE: Our own home.

TOM: We can't afford it.

MAE: I could earn some extra money sewing, we could plant a larger garden, go to fewer movies ...

TOM: (looking up from his newspaper) Have you been arguing with Mama-san?

MAE: No, not at all. We've lived here since we got married. I want to plan the meals and cook for you. I want to ask Alice and Bill over for dinner.

TOM: Ask them over.

MAE: Mama-san wouldn't like it.

TOM: It doesn't matter to her.

MAE: It would embarrass her. She doesn't think our home is good enough to entertain our white friends.

TOM: I realize this arrangement isn't exactly what we had in mind, but we haven't saved enough money.

MAE: Couldn't we borrow some money ... enough for a down payment?

TOM: The fishing may not be as good next year.

MAE: I'm sure there's some way to ...

TOM: We must be practical. (putting down his newspaper) What is it, Mae? There's more to this than just being able to cook your own meals and entertain friends.

MAE: Remember when we got married and moved here, you said it was temporary, until we had our own family. Well ...

TOM: (jumping up from the sofa) You're ...

MAE: Yes, I am.

TOM: When did it happen?

MAE: (laughing) I don't know exactly, but the doctor says my due date is around the first of July.

TOM: I'll have a son next summer. That's great news! Mae, that's terrific!

MAE: It may not be a son.

TOM: His name will be Edward, and his middle name will be Toshio after Papa-san. Have you told anyone else?

MAE: I told Mama-san while we were setting the table, but she said she already knew.

TOM: Mama-san always seems to know these things. Will Papa-san be surprised! A grandson.

MAE: It may be a granddaughter.

TOM: Having a boy first is best.

MAE: Better.

TOM: Having a boy first is better. Your English is better than my English.

MAE: That's one subject I excelled in.

TOM: If Edward inherits our better qualities, he will be industrious ...

MAE: Conscientious ...

TOM: Scientific ...

MAE: Artistic ...

TOM: A wiz in mathematics ...

MAE: Fluent in English ...

TOM: Top of the class ...

MAE: Stop! He's going to be too perfect. I'll be happy if he's an engineer like you.

TOM: (solemnly) You mean a fisherman.

MAE: You'll find an engineering job. It takes time.

TOM: Three years is a long time.

MAE: At least you have a job.

TOM: Mae, I've been fishing with Papa-san since I was a boy and he still treats me that way.

MAE: He can't fish alone.

TOM: Ken is almost old enough to take my place.

MAE: Your friend from university, Fred Shoyama, he found a job, didn't he?

TOM: Yeah, but that's in Toronto. His letters encourage me to come, but it sounds too risky.

MAE: I'm willing to move if you are.

TOM: In your condition, "The Great Adventure" is not for us.

MAE: There must be something we can do.

TOM: I've tried everything, except ... Jim Johnson.

MAE: Your friend at U.B.C.?

TOM: I heard he works for the provincial government. He would certainly be in a position to introduce me to the right people. If so, then a move around the block may be in order.

MAE: You really think so?

TOM: I think we may be able to work something out.

MAE: Tom, I'm so excited ... our own home.

TOM: Let's go see what's for sale.

MAE: There's a white house with a picket fence two blocks from here and another house closer to the waterfront but I didn't like it as much.

TOM: You've already been looking.

MAE: I walked around the neighbourhood after visiting the doctor.

TOM: (hugging MAE) A son!

MAE: Our own home! There's so much to be thankful for.

TOM: And to look forward to.

(Lights dim)

SCENE FOUR

(Lights rise down left on JIM JOHNSON, an employee of the B.C. Security Commission. He is seated at a desk reading a newspaper. TOM enters dressed in a suit and tie.)

TOM: Jim?

JIM: (putting down his newspaper). Tom. Tom Tanaka! How good to see you. It's been ... years. (They shake hands.)

TOM: Three years ... at least.

JIM: Where have you been?

TOM: In Steveston ... fishing with my Father.

JIM: I know you always liked the sea but I thought you'd work as an engineer after we graduated.

TOM: So did I ... but I couldn't find a job.

JIM: That's ... unfortunate.

TOM: What about yourself?

JIM: I got this government job right away. There were lots of openings after the war broke out.

TOM: (wryly) For some people.

JIM: Yes ... well ... ah ... how's the fishing?

TOM: Good ... good enough to make a living.

JIM: That's good. (pause) Tom, when you're fishing, do you ever see any submarines?

TOM: I saw a submarine last week.

JIM: Where? Was it close to shore?

TOM: It was docked.

JIM: Docked?

TOM: It was one of our submarines.

JIM: A Japanese submarine docked here in Vancouver?

TOM: No, it was a Canadian submarine.

JIM: I meant ... have you seen any Japanese submarines?

TOM: No. Why do you ask?

JIM: People are saying that Japanese submarines are landing on the coast ... that Japanese naval officers are living in your fishing villages ... and some of your fishing boats are armed with cannons ... you know ... that sort of thing.

TOM: (chuckling) Do you believe these rumours?

JIM: I don't believe them but I just thought I'd ask.

TOM: I haven't seen any Japanese submarines, naval officers or ... (laughs) cannons. What do the rumours say the Japanese are up to?

JIM: Mapping the west coast.

TOM: Anyone can buy some pretty good maps just down the street, can't they?

JIM: Yes ... I guess they can. Seriously Tom, it's pretty tense right now. Some of my sources are saying that war with Japan is inevitable.

TOM: I surely hope not.

JIM: What do your people in Steveston think?

TOM: Everyone's been busy fishing. I don't think they realize what's going on.

JIM: Do you get any news from Japan?

TOM: Only from relatives.

JIM: What are they saying?

TOM: It's only personal matters ... you wouldn't be interested.

JIM: I mean ...

TOM: As far as I know, there's no collaboration going on, if that's what you mean.

JIM: Tom, I'm sorry if I appear to be prying, but there's a lot of fear about what Japan is up to.

TOM: I have no idea what Japan is up to. The reason I came here was to ask you a favour.

JIM: Of course. Ask away.

TOM: As I said, I've been fishing with my father since we graduated. Jim, I'm an engineer like you. I would give anything to get a job. So far I've tried everything but nothing's happened. Do you know of any openings ... or can you introduce me to some employment officers?

JIM: (pause) Tom, I certainly respect your abilities ... you graduated near the top of the class ... and skilled labour is hard to find these days.

TOM: You know of some openings?

JIM: Perhaps ... however, I must be honest with you ... I don't think anyone will hire you ... not right now.

TOM: Because I'm Japanese.

JIM: People are afraid. I've already told you the kinds of rumours that are going around.

TOM: Rumours are just that ... rumours!

JIM: I know ... and other people don't know you like I do.

TOM: Then tell them what you know about me.

JIM: I don't think it would do any good. Wait until the war's over ... people will soon forget about these things.

TOM: They won't forget ... one look at me and they won't forget.

(Lights dim)

SCENE FIVE

(Saturday, 6 December, 1941. Evening. AIKO is knitting on the sofa. KEN is playing on the floor with some model airplanes near the Buddhist shrine. MAE is at the sewing table. TOSHIO and TOM are playing Hana Fuda, a Japanese card game, at the kitchen table. They begin to count their scores at the same time.)

TOSHIO: Niju, yonju, goju, rokuju, nanaju, nanaju go, hachiju, kuju.

TOM: 20, 40, 50, 60, 80, 100, 120, 140, 145, 150. I win ... again. That's three in a row. You now owe me five dollars. Better luck next week.

TOSHIO: Luck. You have luck but I smarter. Hah!

(MAE looks at TOM, smiles, and motions towards TOSHIO.)

TOM: Oh, by the way Papa, I hear you're going to be an Ojiisan. (TOSHIO startled, looks at TOM, MAE, and back again at TOM. He laughs, jumps up, and slaps TOM on the shoulder.)

TOSHIO: See! What I tell you. (He turns to AIKO.) Oka-a-san wa Oba-a-san ni naru no yo.

AIKO: (smiling) Watashi shiite imashita.

(AIKO shows TOSHIO the blue booties she is knitting.)

TOSHIO: A grandson. More family. (teasingly) Tom, you have to work harder. Catch more fish. No more hole in net.

TOM: I can't work harder. We'll have to eat less. (winks at MAE)

MAE: (to TOM) Tell Papa it may be a granddaughter.

TOM: Not me. Mama's knitting blue booties.

(JUNE enters via the front door.)

JUNE: (somewhat downcast) Evening, everyone.

MAE: How was the movie?

JUNE: (sullenly) Okay, I guess.

MAE: Did he ... did everything go as planned?

JUNE: (still sullen) Yeah. It was a terrific movie.

TOM: It doesn't sound like it.

JUNE: It's what happened after the movie.

MAE: June, we could talk about it later.

JUNE: No, that's okay. We just went for a snack ... but we lost our appetite.

MAE: Lost your appetite?

JUNE: We went to a restaurant called, "The White Lunch." Before we could sit down, a man, I think it was the cook, from the back of the restaurant, waved a big spoon in the air and yelled, "Get out you Japs!" Then Tad got angry and started to sit down but I was frightened and convinced him to leave. "The White Lunch." Isn't that the truth?!

TOSHIO: Tad? Who's Tad?

JUNE: Oh, ah ... Tadashi Sakamoto. A friend of Kumi and Evelyn. We met at the show.

TOSHIO: Don't worry about man with big spoon. Go to different restaurant.

JUNE: Papa, it was humiliating. We have as much right as anyone else to eat at any public restaurant.

TOM: Our rights don't exist here in B.C.

TOSHIO: I remember, it was bad when I come here forty year ago. Many people fish. Japanese, Indian, White. Everyone fight with cannery over price of fish, then everyone fight each other. The White afraid we sell fish for 20¢, not 25¢. White strikers parade here in Steveston, and in Vancouver. I remember sign, "Japanese selling fish at less than union rate will be shot or have boat smashed — the former preferred."

JUNE: What happened?

TOSHIO: Oh, policeman, he patrol Fraser River. But next year, white union try to stop Japanese fishing. One day boat come near boat I work on. We fight with oars. I hit on head. Good thing I young with hard head. (laughs)

JUNE: Then what happened?

TOSHIO: Oh, we get patrol boat to help us.

TOM: It hasn't changed much since 1900.

TOSHIO: We don't hit each other on head.

TOM: No, but the Whites control our activities. They legislate, make it legal, and we can't vote against it.

JUNE: We can't sit in the centre aisle in some movie theatres.

TOM: And I can't get a job as an engineer. I'm just a poor fisherman.

TOSHIO: We not poor! We have house, boat, car, (pats his stomach) food. Poor is when I come to this country.

TOM: Poor is not being treated as an equal in the eyes of the law. Poor is living like a second-class citizen. Papa, why won't anyone hire me? You paid for my education but now I can only fish with you. What good was my education?

TOSHIO: It get better.

TOM: Not unless we do something about it.

TOSHIO: Do what?

TOM: Stand up to the authorities and demand equal treatment and full citizenship. I think Tad had the right idea when he started to sit down at "The White Lunch."

MAE: I think June did the right thing. If we're aggressive we'll get nowhere ... it will only lead to trouble.

TOM: June was afraid ... it's the cook who was aggressive and got his own way. Are we getting anywhere by being polite and obeying the authorities?

MAE: It takes time ... you can't change people overnight.

TOM: Fifty years is hardly overnight.

MAE: Shikata-ga-nai. We must continue to be patient.

TOM: Patience hasn't changed life for our generation and it won't change life for the next generation (motioning towards MAE's stomach). (KEN makes the sounds of an air attack as imaginary bombs strike imaginary targets.)

TOM: Who's winning the war, Ken? The Brits or the Krauts?

KEN: The Brits, with the help of the fearless Canadians. Boom!

TOM: Canadians maybe, but not Japanese Canadians.(mockingly with newspaper in hand) "For our own protection and to prevent the occurrence of 'unfortunate incidents', citizens of Japanese ancestry are exempted from service." So King says. (TOM slams the newspaper down on the kitchen table.)

JUNE: Who is he protecting us from?

TOM: The Whites.

JUNE: We can't fight for Canada because other Canadians will fight us?

TOM: That's what he and his committee are afraid of. I think it's because they don't want us to get the vote.

JUNE: Why?

TOM: Because if we fight for our country, they have to give us the vote. The Japanese that fought in World War One got the vote.

MAE: I'm glad you can't go to war. You're safe here.

TOM: Safe maybe, but with no respect. People like Wilson treat us like second ... worse ... third-class citizens. You know what he's been saying. Segregate all Orientals in the city, make them carry identification cards, move them to other provinces, close the Japanese language schools ...

KEN: That's a great idea!

TOM: (sharply) Ken, this is serious. We already carry identification cards. Wilson's other suggestions may also come true.

MAE: Don't be so pessimistic.

TOM: What will happen to us if there is war with Japan?

TOSHIO: No war with Japan.

TOM: Papa, it's possible. Last year a university professor suggested a war in the Pacific could start as a result of a surprise attack by Japan on Guam, or Pearl Harbour in Hawaii.

TOSHIO: That professor not smart.

TOM: It's possible.

TOSHIO: It not happen.

TOM: How would the Whites react if it happened?

JUNE: They would be afraid of us.

TOM: Exactly, and fear leads to rumours. We've already been accused of fifth column activity.

KEN: What's that?

TOM: That's underground activity behind enemy lines.

JUNE: They think we are helping the Japanese army?

TOM: They think Japanese naval officers are working in disguise in our fishing villages. They think we have cannons in our fishing boats.

KEN: Cannons?

TOM: Yes, cannons. And not little cannons, but big cannons. They don't have the brains to realize that the concussion from these imaginary cannons would blow our boats clear across the Rockies.

TOSHIO: (laughs) Then we fish in Alberta.

MAE: Most people don't believe these stories. They're not stupid.

TOM: Their stupidity and fear may be our worst enemies.

MAE: Tom, you're too serious. This evening was to be a happy time together. Let's not talk about these things.

TOSHIO: Tomorrow I drive everyone in new car. We go look at Christmas lights on Powell Street.

KEN: Great!

AIKO: (getting up from the sofa) Oyasuminasai.

(TOSHIO gets up and follows AIKO stage left.)

KEN, JUNE: Goodnight.

TOSHIO: (motioning to KEN and JUNE) You come too.

(Reluctantly, KEN and JUNE follow TOSHIO. TOM walks to the window in deep thought.)

MAE: (tidying up) It's 11 o'clock. Are you coming to bed?

TOM: In a moment.

MAE: Don't worry ... everything will work out ... it just takes time. You'll find a job and we'll have our own home. (MAE exits) (Lights dim)

(TOM opens the front door and steps outside. He looks onto the dimly lit street.)

TOM: There is not enough light to hide the darkness. Shikata-ga-nai. Shikata-ga-nai.

(Blackout)

SCENE SIX

(Sunday, 7 December 1941. Morning. TOSHIO is kneeling and meditating before the Buddhist shrine. TOM enters stage left. He notices TOSHIO as he goes to the coat rack and searches through some coat pockets. TOM looks out the window and then at TOSHIO, who is just beginning to stand up.)

TOM: Papa, where are the car keys?

TOSHIO: In pocket.

TOM: Which one?

TOSHIO: My pocket (he pulls out a set of keys). You like?

TOM: We're off to church soon.

TOSHIO: Cost you five dollar.

TOM: (laughing) Last night you owed me five dollars.

TOSHIO: (handing keys over to TOM) Now we even. You scratch car, you dead man.

MAE: (entering stage left) Will we need an umbrella?

TOM: The sun's shining.

MAE: That doesn't mean anything. What's the weather report? (MAE starts to put on her coat.)

TOM: I don't know.

(TOM turns on the radio. There is some music and then an interruption in the broadcast.)

RADIO ANNOUNCER: We interrupt this program to bring you a special news bulletin. The Japanese have attacked Pearl Harbour, Hawaii by air, President Roosevelt has just announced. The attack also was made on all naval and military activities on the principal island of Oahu.

(TOM and MAE are speechless. TOSHIO looks perplexed as if he hasn't understood.)

TOM: So they've gone and done it.

TOSHIO: What?

TOM: Japan bombed Pearl Harbour.

TOSHIO: Japan? Bombed?

TOM: Yes, bombed!

TOSHIO: Maybe rumour.

TOM: It's no rumour. It's on the radio!

TOSHIO: Japan?

TOM: Wake up, Papa. Japan bombed Pearl Harbour. A war has started in the Pacific.

MAE: Tom!

TOSHIO: War? Japan?

TOM: (to MAE) I tried to tell him last night. He wouldn't listen. Now he won't believe it.

MAE: No one would listen. We didn't want to believe.

TOM: The government knew it would happen.

MAE: How?

TOM: We were fingerprinted and registered earlier this year, weren't we!? They must have known.

MAE: What's going to happen?

TOM: I'm not sure.

MAE: But Auntie is visiting grandmother in Japan ...

TOM: She can't come home.

MAE: ... and Mama-san was hoping to go home to Nagasaki.

TOM: She can't go home.

TOSHIO: Fight Japan? Fight brother, country?

TOM: Canada is our country.

TOSHIO: Japan home of ancestors, family. I not fight Japan.

TOM: You won't have to. They don't take Japs in the army. I would if I could.

TOSHIO: You fight Japan?

TOM: It's no different than one Anglo-Saxon fighting another.

TOSHIO: But family in Japan.

TOM: I'd fight the Japanese Imperialist Army.

MAE: Now people will really believe the rumours about us. They're afraid of us, and now I'm afraid of them.

TOM: You should have known what would happen. Both of you.

MAE: How were we to know?

TOM: The signs were there. It got clearer every day. You chose to believe in dreams, not reality. Like the immigrants who thought they would make their fortune in Canada and called British Columbia "The Golden Door".

MAE: (near tears) We have to dream or there is no hope, and no future. Not for you, me, or our baby.

TOM: There's no future for our baby.

MAE: Don't talk like that! You're not going to destroy my dreams. I won't let you. (MAE runs out of the room.)

TOSHIO: You fight wife. You fight Japan.

TOM: You taught me to fight for my principles.

TOSHIO: I taught you to respect your family.

TOM: Should I respect blind ignorance?

TOSHIO: You not always smart.

TOM: I'm smart enough to put two and two together and consider the possibility of war in the Pacific. You read Japanese language newspapers that only sympathize with Japan. You plan to visit Japan and don't think about what is really happening there. You tolerate prejudice and expect things to change. You live in the past and say it can't happen. Well, it has happened. You are wrong about Japan and you are wrong about democracy. (TOSHIO slumps down on the sofa, covers his face with his hands, and weeps.)

TOM: (realizing he has been too outspoken) Papa, I ...

(TOM's hand is extended towards TOSHIO.)

(Blackout)

ACT TWO, SCENE ONE

(Spring, 1942. Afternoon. The Tanaka living room. The radio is conspicuously absent. AIKO is arranging cherry blossoms and tulips in a vase at the kitchen table. There is a knock at the front door followed by a second knock in quick succession.)

AIKO: Choto ma-a-te kudasai.

TAD: (out of breath) Konnichiwa. June wa orimasu ka?

AIKO: Hai ohairi nasai.

(AIKO gives a second glance at TAD as she exits stage left. There is some whispering stage left as TAD is left standing by the front door, fidgeting and looking out the window. JUNE enters.)

JUNE: Tad, what are you doing here?

TAD: Well, I ... (glances out the window) Is your Father home?

JUNE: No. What is it?

TAD: I need to talk to you.

JUNE: What happened?

(TAD notices AIKO peeking through the bedroom door. After being seen by TAD, AIKO shuffles to the kitchen.)

AIKO: Watakushi ga shimasu. (AIKO exits stage right.)

JUNE: Well, what happened?

TAD: I got a notice from the RCMP yesterday.

JUNE: What did it say?

TAD: It said to report to the Immigration Building this morning.

JUNE: This morning?

TAD: I didn't go.

JUNE: Are you crazy?

TAD: I can't go now. I have to help my Mother sell our house.

JUNE: Sell? But ...

TAD: Since they took my Father, it's my responsibility.

JUNE: If you get caught, they'll send you to a concentration camp.

TAD: I'll turn myself in after I sell the house.

JUNE: How can you do that without getting caught?

TAD: I'm hiding at a friend's house. He's white. They won't look there.

JUNE: Don't be so sure. There are lots of informers these days.

TAD: I have to take that chance. How are you doing?

JUNE: I'm okay, I guess.

TAD: What's happening to your family?

JUNE: Nothing, yet. Papa-san and Mama-san don't know what to do. Mae's writing letters everywhere trying to find a place for us to go. Tom attends lots of meetings. They're afraid our family will be split apart, like yours.

TAD: Are you going to sell your house?

JUNE: I don't think so. Papa-san wants to keep it so we have something to come back to after the war.

TAD: (looking out the window) I better go before the sun sets.

JUNE: When will I see you again?

TAD: After I sell the house. Before I turn myself in.

JUNE: Where can I find you, in case ...

TAD: My Mother will know where I am. I sure miss taking you to the movies. (TAD holds JUNE's hand after glancing at the kitchen door.)

JUNE: Me too. This curfew is sure spoiling our social life.

(TAD and JUNE glance again at the kitchen door and then kiss.)

TAD: Bye. (TAD exits. JUNE looks out the window and waves as MAE enters stage left.)

MAE: Who are you waving to?

JUNE: Tad.

MAE: He's here?

JUNE: He just left.

MAE: What was he doing here?

JUNE: He wanted to tell me that the RCMP sent him an evacuation notice yesterday.

MAE: At his age?

JUNE: He turned 18 last month.

MAE: When does he have to leave?

JUNE: Today ... but he's not going anywhere, except in hiding.

MAE: In hiding?!

JUNE: He won't report to the RCMP until his house is sold.

MAE: How can the Security Commission send someone a notice and expect them to report within 24 hours? It's unfair.

JUNE: I hate this war! Life is so boring. We can't even listen to the radio.

MAE: At least we're not in the war zone.

JUNE: Yeah ... but now we have to leave the so-called "protected zone" in order to protect the whites from us enemy aliens. Mae, I was down at the tracks yesterday. A trainload of men were headed for the interior. They were all dressed in their Sunday clothes as if they were going to a funeral. Women and children were running down the platform waving and crying. It was so sad.

MAE: I feel sorry for the women who have children. Some days I wish I wasn't having this baby.

JUNE: Mae, don't talk like that.

MAE: I don't know where it will be born, or even if Tom will be there. It's all so uncertain. Not knowing is the worst part.

JUNE: Maybe we'll find a place in the east. They say we can stay together if we go and work in the sugar beet fields in Alberta or Manitoba.

MAE: What do we know about sugar beet farming?

JUNE: What about your friends in Ontario? They said they'd try and help.

MAE: It all takes time. I'm afraid time will run out before we know what to do.

(The door opens and KEN enters. His clothes are dirty, his shirt is ripped, and it is obvious that he has been in a fight. He kicks off his shoes and proceeds to walk towards the bedroom door, not looking at anyone.)

MAE: Ken, what's the matter?

KEN: Nothing.

MAE: You've been fighting.

KEN: Yeah.

MAE: Are you okay?

KEN: Yeah.

MAE: Do you want to talk about it?

KEN: No.

MAE: Well, change your clothes and wash up. We can talk about it when you feel better. Okay?

KEN: Okay. (KEN exits)

JUNE: Some of those kids at school are sure mean ... just like their parents.

MAE: Prejudice is learned at home. (The front door opens and TOM enters.) Hi. How was your meeting?

TOM: Not great. Most of the Council are in favour of co-operating with the Security Commission ... even if it means splitting up the family.

MAE: Splitting up the family?

TOM: The Security Commission wants to send all Japanese men to work camps, and women and children to interior housing projects ... which is a fancy way of saying internment camps.

JUNE: Why are they separating the men from the women ... so we can't reproduce?

MAE: We can't live together?

TOM: If the Security Commission gets its way, that's what will happen.

MAE: But Tom, I need you.

TOM: I protested. I said our willingness to go along with the Security Commission's orders had gone far enough.

MAE: The Council didn't agree with you?

TOM: The Council wants us to accept the loss of all our civil rights just to prove we are loyal to Canada.

MAE: What are we going to do?

TOM: I'm not sure ... but those who agreed with me talked about forming another group.

MAE: To do what?

TOM: To write to Austin Taylor, the Chairman of the Security Commission, and state our reasons for not agreeing with his proposal.

MAE: If you resist, they'll say you're a trouble-maker and send you to a concentration camp.

TOM: If I don't resist, we'll be separated anyway.

JUNE: Where's Papa-san?

TOM: He left the meeting early.

MAE: Why?

TOM: I don't think he liked my idea about forming another group.

JUNE: Why not?

TOM: I voted against the Council. I guess I disgraced him. I could see the look in his eyes as he walked out the door.

MAE: He's probably down at Annieville Dyke. Ever since they took his boat, he goes down and looks at it every day.

JUNE: He misses it more than his car.

TOM: He'd better get home soon. The sun sets within the hour.

(KEN enters wearing a sign around his neck which reads, "I am Chinese".)

JUNE: Ken, what are you doing?

KEN: I'm changing my identity.

JUNE: You can't do that.

KEN: The whites can't tell the difference.

TOM: Ken, take it off. (KEN parades around the room.) Take it off before Papa-san comes home.

KEN: I'm sick of being a Jap ... at least they don't bother the Chinks.

TOM: I said take it off!

KEN: No!

MAE: Ken, I know what you're going through, but ...

KEN: No you don't!

MAE: ... but you can't change who you are.

TOM: Ken, for the last time ... take it off!

KEN: I'm not a Jap ... I'm a Chink.

MAE: Nothing you do can change that ... shikata-ga-nai.

KEN: Shit on your shikata-ga-nai!

(MAE is shocked while TOM is outraged and slaps KEN in the face. KEN falls to the floor. JUNE screams.)

TOM: Don't you swear at my wife ... in this house ... you little ...

(MAE rushes forward, bends down and holds KEN.)

MAE: He didn't mean it.

(KEN is crying in Mae's arms. TOM turns away, trying to control his anger.)

MAE: It's alright ... don't cry.

KEN: I'm ... sorry ...

MAE: I know ... it's okay.

(JUNE and MAE help KEN to his feet.)

MAE: Now go and wash up for dinner.

(KEN, with JUNE's assistance, walks slowly towards stage left. KEN takes off the sign from around his neck as they exit.)

MAE: He was in another fight at school.

TOM: I didn't know ... I'm sorry.

MAE: You'd better talk to him ... he needs your help ... and he idolizes you.

TOM: He does?

MAE: He brags about you to his friends ... how you've gone to university ... how you're going to build the biggest fishing boat on the West Coast.

(TOM slumps down on the sofa and holds his head.)

TOM: What's happening to us?

MAE: It's the uncertainty ... we don't really know who we are ... or where we're going.

(TOSHIO enters via the front door. He ignores TOM and exits stage right into the kitchen.)

TOM: Papa ... I ... (to MAE) If only he'd listen to me.

MAE: He's worried ... he doesn't want us to be split apart either.

TOM: Then he should stand up to the authorities.

MAE: He's part of the Japanese community.

TOM: The Japanese community has got to stand up to the authorities and demand our rights ... now!

MAE: Maybe now is too late ... or too early. (pause) You and Papa-san will have to agree on what to do.

TOM: We can't agree on anything.

MAE: If only somebody would answer my letters.

TOM: I almost forgot ... I dropped by the post office on the way home. Here's a letter from your Mother.

(MAE takes the letter and opens it.) I'll talk to Ken. Maybe all of us can play Hana Fuda after dinner. (TOM gets up and begins to walk stage left.)

MAE: My parents were ordered to leave their home! Mother wrote the day they left.

TOM: Where did they go?

MAE: Hastings Park. I have to go there right away.

(MAE rushes to the coat rack and begins to put on her coat.)

TOM: You can't go now. The sun is setting. You'll have to wait until tomorrow.

MAE: Wait! Wait! All we do these days is wait!

(MAE slumps down in a chair by the front door. TOM walks towards the window and stares outside.) (Lights dim)

TOM: When the sun goes down, it takes with it light and freedom, and makes us criminals if we dare venture out of our homes onto the street.

(Fade to Black)

SCENE TWO

(Down left, a woman, SETSUKO, is sitting on the edge of a cot which is surrounded on all sides by hanging blankets. The woman is staring at the floor as if in a trance. There is the sound of small children crying in the background. One of the blankets is pulled back to reveal MAE carrying a basket. She quickly kneels beside her Mother.)

MAE: Mother! Mother! It's me ... Mae. I came as quickly as I could. (SETSUKO, startled, looks at MAE, hugs her, and begins to sob.) Mother. Are you alright? Are you well?

(SETSUKO nods.) Here. Take this handkerchief.

SETSUKO: (wiping her eyes) Mae ... Mae ... I ... I'm so happy you're here.

MAE: I would have come yesterday but I got your letter too late. Are you well, Mother ... are you well?

SETSUKO: Yes ... I'm well ... enough.

MAE: When did you get here? Where's Father? Have you seen him?

SETSUKO: Your Father ... they took him to another building.

MAE: Have you seen him?

SETSUKO: Not since we came here. That was three ... no ... four days ago. I can't visit without a pass.

MAE: You said in your letter there wasn't time to ...

SETSUKO: How are you, Mae? And the baby?

MAE: Fine Mother. Just fine. What happened? Why did you have to leave in such a hurry?

SETSUKO: The police came and told us we had to go ... right away. Pack your bags, they said. Only bring what you can carry. We'll be back in a couple of hours.

MAE: A couple of hours?! Wasn't there more warning than that?

SETSUKO: No. They just came and told us we had to go. It was dinnertime. We left our food sitting on the table and started to pack. I didn't know what to take. Where were we going? For how long? I didn't know.

MAE: (looking around the room) Did you only bring one small suitcase?

SETSUKO: No. I filled a pillowcase with clothes and a couple of blankets ... the ones hanging up there. Your Father brought two large suitcases and a dufflebag. I don't know how he managed to carry everything ... they were so heavy. He brought our set of wedding dishes. I hope they didn't break.

MAE: What about the furniture ... and your sewing machine?

SETSUKO: We left them behind.

MAE: In storage?

SETSUKO: There wasn't enough time ...

(SETSUKO bows her head and begins to sob again.)

MAE: Mother. It'll be alright. Don't cry.

(SETSUKO composes herself and looks around the room.)

SETSUKO: (in disgust) Look where they put us. In stalls where they put cattle and horses. The smell is awful ... just awful. We're not animals.

MAE: Don't they clean this place?

SETSUKO: They try but you can't get rid of animal smells. Yesterday they dug up an area over there. It was full of maggots. It's the women with small children that I really feel sorry for ... the woman on the other side of this blanket has three children under the age of five ... everyone of them is sick. They cry all night. She can't get any sleep ... neither can I.

MAE: That's awful.

SETSUKO: It must be the food. Potatoes and stew. We don't like potatoes and stew. We're not used to it.

(MAE opens a basket and presents SETSUKO with some food.)

MAE: I brought you some rice cakes and pickles.

SETSUKO: It smells heavenly.

MAE: It tastes even better.

(SETSUKO takes a small bite and savours it.)

SETSUKO: Now I won't have to stand in line for dinner.

MAE: What do people eat besides potatoes and stew?

SETSUKO: Chocolate bars and Coca-Cola. You can buy them at the store.

MAE: Do you know any of the women here?

SETSUKO: No. Some people from the United Church came last night. They asked me how I was doing … if I needed any help.

MAE: Did the authorities say how long you'd have to stay here?

SETSUKO: No. No one says anything. I'm afraid for your Father. Every evening they call out some registration numbers. If your number is called, you're shipped to a road camp within three days.

MAE: Why do they always give such short notice?

SETSUKO: It's the war. Shikata-ga-nai.

MAE: Mother, I've got to get you and Father out of here. Maybe you can come and live with me. I'll get Tom to go to the authorities tomorrow and tell them that we'll be responsible for you.

SETSUKO: Do what you can Mae … but don't be rash. I wouldn't want them to send TOM to a concentration camp.

MAE: (getting up to leave) Don't worry Mother. I'll be back as soon as TOM has talked with the authorities.

(MAE and SETSUKO kiss each other on the cheek. SETSUKO feebly waves goodbye and returns to staring at the floor. (pause) SETSUKO slowly stands up and reaches for the basket of food. She carries it and enters the cubicle behind her cot where the Mother with three small children is living.)

(Fade to black)

SCENE THREE

(Down right, two men are in an office of the B.C. Security Commission. MR. JONES, the senior supervisor with an English accent, is standing beside a filing cabinet. JIM is seated at a desk and frantically looking through some files. The desk is littered with papers and books and is surrounded by a chair, a picture of King George VI, and the Red Ensign flag.)

JIM: (flustered) It has to be here ... somewhere.

MR. JONES: (intimidating) I just gave it to you this morning.

JIM: It's here, it's definitely here ... somewhere.

MR. JONES: I need it for the meeting this afternoon.

JIM: What time?

MR. JONES: Two o'clock. (sarcastically) Do you think you can find it within the next (looking at his chain watch)... four hours?

JIM: Oh yes, sir. It's here, it's definitely here ... somewhere.

MR. JONES: It's a threat ... a very serious threat. Before you know it, we'll have a riot on our hands.

JIM: I hope not.

MR. JONES: Hope won't help. Our actions will! But we can't do a thing until you find that Jap letter from the "Nigh-see what-you-ma-call-it."

JIM: Nisei Mass Evacuation Group.

MR. JONES: Nisei ... what the hell does that mean?

JIM: It means second-generation Japanese ... Japanese born in Canada.

MR. JONES: What the hell difference does that make? A Jap's a Jap!

JIM: Ahhh ... here it is. I knew it was here, somewhere. (MR. JONES grabs the letter and quickly skims its contents.)

MR. JONES: What audacity! Blatantly saying no to our last order. Trouble-makers, that's what they are ... trouble- makers. The RCMP will know who all these "Nigh-see" trouble-makers are.

JIM: Nisei.

MR. JONES: We should ship the lot of them back to Japan. That'll teach them for invading out British posts in Hong Kong and Singapore. They're a menace. An absolute menace. (MR. JONES stomps out of the room stage right. JIM wipes his brow and sighs. He stands up and puts some of the files back into the filing cabinet. There is a knock at the door.)

JIM: (not looking around) Come in.

(TOM enters stage left.)

TOM: I was told to come here. (JIM turns around.) Jim? What are you doing here?

JIM: Tom! Well ... I was transferred here a few weeks ago. I'm coordinating the evacuation of ... of the people of Japanese origin.

TOM: Like me.

JIM: (uneasily) Yeah ... well ... what brings you here? I'm sorry I wasn't able to find you a job. (JIM sits down.)

TOM: I'm not looking for a job. Under the circumstances, no one would hire me, would they? (JIM shifts uneasily in his chair.) It's about my in-laws. They're in Hastings Park and ...

JIM: Hastings Park has made our office extremely busy.

TOM: ... and they had to leave their farm on Vancouver Island on very short notice, and ...

JIM: Everything's a rush these days.

TOM: ... and there wasn't enough time to store their belongings or get someone to look after their farm.

JIM: Don't worry. Their property automatically comes under the protection of the Custodian of Enemy Alien Property.

TOM: For how long?

JIM: Until the war ends, I guess. Please Tom, have a seat.

TOM: (sitting down) I also came here to find out if my in-laws could stay with us in Steveston.

JIM: I'm afraid that's not possible.

TOM: It's not far away and we'd be responsible for them.

JIM: If we made exceptions, the evacuation program would become an administrative nightmare.

TOM: But Jim ... they're part of my family, and ...

JIM: Tom ... I understand what you're going through ... and I sympathize ... but there's nothing I can do.

TOM: What's going to happen to them?

JIM: Your father-in-law will probably go to a road camp. We're creating employment for the Japanese while the war's on.

TOM: We were employed.

JIM: Yes ... well ... ah ...

TOM: Which road camp?

JIM: The one near Jasper. We planned to send them to Ontario but there were too many protests from the people there.

TOM: What about my mother-in-law?

JIM: She'll have to stay in Hastings Park until the interior housing projects are completed.

TOM: How long will that take?

JIM: It could take months ... the logistics of moving 20,000 people are incredible, just incredible ... but we're working as quickly as we can to comply with Order-in-Council P.C. 1486 and remove all Japanese from the "Protected Area".

TOM: You mean Japanese Nationals and Japanese Canadians.

JIM: Yes ... well ...

TOM: What are my in-laws going to live on?

JIM: The work camps pay 25¢ an hour.

TOM: That's not much.

JIM: I agree ... but some people don't think the Japanese need much money to live on. Your father-in-law will have to send your mother-in-law some money so that she can pay the Hastings Park boarding fee of $10 a month.

TOM: She has to pay to stay there?!

JIM: It's costing the government a lot of money to house and transport these ... ah ... your people.

(TOM stands up and turns away in disbelief.)

TOM: Why are you doing this?

JIM: It's my job.

TOM: At university I thought we were friends ... equals.

JIM: We were ... I mean ... we are ...

TOM: Then why are you involved with this evacuation?

JIM: It's my job. It's what the government has legislated. Tom, it's for your own protection.

TOM: Protection? From who?

JIM: From other people. If you stay you'll create feelings of racial hostility.

TOM: Are you saying that since I'm the victim of racism I'm also the cause of racism?

JIM: Well ... no ... I ...

TOM: And I have to be removed from people with racist attitudes?

JIM: No ... I ...

(MR. JONES enters the room with a letter in his hand.)

MR. JONES: File this letter ... (MR. JONES stops dead in his tracks when he sees TOM. He drops the letter on JIM'S desk.) ... and don't lose it! (MR. JONES stomps back into his office.)

JIM: That's my boss. It's a good thing everyone around here's not like him.

TOM: The government's line of reasoning is preposterous.

JIM: Yes ... well ... ah ... you have to admit ... it's for your own good. Everybody says so. Even your own people.

TOM: They're only going along with your orders to show their loyalty to Canada. That doesn't mean they agree with what's happening to them.

JIM: Well ... we have to abide by King's orders.

TOM: I imagine he's under pressure to make the most of the situation.

JIM: What do you mean?

TOM: People have been trying to get rid of us since we came to this country. Now's their golden opportunity.

JIM: It's because of the war ... you're Japanese. Some of you could be involved in subversive activities, and your presence increases the threat of civil violence.

TOM: Have you caught anyone involved in subversive activities?

JIM: Well ... no ... but ...

TOM: As a Canadian citizen, the government should protect me from civil violence.

JIM: It is protecting you.

TOM: How?

JIM: By moving you to another part of Canada.

TOM: (throwing up his hands) That policy is playing right into the hands of the racist bigots who want to get rid of us.

JIM: It's only until the war ends. Please Tom, sit down.

TOM: (sitting down) And is it the government's policy to split our families apart until the war ends?

JIM: I ... I don't know.

TOM: It looks that way ... unless your Commission goes along with our request.

JIM: Request?

TOM: The Nisei Mass Evacuation Group ... our request for mass evacuation in family groups.

JIM: You're part of that group? We just received the letter this morning ... I remember it well. (looks towards MR. JONES' door)

TOM: Will you accept our request?

JIM: Well ... ah ... I don't know ... there's a meeting this afternoon.

TOM: We should at least have the freedom to live with our families, don't you think?

JIM: Why yes ... of course ... but I don't get to vote on the matter.

TOM: I don't get to vote, period! (TOM gets up to leave.)

JIM: I'm sorry Tom. I wish I could help you. I really do. I'll see if there's any chance at all to get your in-laws out of Hastings Park.

TOM: (not very hopefully) Sure. Thanks. (TOM walks towards the door and turns.) By the way Jim, there's another matter I'm puzzled about.

JIM: What's that?

TOM: Why has the Commission and the RCMP employed Morii to speak on behalf of the Japanese community?

JIM: Morii? I have no idea.

TOM: I think he's a crook.

JIM: Really?!

TOM: He's been involved in some shady dealings. He even supports Japan's aggression in Asia. He said so in public speeches prior to Pearl Harbour.

JIM: Well ... I guess in wartime all types of people are needed.

TOM: (staring at JIM) Yeah, I guess so.

JIM: The important thing, Tom, is for you and your group to cooperate. If we can count on your cooperation, there's nothing to worry about.

TOM: Goodbye Jim. (TOM exits stage left.)

JIM: Poor fellow.

(MR. JONES enters with another letter in his hand.)

MR. JONES:(looking around the room) Good. The Jap's gone. What did he want?

JIM: Ah ... he wanted to find out what would happen to his in-laws and I said I would ...

MR. JONES:Here's another letter to file. It's from Mr. Ian MacKenzie. He's proposing to confiscate all those Jap farms ... sell them to the war vets ... great idea. Now don't misfile it. (MR. JONES exits stage right.)

JIM: But ... (JIM stands by his desk with letter in hand which advocates a policy contrary to the assurances he just gave TOM.)

(Blackout)

SCENE FOUR

(Evening. The Tanaka living room. It is dimly lit by a coleman lamp and two candles. Blackout blinds cover the windows. TOSHIO and TOM are seated on the sofa that has been moved stage centre while MAE and JUNE do some housework stage left. AIKO is beginning to serve tea. KEN is at the kitchen table doing his homework.)

MAE: (to JUNE) I never thought we'd be doing housework at night.

JUNE: What else is there to do?

MAE: At least it gives us more time to visit during the day.

(MAE and JUNE begin to put away their brooms, dustpans, and dustcloths.)

TOM: (to TOSHIO) We have to make some decisions!

TOSHIO: How long we got?

TOM: A couple of months ... at the most.

TOSHIO: What choice we got?

TOM: Move to eastern Canada, work in the sugar beet fields on the Prairies, or go to one of those ghost towns in the interior.

MAE: (wryly) Go east young man, go east.

TOSHIO: (half-seriously) I not young man. Maybe I go west, to Japan.

TOM: That's not a choice.

TOSHIO: Maybe ... after war.

TOM: Your choice is east. How far east are we going to go?

MAE: Ontario may not be a choice. We still need a job offer, letters of recommendation, and a permit to travel there. That takes time.

TOM: And time is running out. As far as I'm concerned, the beet fields are also out.

MAE: I agree.

TOSHIO: Why?

TOM: What do we know about farming?

TOSHIO: (teasingly) Mae farmer's daughter.

TOM: (gesturing towards MAE's stomach) I can't let her work in that condition.

MAE: And I can't see either of you as farmers.

TOSHIO: You teach.

MAE: What I know doesn't apply to sugar beets.

TOM: The only advantage is that we could stay together as a family.

TOSHIO: That important.

TOM: I think we can at least agree on that point.

KEN: (eerily) What about the ghost towns?

TOM: The government's been sending work crews to fix them up. Some people are moving there already.

TOSHIO: People from Steveston go to Greenwood. Maybe we go there too.

MAE: I heard Kaslo was the best place.

JUNE: Don't go to Sandon. I hear it floods every spring and the mountains are so high the sun never gets to it.

TOM: There's also New Denver, Slocan City ...

MAE: We don't know anything about these places. How can we choose? Anyway, I don't like the idea of going to a ghost town. It means you would have to work in a road camp, somewhere.

TOM: (sarcastically) A job. At last I'd have a job.

MAE: But not as an engineer.

TOM: At least I'd be building something. What about our house, Papa? Do we sell or rent? (AIKO stops what she's doing and listens attentively.)

TOSHIO: Rent.

TOM: I think we should sell.

TOSHIO: House important.

TOM: I agree, but we don't know what's going to happen to us.

TOSHIO: We come back after war.

TOM: Maybe not. Who knows? It's more practical to sell.

JUNE: I don't want to sell our house.

KEN: Me neither.

TOSHIO: My children born here.

MAE: This house is Mama's life.

TOM: I don't want to sell either, but ...

TOSHIO: Too many people sell. Price too low.

TOM: June, what about Tad's house?

JUNE: It's not sold yet. His mother doesn't ... (fighting back the tears) ... doesn't know what to do. She can't speak English.

TOM: I thought Tad was in charge of ...

JUNE: They found him. He's gone!

TOM: Gone?

MAE: We think he's been sent to Petawawa, in Ontario. June just found out this afternoon.

TOM: A concentration camp?

MAE: He shouldn't have tried to evade the authorities.

JUNE: He was going to turn himself in ... he wasn't harming anyone ... he was just trying to sell his house.

TOM: That's why we have to decide, Papa. Time is running out.(AIKO is near the kitchen. She pulls aside the blind and looks out the window.)

AIKO: Otoko no hito ga kimasu. (AIKO scurries into the kitchen. The coleman lamp and candles are quickly extinguished by TOSHIO and TOM. There is a loud knock at the door. No one moves. There is a second loud knock.)

VOICE: Is anyone home? RCMP.

(TOM opens the front door. An RCMP OFFICER stands in the doorway and shines a flashlight in TOM's face.)

RCMP OFFICER: (polite but firm) Is this the Tanaka residence?

TOM: Yes sir.

RCMP OFFICER: Are you TOM Tanaka?

TOM: Yes sir.

RCMP OFFICER: May I see your registration card?

(TOM pulls out his wallet and shows him a card.)

RCMP OFFICER: (handing TOM a piece of paper) This notice is for you. Your deferment permit to stay here is cancelled. As an enemy alien you are to leave the Protected Area by the 30th of April, 1942. You are to report to the police barracks at 33rd and Heather. Failing to appear will lead to your internment. Do you understand?

TOM: Yes sir.

RCMP OFFICER: Do you have any questions?

TOM: Why was my deferment permit cancelled?

RCMP OFFICER: Orders.

TOM: Orders? From who?

RCMP OFFICER: I'm just obeying orders. Any more questions?

TOM: No sir.

RCMP OFFICER: You have until the 30th of April. Good evening.

(The RCMP OFFICER exits. TOM shuts the door. The coleman lamp is turned on. AIKO enters from the kitchen.)

TOM: (with much irony) Maintain the right.

MAE: You have to leave in a couple of days. That's unfair.

TOM: Papa, look after Mae while I'm gone.

TOSHIO: Yes Tom ... my son.

TOM: (to MAE) Don't worry about me. I'll be okay. Think of the baby.

MAE: I don't want to be alone.

TOM: You're not alone.

MAE: What more are we supposed to endure?

TOM: We must endure. Whatever happens, we must endure.

MAE: What's going to happen? What's going to happen to all of us?

(Stage lighting focuses on TOM and fades away from the other characters. TOM begins to walk slowly down stage.)

TOM: What's happening? Is this a dream? I'm not a criminal. I was born here. Would I sabotage my own home? What determines my loyalty ... my black hair and yellow skin? Is the value of my Canadian citizenship worthless? Canada ... I believed in you but you have betrayed me. You allow hateful prejudice and propaganda to exist under the banner of democracy. Do you expect me to shrug my shoulders and say shikata-ga-nai, this is wartime? What's happening is shameful ... I no longer have pride in you. I am bitter, with a bitterness I will never forget!

(Blackout)

SCENE FIVE

(Evening. A bedroom. Lights rise on MAE who is sitting on the floor stage left and rocking a basket. She is singing an old Japanese lullaby, *Nen-nen-koro-ri*. Offstage there is the sound of someone knocking at a door.)

MAE: (softly) Who is it?

TOM: (offstage) Mae? Is that you?

MAE: Tom?

(MAE gets up as TOM enters. They embrace.)

TOM: Mae, I'm back.

MAE: Tom ... I was so scared.

TOM: How are you?

MAE: I'm fine, now that you're here.

TOM: Where's Edward?

MAE: He's here, sleeping.

TOM: (looking in the basket) My son! (touching Edward's face) Edward Toshio Tanaka.

MAE: Tom, how did you get here? Did you escape? Did anyone see you? You'll have to go back ...

TOM: No, don't worry. They let me go.

MAE: Let you go?

TOM: They let all married men in the work camps go home ... (looking around)... I mean, go back to their families. Does everyone sleep in this small room?

MAE: Yes. At least we're in a shack ... some people have to live in a tent.

TOM: This is awful! When winter comes we'll freeze to death.

MAE: Don't forget our dreams, Tom.

TOM: What can you dream about here in this shack?

MAE: (bending down and touching Edward) I dream ... I dream about the future.

(Lights dim)

SCENE SIX

(Slocan Valley, interior of British Columbia. Spring, 1945. Afternoon. The set focuses on a communal kitchen. A large stove is located stage right. A kitchen table and chairs are located stage left. There are numerous pots and pans, and hanging dishtowels. The room has a very crowded appearance. A front door leading outside is centre stage. Doors lead offstage to the right and left. The Tanaka family bedroom is offstage left. A couple argues in Japanese offstage right. A young child cries offstage left. AIKO is preparing dinner while JUNE is setting the table.)

AIKO: Koko ni heiwa nashi.

JUNE: Oka-a-san mizuumi made arukinasai.

AIKO: Iie Oka-a-san ga takimasu.

JUNE: Oka-a-san ita.

AIKO: Arigato.

(AIKO takes off her apron, puts on her coat, and exits via the front door. JUNE stirs the contents of the pots on the stove. A man, GEORGE, enters stage right and slams the door. JUNE pretends not to notice and continues stirring. GEORGE paces about the room before exiting the front door and also slamming it shut. MAE enters stage left.)

MAE: Who's slamming doors?

JUNE: George.

MAE: It's no wonder Edward won't go to sleep.

JUNE: (almost whispering) They're fighting again.

MAE: What about, now?

JUNE: The same thing.

MAE: I'd complain too if Tom drank and gambled like George. (looking stage right) We don't have much privacy, do we?

JUNE: I'm tired of cleaning up after them. This place is always a mess.

MAE: Where's Mama-san?

JUNE: She's gone for a walk by the lake. I think she needed some peace and quiet.

MAE: She really misses her own kitchen.

JUNE: It was her retreat.

MAE: I really worried about her when we found out our house was sold. She seemed to age ten years overnight.

JUNE: She had her heart set on going back home.

MAE: How could the Custodian decide to sell all our property without our consent? (pause) What's for dinner?

JUNE: Noodles and vegetables, the same as yesterday ... unless Papa-san and Tom catch some fish.

MAE: I don't like it when they go fishing. Someday the RCMP will catch them.

JUNE: This valley is full of lakes and the authorities make fishing illegal ... how stupid.

MAE: They don't want us roaming around the countryside.

JUNE: There's no place to go. The mountains are so high it's like living behind a barbed wire fence.(The crying in the background has stopped.) Sounds like Edward has finally gone to sleep.

MAE: If it wasn't for him I'd have no hope for the future. Some day we'll have our own home, and he'll have his own bedroom.

JUNE: Are we going east or west? We have to decide by tomorrow.

MAE: I know you want to go east.

JUNE: I miss him.

MAE: I know.

JUNE: I think about him all the time.

MAE: How's he doing?

JUNE: Okay, I guess. It's hard to tell. Most of his letters are censored.

MAE: I thought if Tad accepted a job in Ontario he could become a free man.

JUNE: If they won't send him back to B.C., he'd rather stay in Petawawa as a prisoner and let the government take care of him.

MAE: We sure suffer because of our pride, don't we?

JUNE: I wonder if I'll ever see him again?

MAE: Of course you will.

JUNE: You must convince Papa-san to go east. All this talk about going back to Japan is frightening. I'm not going. I can't.

MAE: I want to do what's best for Edward. (KEN enters via the front door. He's wearing a baseball uniform, with cap and glove.)

JUNE: Did you win?

KEN: Nah!

MAE: Are the Doukhobors that good?

KEN: They're bigger than us.

MAE: Be quiet. Edward's sleeping.

KEN: Yeah! (KEN exits stage left.)

MAE: If it wasn't for baseball, I don't know what he'd do.

JUNE: I don't like the guys he's hanging around with. Some of them are just looking for trouble.

MAE: There's not much for them to do.

JUNE: They don't try. I see them at school just fooling around.

MAE: There's not much motivation ...

(KEN re-enters the room after depositing his cap and glove.)

KEN: What's there to eat?

JUNE: (teasingly) Nothing you'd like.

KEN: I eat anything.

JUNE: And everything. Typical teenager.

(AIKO rushes through the front door and scurries stage left.)

AIKO: (excitedly) RCMP to Papa-san to Tom kimasu! (AIKO exits)

MAE: I knew something like this would happen.

(TOSHIO and TOM enter through the front door carrying fishing rods and a basket. Behind them is an RCMP OFFICER.)

RCMP OFFICER: You know fishing is illegal.

TOM: Yes sir.

RCMP OFFICER: You fished too close to town ... someone saw you and complained.(examining TOSHIO'S fishing rod) This is a fine piece of equipment. I've never seen a reel like this one.

TOM: It's automatic.

RCMP OFFICER: I wish I had one like this. Since I received a complaint, I have to confiscate your fishing rod. (continuing to admire the fishing rod) I really don't want to take this from you. Do you have anything else I can take back with me, instead?

KEN: I have a fishing rod.

(KEN exits stage left and enters holding a stick with a hook, line and sinker. He gives it to the RCMP OFFICER.)

RCMP OFFICER: That'll do. Good day.

(The RCMP OFFICER exits. TOSHIO and TOM look at each other in amazement. AIKO peeks out from behind the bedroom door before entering the room.)

KEN: Catch any fish?

TOSHIO: Sure.

KEN: How many?

TOSHIO: Two big whitefish and a troot.

KEN: Trout.

TOSHIO: That what I say ... troot.

TOM: We'll have sashimi tonight.

TOSHIO: Ken, *kyo gakko de otonashiku shite itaka?*

KEN: Some things never change. Yes, I was a good boy in school, Papa.

TOSHIO: Good, then you translate newspaper for Mama.

KEN: My Japanese isn't that good.

TOSHIO: You translate newspaper, it get better.

KEN: Do I have to?

JUNE: Here's the paper.

MAE: Take Mama outside and we'll call you when dinner's ready.

KEN: I'll translate the sports page.

(KEN and AIKO exit through the front door.)

TOSHIO: I come too. I listen. (TOSHIO exits as MAE whispers something to JUNE.)

JUNE: I'll check on Edward. (JUNE exits stage left as TOM sits down at the kitchen table with part of the newspaper.)

MAE: They want our decision tomorrow.

TOM: I know.

MAE: What's it going to be?

TOM: We have to talk to Papa-san.

MAE: We have to decide what's best for Edward.

TOM: That's just it ... we don't know what's best. Every time we try to decide, they change the rules.

MAE: Then we decide on faith.

TOM: Faith?! Do we have any faith left?

MAE: We must have faith in ourselves, faith in our country.

TOM: (bitterly) Our country has taken everything from us. Our families have been split apart, we've been moved around like cattle, and I couldn't even be with you when Edward was born.

MAE: But we're together now. I think it will be better for us in the east.

TOM: Look at the headlines ... "Who Wants Japs?"... "No Takers" ... we're still treated like enemy aliens.

MAE: It will change.

TOM: How many generations will it take?

MAE: I don't know, but my heart says it's best for Edward if we stay in Canada.

TOM: What about your parents?

MAE: I don't know what they're going to do. There hasn't been enough time to write and get a reply.

TOM: You know I'm responsible for Papa-san and Mama-san. If they decide to go back to Japan ...

MAE: You must convince them to stay.

TOM: If only I had a job ... a decent job.

MAE: The man from the Department of Labour said he'd help you get a job in the east.

TOM: Some help! If it wasn't for the labour shortage, he wouldn't care in the least. We can't rely on his promises, and I'd have to accept whatever he offers me.

MAE: Accept it. It doesn't have to be forever. You can contact your engineering friends once we get there.

TOM: There's a great deal of risk ...

MAE: There's just as much risk in going to Japan. June and Ken wouldn't fit into Japanese society. Neither would we.

TOM: Where do we fit?

MAE: We were born here. We were taught to think as Canadians.

TOM: Most of our people have decided to repatriate.

MAE: We can't just follow the crowd and do something we'll regret later on.

TOM: Mae, I'm tired of all this discrimination.

MAE: There's just as much discrimination right here in the Slocan Valley. We're no better than anyone else. My friend Irene works as a secretary for the Administration. Most of the other women won't even talk to her. People deciding to stay in Canada are ostracized and called dogs.

TOM: As Japanese, we're taught that our society as a whole is more important than our individualism.

MAE: We're not Japanese, we're Canadian. This is our country, even if it has failed us.

TOM: We entered the Golden Door and now we're booted out the back door.(pause) Mae, I know you're right ... in spite of what's happened.

MAE: You must convince Papa-san.

TOM: It could split our family apart.

(GEORGE enters via the front door)

GEORGE: Want a game of cards?

TOM: No thanks. We're eating dinner soon.(GEORGE shuffles about the room and looks stage right, not wanting to enter.)

GEORGE: I was in town. Everyone's talking about going back to Japan, except for some dogs! What are you doing?

TOM: Haven't decided.

GEORGE: There's nothing to decide ... repatriate.

TOM: Why should we repatriate ... we've never been to Japan.

GEORGE: Japan's winning the war.

TOM: That's not what I've been reading.

GEORGE: Propaganda. Just wait 'til Japan lands on the coast, then things will change. This country's no good.

TOM: We were born here. It's our country.

GEORGE: We're enemy aliens. All the notices say so.

TOM: That's how we're treated but it's not the way we feel.

GEORGE: They took everything. Why should we go east just to prove we're loyal to Canada. Stay here. Let the government take care of us.

TOM: I don't want to be on welfare.

GEORGE: The government is paying more for us to repatriate than move east. Let them pay our way back to Japan.

TOM: But we don't belong in Japan.

(KEN, AIKO and TOSHIO enter via the front door.)

KEN: Dinner must be ready by now.

(JUNE enters stage left and helps MAE and AIKO at the stove.)

GEORGE: We don't belong here.

TOSHIO: What you talk about?

TOM: Repatriate. Should we repatriate or not?

GEORGE: If you don't repatriate, they'll throw you out of this house and let you starve.

TOM: Who told you that?

GEORGE: Some guys in town.

TOM: Well, I don't believe it.

TOSHIO: We not have much money. (TOSHIO sits down at the table.)

GEORGE: Repatriate, then you don't have to worry.

TOM: It may seem easier to repatriate but it will be harder later on.

GEORGE: It will be easier later on. We speak Japanese and English. We can get a good job in Japan, and we will be free from racist propaganda.

TOM: But not discrimination.

GEORGE: What?

TOM: Our western ways represent the enemy. We won't fit into their way of life.

GEORGE: Maybe you won't! (to TOSHIO) You spent your whole life working in this country. Where did it get you? They took everything. Now you're rotting in this hole!

TOSHIO: (pause) Repatriate ... family stay together. (GEORGE nods his approval, while MAE, JUNE and KEN look on in dismay.)

JUNE: But Papa ...

TOM: We can stay together if we move east.

TOSHIO: I too old to start over.

TOM: Papa, I'm not too old to start over.

TOHIO: What you do?

TOM: I can get a job in Ontario.

TOSHIO: Good job?

TOM: Not at first, but I'll find an engineering job sooner or later.

TOSHIO: What I do?

TOM: Papa, you've worked hard all your life ... now it's my turn.

TOSHIO: You support me?

TOM: Yes, I'll support you.

TOSHIO: Me support me.

TOM: But, it's my turn to support you.

TOSHIO: You boss? I not like that.

TOM: Papa, you'll always be the boss around here.

TOSHIO: You make money, you boss. Can I fish in Ontario?

TOM: It's not the same as fishing in Steveston, but there are the Great Lakes.

TOSHIO: What's great about them?

TOM: They're large inland seas. Maybe someday you'll have your own fishing boat again and fish in the Great Lakes.

TOSHIO: I like fish in ocean.

TOM: The Great Lakes are like an ocean.

TOSHIO: Lake not ocean. Japan has ocean.

TOM: Japan ... why should we go to Japan?

TOSHIO: Home in Japan.

TOM: You made your home in Canada. This is home to your children. Papa, remember what you said after those guys at the dock yelled, "The Japs are ruining the fishing industry!" You said,

"Don't worry, people change, it'll get better."

TOSHIO: It got worse.

TOM: But you were optimistic that it would get better. We must try and be optimistic now; if not for us, then for Edward.

TOSHIO: I live here more than 40 year. All my children born here. You go to good school ... to university ... you educated. In Japan we poor ... very poor ... too poor for much school. You want to stay here ... all my children want to stay here ... I know ... maybe here you have future ... I don't know ... family must stay together ... be happy together ... your life here ... Edward life here. You stay ... Mama and I stay.

TOM: It means starting over.

TOSHIO: We start over ... you educated ... you smart ... Hah! My son the engineer!

GEORGE: How can you stay here, in this country? You're all traitors ... no better than dogs!

(GEORGE exits stage right and slams the door.)

TOSHIO: Now we eat in peace. (to AIKO) Oka-a-san watashi tachi Ontario ikimasho.

(AIKO nods but does not visibly show whether or not she is in favour of the decision. She remains at the stove while MAE serves the others who are seated at the table.)

KEN: I'll learn more Japanese if you like.

TOSHIO: I like.

JUNE: I can't wait to go to Ontario.

TOSHIO: Why?

JUNE: Ahhh ... no special reason. I hear the winters are warmer.

TOSHIO: I hear boys nicer, too. (JUNE blushes.)

MAE: (looking at AIKO) I don't think Mama's very happy about going east.

TOM: It'll be a long time before we can afford to send her home for a visit.

TOSHIO: We work hard. She go home ... someday. (TOSHIO reaches into his pocket and brings out a small bottle.) We toast to future ... I have sake.

TOM: Where did you get that? It's illegal!

TOSHIO: My secret.(to AIKO) Oka-a-san téburu ni kita.

(AIKO sits down at the table. TOSHIO pours sake for everyone. He lifts up his glass.)

TOSHIO: To Edward.

(Everyone except AIKO lifts up their glasses.)

EVERYONE: To Edward.

(AIKO slowly lifts up her glass. Her hand trembles.)

AIKO: To Edward.

(Fade to Black)

THE END

GLOSSARY

Japanese:	Arigato
Phonetically:	*ah-ree-gah-toh.*
Translation:	Thank you.

Japanese:	Choto ma-a-te kudasai
Phonetically:	*choh-toh mah-ah-teh koo-dah-sah-ee.*
Translation:	I'm coming.

Japanese:	Doshite shite ta no?
Phonetically:	*doh-shee-tah shee-tah tah-noh?*
Translation:	How did you know?

Japanese:	Hai ohairi nasai.
Phonetically:	*Hah-ee oh-hah-ee-ree nah-sah-ee.*
Translation:	Yes, come in.

Japanese:	Hana Fuda
Phonetically:	*hah-nah foo-dah*
Translation:	Japanese card game

Japanese:	Iie Oka-a-san ga takimasu.
Phonetically:	*ee-eh oh-kah-sahn gah tah-kee-mahs.*
Translation:	No, Mother, I'll cook.

Japanese:	Ken, kyo gakko de otonashiku shite itaka?
Phonetically:	*Ken, kyoh gahk-koh deh oh-tohn-ah-shee-koo shteh ee-tah-kah?*
Translation:	Ken, were you a good boy in school today?

Japanese:	Koko ni heiwa nashi.
Phonetically:	*koh-koh nee heh-wah nah-shee.*
Translation:	There is no peace here.

Japanese:	Konnichiwa. June wa orimasu ka?
Phonetically:	*kohn-nee-chee-wah. June wah or-ee-mah-soo kah?*
Translation:	Good afternoon. Is June home?

Japanese:	Niju, yonju, goju, rokuju, nanaju, nanaju go, hachiju, kuju.
Phonetically:	*nee-joo, yohn-joo, goh-joo, roh-koo-joo, nah-nah joo, nah-nah-joo goh, hah-chee-joo, kyoo-joo.*
Translation:	20, 40, 50, 60, 70, 75, 80, 90.

Japanese: Nisei
Phonetically: *nee-seh*
Translation: Second generation Japanese Canadian

Japanese: Ojiisan
Phonetically: *oh-jee-sahn*
Translation: Grandfather

Japanese: Oka-a-san ita.
Phonetically: *oh-kah-sahn ee-teh.*
Translation: Mother, go ahead.

Japanese: Oka-a-san mizuumi made arukinasai.
Phonetically: *oh-kah-sahn mee-zoo-oo-mee mah-deh ah-roo-kee-nah-sah-ee.*
Translation: Mother, go for a walk by the lake.

Japanese: Oka-a-san téburu ni kita.
Phonetically: *oh-kah-sahn teh-boo-roo nee kee-teh.*
Translation: Mother, come to the table.

Japanese: Oka-a-san, wa Oba-a-san ni naru no yo.
Phonetically: *oh-kah-sahn wah oh-bah-sahn nee nah-roo noh yoh.*
Translation: Mother, you are going to be a grandmother.

Japanese: Oka-a-san watashi tachi Ontario ikimasho.
Phonetically: *oh-kah-sahn wah-tah-shee tah-chee Ontario ee-kee-mah-shoh.*
Translation: Mother, we are going to Ontario.

Japanese: Otoko no hito ga kimasu.
Phonetically: *oh-toh-koh noh hee-toh gah kee-mahs.*
Translation: A man is coming.

Japanese: Oyasuminasai.
Phonetically: *oh-yah-soo-mee-nah-sah-ee.*
Translation: Goodnight.

Japanese: RCMP to Papa-san to TOM kimasu!
Phonetically: *RCMP toh Papa-sahn toh TOM kee-mahs!*
Translation: The RCMP and Father and TOM are coming!

Japanese: Sake
Phonetically: *sah-keh*
Translation: Rice wine

Japanese: Shikata-ga-nai.
Phonetically: *shee-kah-tah-gah-nah-ee.*
Translation: It can't be helped.

Japanese: Watakushi ga shimasu.
Phonetically: *wah-tah-koo-shee gah shee-mahs.*
Translation: I'll start dinner.

Japanese: Watakushi shi-te imashita.
Phonetically: *wah-tah-koo-shee shee-teh ee-mah-shee-teh.*
Translation: I know.

Questions

Beautiful Deeds/De beaux gestes
by Marie-Lynn Hammond

1. In what ways are Corinne and Elsie similar?

2. In what ways are they different?

3. To what extent do you think their dissimilarities are attributable to their varied cultural and socio-economic backgrounds?

4. How might the lives of Elsie and Corinne have been different had they been born, say, thirty years ago instead of over a hundred years ago?

5. It's easy sometimes to forget that elderly people were once young too. What do you know about your own grandparents' histories?

6. Write a short monologue in the "voice" of an elderly person you know about an important event in his or her life. (As the author of this play has done, you are allowed to use your imagination to fill in bits of missing information!)

7. The Marie-Lynn character in *Beautiful Deeds/De beaux gestes* sings, at the very beginning of the play, that she feels "prise au milieu/ entre les deux" — i.e., caught between her French and English selves. By the end of the play has she resolved her conflicted identity in any way, and if so, how?

8. How does the structure of this play differ from a more classic, traditional drama?

9. This play includes the stories of four legal marriages and one common-law marriage. Compare the reasons behind each of these unions. Do you think any of these marriages were successful? Why? Which ones failed? Why?

Like the Sun

by Veralyn Warketin

1. Describe the average home of an Irish peasant in the 1840's. Compare their way of life with your own by a written description or an illustration. Discuss with your class.

2. Imagine that you are one of the characters in the play (John, Kathleen, the Priest etc.). Perhaps you are Thomas just after the eviction when your house has been burnt to the ground and you have seen your mother cry. Write a journal entry on your feelings.

3. Discuss the image of the "cursing stone" in the play. How does it relate to the theme? What is the play's theme?

4. "The tragedy of the famine cannot be reduced to a morality play, with an evil British government and heartless landlords on the one side, and a virtuous people on the other. The reality is messier, more complex, more ambiguous." Discuss.

5. There are still famines today. Why?

6. One production of the play opened with a slide projection of a photograph of Irish president Mary Robinson with the famine victims in Somalia. The play closed with a photograph of Mary Robinson on Grosse Ile (she was the first Irish head of state to visit the gravesites in August of 1994). Why was this parallel drawn?

7. Describe the conditions aboard the emigrant "coffin ships." How do they compare with refugees fleeing countries today?

8. Why did the Irish in Canada and Ireland react so strongly against the Parks Canada plan to turn Grosse Ile into the theme park "Canada: Land of Welcome and Hope"?

9. Is there a local foodbank in your area? With your class investigate and find ways to become involved with the needy/hungry where you live.

"Mom, Dad, I'm Living with a White Girl"
by Marty Chan

1. What drives Mark to his decision to stay with his parents? Would you make the same decision? Why or why not?

2. Is the ending a happy one or a tragic one? Why?

3. Do you think the play needs the fantasy scenes? Why or why not?

4. Examine some of the fantasy sequences. What do they contribute to the reality scenes?

5. The play shows glimpses of Chinese culture. Find some examples and discuss how these helped shape the world of the Gee family.

6. The play uses subtext throughout. Find an example of subtext and discuss what the characters are really talking about.

7. The play explores Asian stereotypes in pop culture. What examples of other stereotypes can you find in today's movies and television shows?

8. The Yellow Claw is usually a male figure. Why did the playwright make Li Fen the Yellow Claw?

9. Do you know of anyone in a situation similar to Mark's? Ask them why they are afraid to tell their parents.

10. If you were acting one of the roles, how would you handle the shifts from one character to another?

11. If you were directing this play, how would you handle the transitions? Can you think of another device besides the gong?

Gently Down the Stream
by Aviva Ravel

1. What is the significance of the play's title?

2. Provide character sketches of Moish and Alex. Would they have been companions in their youth?

3. Alex often insults Moish. Yet why does Moish seek him out?

4. Describe and discuss the various characters who pass by in the park, and the old men's reaction to each one.

5. The men explore a number of philosophical questions. Select a few and discuss.

6. What social and ethical issues does the presence of the dead man raise?

7. The "Theatre of the Absurd" expresses the belief that man's life is essentially without meaning or purpose and that human beings cannot communicate rationally. This concept is contained in the works of playwrights such as Pinter, Ionesco and Beckett. What are the differences and similarities between *Gently Down the Stream* and "The Theatre of the Absurd"?

8. What challenges does the actor face in creating either one of the two characters?

9. What guidelines would you offer to the director?

The House on Hermitage Road
by Dirk McLean

1. What were Jacqueline's personal and sociological reasons for leaving Trinidad for England?

2. What are the family's feeling about Jacqueline's move?

3. Describe the activities surrounding Trinidad's Independence.

4. Discuss the decree pertaining to dogs and what impact it would it have on the environment.

5. How important is the passing of the school exam to the children in Trinidad? How does Dirk cope with his failure?

6. What was the impact of Nursey's illness and death on Dirk?

7. Compare Christian funeral rites in Trinidad with those in Canada.

8. Do you believe Dirk will adjust well to Canada? What problems might he encounter in the new country?

9. Do you believe that the absence of a parent for a long period of time has a lasting effect on the child?

The Golden Door
by W. Ray Towle

1. In retrospect, it is clear that Japanese Canadians were no threat during the Second World War. However, from the point of view of other people living at that time, was the Canadian Government justified in controlling the activities of Japanese Canadians?

2. Why did people fear the Japanese Canadians during the Second World War? Was it simple ignorance based on a lack of interaction between cultural groups, or was it government propaganda?

3. Should ethnic groups attempt to retain their original culture, traditions, and language when they move to another country?

4. Does a multi-ethnic identity enrich a society or lead to social unrest?

5. What recourse does the individual citizen have to protest discriminatory laws?

6. How should we react to derogatory slang used to deprecate minority cultural groups?

7. Why are visible minorities easy targets for discrimination?

8. What are the similarities between the racial discrimination experienced by immigrants of various ethnic backgrounds during the Second World War and more recent times?

9. Do you think that $21,000 per person in 1988 was fair compensation from the Canadian Government to surviving Japanese Canadians interned during the Second World War? Why did it take 46 years for a formal Government apology?